Inside Copilot

Inside Copilot is designed to teach users to master Copilot, Microsoft's generative AI assistant. Learn prompt engineering and use cases for Copilot in many Microsoft products at beginner, intermediate, and expert levels. Perfect for any professionals who find their schedules packed with repetitive computer tasks, Copilot can automatically generate PowerPoint presentations, draft emails on Outlook, write code on GitHub, and more. Both companies and individuals can learn to utilize Copilot to significantly speed up processes and gain an advantage.

More information about this series at https://link.springer.com/bookseries/17432.

GovOps with Microsoft Power Platform and Copilot

Automating Governance

Sarat Piridi

Apress®

GovOps with Microsoft Power Platform and Copilot: Automating Governance

Sarat Piridi
Lathrop, CA, USA

ISBN-13 (pbk): 979-8-8688-1795-3　　　　　　ISBN-13 (electronic): 979-8-8688-1796-0
https://doi.org/10.1007/979-8-8688-1796-0

Managing Director, Apress Media LLC: Welmoed Spahr
Acquisitions Editor: Ryan Byrnes
Coordinating Editor: Gryffin Winkler

Cover image by eStudioCalamar

Distributed to the book trade worldwide by Springer Science+Business Media New York, 1 New York Plaza, New York, NY 10004. Phone 1-800-SPRINGER, fax (201) 348-4505, e-mail orders-ny@springer-sbm.com, or visit www.springeronline.com. Apress Media, LLC is a Delaware LLC and the sole member (owner) is Springer Science + Business Media Finance Inc (SSBM Finance Inc). SSBM Finance Inc is a **Delaware** corporation.

For information on translations, please e-mail booktranslations@springernature.com; for reprint, paperback, or audio rights, please e-mail bookpermissions@springernature.com.

Apress titles may be purchased in bulk for academic, corporate, or promotional use. eBook versions and licenses are also available for most titles. For more information, reference our Print and eBook Bulk Sales web page at http://www.apress.com/bulk-sales.

Any source code or other supplementary material referenced by the author in this book is available to readers on GitHub (https://github.com/Apress). For more detailed information, please visit https://www.apress.com/gp/services/source-code.

If disposing of this product, please recycle the paper

*To my wife, **Bhanu**, for her endless love, patience,
and encouragement. Your unwavering belief in
me made this journey possible and gave me the strength to
pursue my passion.*

*To my son, **Dennis**, whose curiosity and boundless
imagination inspire me to keep learning and
innovating. May this book one day remind you
that knowledge and creativity can truly shape the world.*

*To the incredible team at **CalOES**, whose collaboration,
insights, and commitment to public service helped shape
many of the ideas and frameworks in this book.
Your dedication to modernizing government for the
people of California continues to inspire me every day.*

*And to **public-sector innovators everywhere**—May this
book serve as a guide and encouragement in your
mission to build better, smarter, and more
human-centered government services.*

Table of Contents

Chapter 10: Resources and Templates 337

Chapter 11: Azure AI + AI Builder High-Level AI Model Development...341

Chapter 12: Copilot Studio In-Depth Tutorial: Bots, Prompts, and Custom Skills...345

Chapter 17: Monitoring and Logging with Azure Monitor and Power Platform Admin Center 365

Chapter 18: Disaster Recovery and Business Continuity Planning...369

Chapter 19: The Future of Digital Government: Trends to Watch......373

Chapter 20: Developing a Culture of Low-Code Innovation in Government Sector 377

About the Author

Sarat Piridi is a Microsoft-certified Solution Architect (Power Platform Solution Architect Expert, Azure Solutions Architect Expert, and Power Automate RPA Developer) with more than 14 years of global experience designing and delivering large-scale, enterprise-grade automation solutions. He has led numerous multimillion-dollar digital transformation projects across both public and private sectors. Sarat's career includes leadership roles at Microsoft, where he architected the Unified Premier global-scale automation program; Facebook (Meta) Global Security Team, delivering AI-driven automation for critical security operations; Fidelity Investments; State of California; Huawei; Silicon Valley Bank (SVB); and Microsoft's Xbox and Surface Teams. He currently drives public-sector innovation at Cal OES. In addition to his solution delivery expertise, Sarat is a published thought leader. He has coauthored the book *Rise of AI Bureaucrats*, contributed to multiple peer-reviewed research papers on AI-driven government transformation, and regularly speaks at industry conferences. He also serves on technical advisory boards focused on advancing public-sector digital transformation.

Author's Note

GovOps 2.0: Automating Government with Power Platform represents over a decade of experience in public sector transformation, combined with ongoing work in AI, automation, and low-code technologies.

All architectural patterns, use cases, and best practices presented here are based on real-world projects or repeatable frameworks successfully implemented across various US government agencies.

Any reference to government departments in this book is for educational and illustrative purposes only, and does not represent official endorsements by those agencies.

About the Technical Reviewer

Fabio Claudio Ferracchiati is a Senior Consultant and Senior Analyst/Developer specializing in Microsoft technologies. He currently works at Telecom Italia (`www.telecomitalia.it`). Fabio holds several Microsoft certifications, including Microsoft Certified Solutions Developer (MCSD) for .NET, Microsoft Certified Application Developer (MCAD) for .NET, and Microsoft Certified Professional (MCP). He is also a prolific author and technical reviewer. Over the past decade, he has contributed numerous articles to both Italian and international technology magazines and has coauthored more than ten books covering a wide range of computing topics.

Acknowledgments

I would like to express my deepest gratitude to the following contributors and supporters.

Satyanarayana Asundi, Senior Software Engineer, Satyanarayana is my senior from college and a long-time collaborator. As a co-author on several research publications, he contributed significantly to the concepts and frameworks in this book. His expertise in AI, automation, and solution architecture helped shape many of the models and strategies presented in GovOps 2.0.

Durga Bhavani Teki, Solutions Specialist, CalOES, Durga is my colleague at CalOES and provided valuable contributions to the design, testing, and rollout of automation use cases featured in this book. Her practical insights and detailed feedback helped align the solutions with real-world public sector needs.

Bharath Alluri, Senior Developer, CalOES, Bharath is a key development lead at CalOES and has worked closely with me on building and deploying several mission-critical applications included in this book. His deep understanding of Power Platform, API integrations, and deployment pipelines was essential in translating ideas into scalable government solutions.

Endorsement

GovOps 2.0 offers a timely and practical framework for how government agencies can approach automation and digital transformation using modern low-code tools.

Sarat Piridi's work translates complex modernization goals into actionable strategies that are especially relevant to public-sector IT leaders and program teams working to streamline operations and improve service delivery.

This book stands out as a resource that bridges technology and implementation in a meaningful, accessible way.

—**Ravi Bhadana,** Digital Transformation Leader
California Governor's Office of Emergency Services

Foreword

Government transformation depends not just on technology but on repeatable, scalable frameworks that work in real-world settings.

GovOps 2.0 is one such guide—it outlines practical strategies that reflect how agencies can modernize using low-code platforms like Microsoft Power Platform and RPA.

This work contributes meaningfully to the public-sector toolkit and offers valuable guidance for teams looking to build secure, efficient, and adaptable digital services.

—**Ravi Bhadana,** Digital Transformation Leader
California Governor's Office of Emergency Services

Preface

Public-sector organizations across the globe are being asked to do more with less—deliver services faster, more transparently, and with a citizen-first approach. Over the past decade, I've worked closely with agencies and government partners to witness firsthand the challenges they face: aging systems, slow processes, and limited budgets. Yet, the potential to revolutionize how governments operate has never been greater.

This book is the culmination of real-world experience, research, and my passion for empowering government with low-code technology. It is designed for architects, developers, leaders, and public servants ready to make an impact using Microsoft Power Platform and Azure AI.

CHAPTER 1

Introduction to Government Modernization

1.1 The Need for Change

Governments worldwide have reached a critical juncture in their digital transformation journey. As citizens increasingly expect better services, public institutions need to incorporate modern technologies to maintain their effectiveness, transparency, and service quality. The era of lengthy queues, paper documentation, and complicated bureaucratic processes is becoming incompatible with the expectations of today's technology-savvy population.

Citizens expect their government interactions to be as instinctive as their experiences with modern tech companies. They should be in real-time/personalized and mobile-accessible. However, delivering this level of service is challenging. The reasons behind this are entrenched legacy systems, siloed data repositories, and paper-heavy manual processes.

© Sarat Piridi 2025
S. Piridi, *GovOps with Microsoft Power Platform and Copilot*, Inside Copilot,
https://doi.org/10.1007/979-8-8688-1796-0_1

At the same time, governments face increasing demands with fewer resources. Budgets are tightening, but the demand for public services continues to rise. Agencies must do more with less. They cannot compromise security/compliance or service quality.

The answer lies in reforming the basis of government service delivery. This encompasses digitizing current processes and, additionally, recasting them through cloud-native platforms and automation tools. Low-code platforms facilitate rapid innovation. They achieve this by limiting the reliance on conventional development cycles.

Modernization is no longer a choice but a requirement. Government agencies ought to embrace flexible and user-friendly platforms such as Microsoft Power Platform. This can assist them

- Reorganize internal operations

- Provide faster, more transparent services

- Reduce manual workload

- Increase accountability

- Enable data-driven decision-making

The journey begins with recognizing the urgency and opportunity of change.

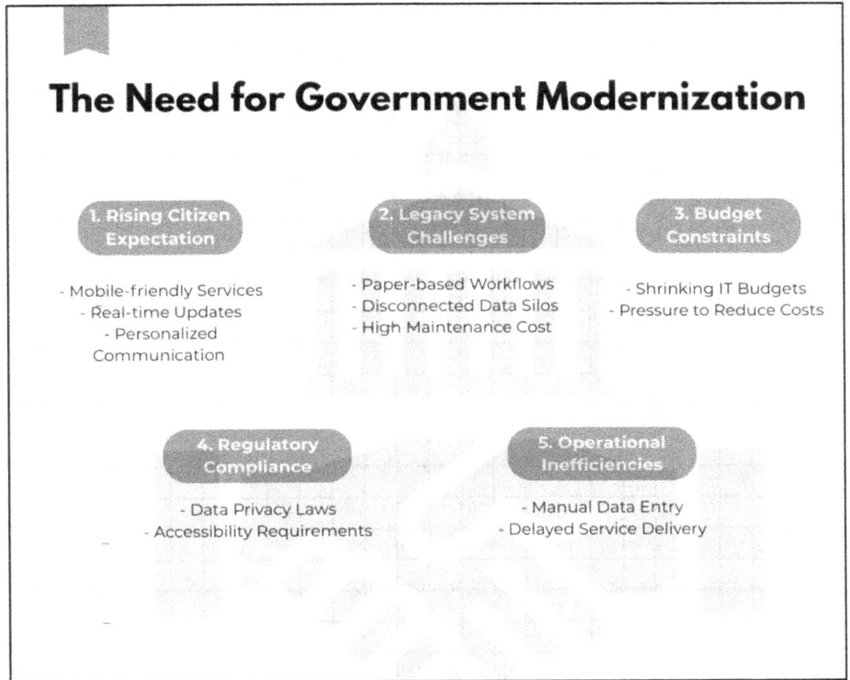

Figure 1-1. *The Need for Government Modernization*

1.2 Challenges in Traditional Government IT

Government IT systems continue to operate on decades-old infrastructure despite digital transformation efforts. These legacy systems create significant barriers to modernization and service delivery. It results in slow/expensive and complicated change processes.

These are some of the challenges:

1. **Lengthy Procurement Cycles**

    The process of procurement by the government is usually slowed down. This is because they have to follow many laws, require approval from different levels, and have strict rules for choosing the supplier. These processes can last a long time, sometimes months or even years which makes it hard to react fast to new requirements or changing expectations from people.

    Example: The department for Public Health has a plan to introduce a new system for vaccination appointments. However, they need more than six months' time to finish choosing the supplier and approve contracts. During this waiting period, the demands of citizens have changed already.

2. **High Development and Maintenance Costs**

    Public sector traditional application development is characterized by custom-built software with drawn-out development cycles. There's moreover a hefty maintenance cost associated. To keep such systems operating and abiding by regulations demands specific expertise and considerable financial commitment. This can divert resources from innovation.

    Insight: Many agencies spend more than 70% of their IT budget on maintenance alone. This leaves little room for new digital initiatives.

3. **Regulatory and Compliance Constraints**

   The regulations around accessibility (e.g., Section 508), data protection measures like GDPR and HIPAA, as well as cybersecurity standards such as NIST and FedRAMP need to be adhered to by government systems. These requirements add more complexity levels in designing/developing the system along with its deployment. This holds a greater relevance for those systems which are not natively built on cloud technology.

4. **Difficulty in Scaling or Adapting Systems Quickly**

   Legacy platforms were not designed for agility. Scaling an application or adding new features requires deep architectural changes. This inflexibility prevents fast response to emerging situations, for example, public health crises, natural disasters, or economic relief programs.

   Case in point: During the COVID-19 pandemic, several state unemployment systems crashed under demand. This is because they could not scale.

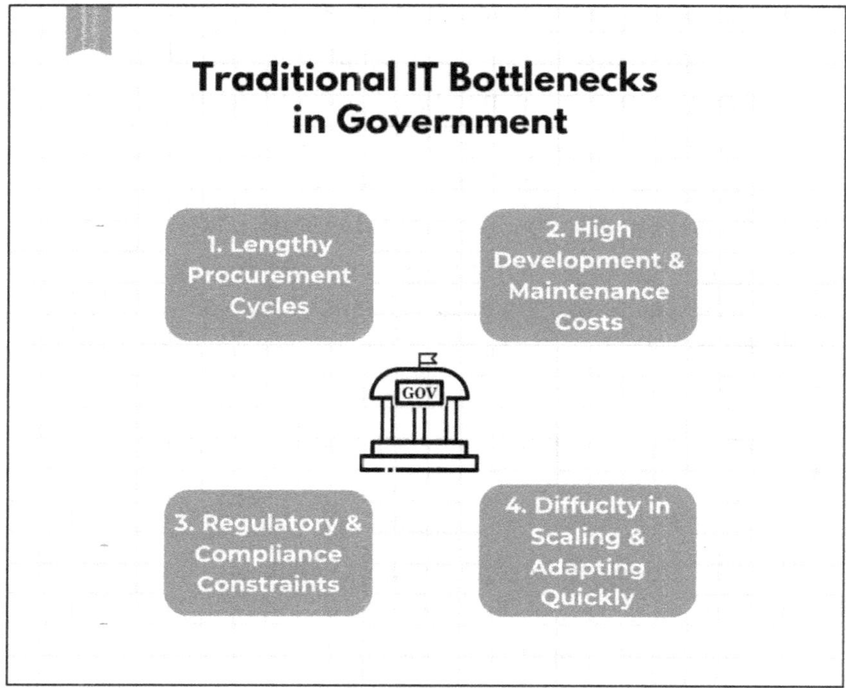

Figure 1-2. *Traditional IT Bottlenecks in Government*

1.3 The Low-Code Advantage

Low-code platforms are revolutionizing government agency development and deployment of digital services. Contrary to conventional development, involving the writing of thousands of lines of code and specialized skills, low-code platforms offer visual interfaces, preconfigured components, and drag-and-drop tools—radically streamlining solution delivery.

Benefits for Government Agencies

1. **Rapid Application Development**

   Platforms of low-code give a chance to groups in IT and users without technical skills to create applications within days or weeks. Speed like this is very important when needing fast response for changes in public requirements/emergencies or shifts in policy.

   Example: A city department launches a flood assistance app within two weeks using Power Apps. This is to collect claims and track damage assessments.

2. **Empowering Citizen Developers**

   Low-code empowers staff outside the IT department. They could be analysts, administrators, and field personnel. They are able to create solutions that improve their own workflows. These "citizen developers" can prototype/test and refine applications with minimal reliance on central IT.

   Note: Governance remains critical to balance innovation with control (covered in later chapters).

3. **Better Collaboration Between IT and Business Units**

   With low-code, IT does not have to create each solution from the ground up. Rather, they can concentrate on platform governance, security, and integration, while business users assist with app design, logic, and data input. This shared model accelerates innovation and guarantees solutions meet real-world requirements.

4. **Scalability, Security, and Compliance**

   Today's low-code platforms like Microsoft Power Platform are made on secure and cloud-native architectures. They meet government-grade security standards. They consist of features like RBAC, audit trails, and environment isolation. They ensure compliance with accessibility, privacy, and regulatory policies.

   For instance, *Microsoft Power Platform* supports FedRAMP, HIPAA, and GDPR. This makes it suitable for US and international public sector use.

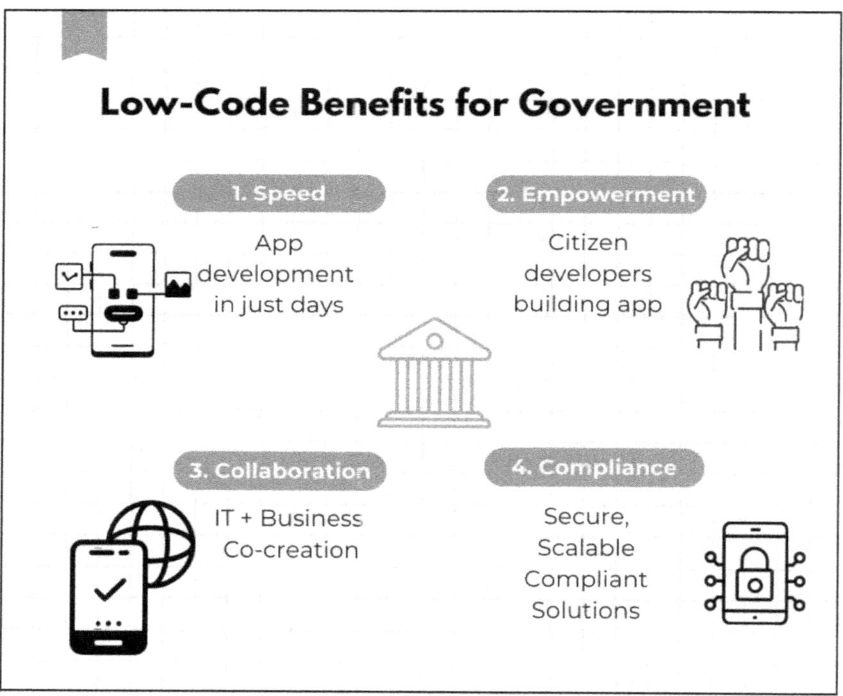

Figure 1-3. *Low-Code Benefits for Government*

1.4 Role of Microsoft Power Platform

This power-packed solution is at the forefront of low-code digital transformation in the public sector. It provides a unified, scalable suite of tools that enable government agencies to modernize processes and build responsive applications. They can also use it to automate manual tasks and gain actionable insights. You can achieve these goals while ensuring compliance, security, and accessibility at the same time.

Important Components of the Power Platform

- **Power Apps:** Create user-friendly web and mobile applications without extensive programming knowledge. Perfect for converting paper forms to digital, managing workflows, and supporting mobile field operations.

- **Power Automate:** Enables seamless process automation across both modern and legacy systems. Cloud flows automate cloud-based apps and services using triggers and connectors. Desktop flows (RPA) automate legacy applications through UI-based robotic process automation. Together, they streamline workflows, eliminate manual tasks, and accelerate digital transformation.

- **Power BI:** Convert raw data into real-time dashboards, trend reports, and compliance visualizations for leadership and staff users.

- **Power Pages:** Build secure and public-facing portals. They can handle citizen services such as permit applications, license renewals, and service requests.

- **Dataverse:** It functions as a secure and scalable data foundation. It supports relational data modeling, role-based access control, audit trails, etc.

- **AI Builder:** Empowers automation of tasks like form processing, document understanding, object detection, and predictions without requiring data science skills.

- **Copilot:** Facilitates the creation of apps, flows, and reports through natural language descriptions, expediting solution development.

1.5 Why Microsoft Power Platform Stands Out in Government

- **Fusing with Existing Tools:** Seamless compatibility with Office 365, Teams, Azure, and Dynamics 365 allows agencies to build on their current systems. They don't have to spend on costly restructuring.

- **Government-Ready Security:** Supported by FedRAMP High, HIPAA, ISO, and NIST standards, the platform satisfies the security needs of federal, state, and local governments.

- **Scalability and Extensibility:** The platform supports everything from small departmental solutions to full-scale enterprise modernization efforts.

- **Innovation Without Disruption:** Agencies can incrementally modernize legacy systems by layering Power Platform on top, reducing risk, and maximizing ROI.

Use Case Snapshot

The Department of Motor Vehicles (DMV) uses Power Apps to create a mobile check-in system, Power Automate for queue management, Power BI to monitor wait times, and Power Pages to provide citizens with real-time status updates—all in under three months.

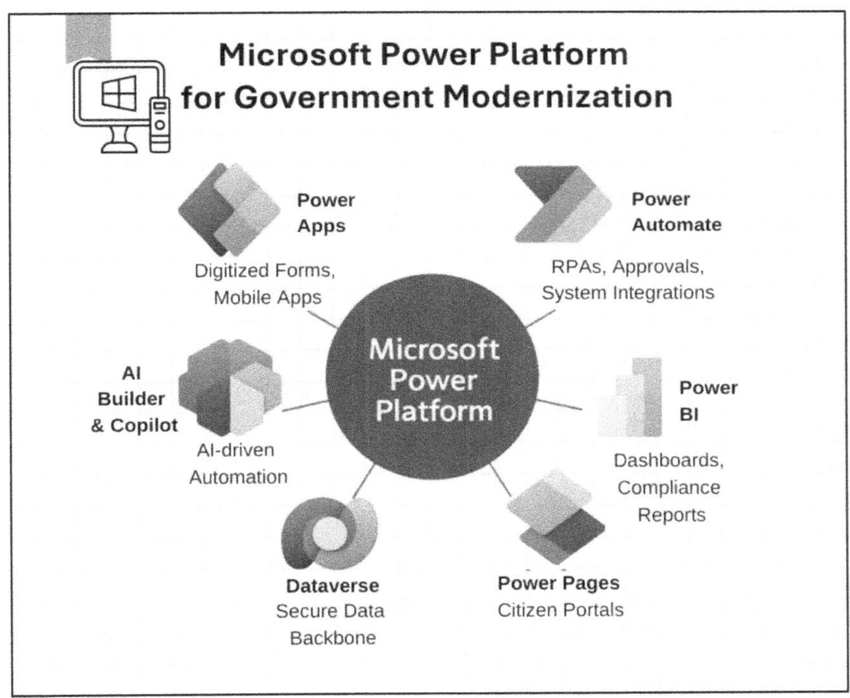

Figure 1-4. *Power Platform for Government Modernization*

CHAPTER 2

Overview of Microsoft Power Platform

2.1 Power Apps

Power Apps is Microsoft Power Platform's application-building component that permits users to custom-build apps based on a low-code/no-code interface. Government agencies can leverage Power Apps in order to streamline paper forms into automated processes. They can deliver mobile-facilitated tools that build staff and resident experiences.

There are two main types of Power Apps.

Canvas Apps

They offer a pixel-perfect, drag-and-drop experience where users can build the user interface from scratch on a blank canvas. They are very flexible and ideal for apps where a custom user experience is required.

© Sarat Piridi 2025

S. Piridi, *GovOps with Microsoft Power Platform and Copilot*, Inside Copilot,
https://doi.org/10.1007/979-8-8688-1796-0_2

Key Features

- **Responsive layouts** for phones, tablets, and desktops

- **Control gallery** with hundreds of UI components

- **Custom forms and logic** using Power Fx formulas

- **Offline capabilities** for field operations

- **Integration with REST APIs and custom connectors**

Use Cases

- Field inspection apps (e.g., for environmental or safety compliance)

- HR self-service portals

- Mobile workforce time tracking

- Emergency response coordination

Model-Driven Apps

They are based on data models in Dataverse. These are ideal for scenarios that require complex business logic and data relationships. They are great for built-in components like forms, views, dashboards, and workflows.

Key Features

- Auto-generated UI from data model

- Built-in navigation, views, and forms

- Business rules and validation

- Role-based access control

- Scalability for large datasets

Use Cases

- Case management systems (e.g., public complaints or permit processing)

- Grant or subsidy tracking portals

- Inspection and audit tracking systems

- Licensing systems for contractors or vehicles

Integration with Dataverse and External APIs

Both the app types can use **Microsoft Dataverse** as their primary data source. This will offer secure storage, auditing, and RBAC. Additionally, Power Apps integrates with **over 1,000 connectors.** This includes

- **Government systems** (e.g., SharePoint, Dynamics 365, SAP, Oracle)

- **Cloud platforms** (e.g., Azure, AWS, Google)

- **APIs and custom endpoints** through custom connectors

Canvas vs Model-Driven Power Apps

Feature	Canvas Apps	Model-Driven Apps
UI Design	Fully customizable	Auto-generated from data model
Best For	Task-based, user-centric apps	Data-centric, process-heavy systems
Learning Curve	Easier for designers	Structured and guided
Use Case Examples	Field apps, inspections	Case management, licensing
Data Source	Flexible (any connector/API)	Primarily Dataverse

Figure 2-1. *Canvas vs. Model-Driven Apps*

2.2 Power Automate

Power Automate is Microsoft's robust automation platform. It allows government agencies to automate business processes in on-premises and cloud environments. It decreases manual effort, removes repetitive work, and integrates modern and old systems to enhance efficiency and delivery of services.

Power Automate has two primary automation types.

Cloud Flows

They are designed to connect cloud-based services using triggers and actions. These flows are ideal for automating approval processes and integrating apps. Also, useful for syncing data and managing notifications.

Key Capabilities

- Event-based triggers (e.g., email received, form submitted)

- Thousands of connectors (Outlook, SharePoint, Teams, SAP, SQL, etc.)

- Parallel branches and conditional logic

- Approval routing with integration into Teams and Outlook

- Scheduled and instant flows

Use Cases

- Automating invoice approval processes

- Notifying supervisors of incident reports

- Synchronizing citizen records between systems

- Archiving public records automatically

Desktop Flows (RPA)

These bring Robotic Process Automation into the Power Platform. These flows are used to automate tasks on legacy systems that do not have APIs, using UI automation.

Key Capabilities

- Automate mouse clicks, keystrokes, and screen scraping.

- Integration with legacy systems, mainframes, and local apps.

- Use of browser and desktop automation agents.

- Attended and unattended automation support.

- Error handling and retry policies.

Cloud Connectors in Desktop Flows (Preview)

Integrates cloud-based connectors within desktop flows to bridge legacy systems with modern cloud services.

Record with Copilot (AI Recorder)

Allows users to build desktop flows by describing tasks through voice or text. Copilot automatically generates automation steps, reducing setup time.

Use Cases

- Data entry into legacy tax filing systems

- Automating reports from desktop-only government apps

- Migrating records from Excel to a government ERP system

Connectors

Power Automate connects to over **1,500+ services**. This includes

- **Microsoft Services:** SharePoint, Outlook, Teams, Dynamics 365, Excel, Forms

- **Enterprise Systems:** Oracle, SAP, SQL Server

- **Government Platforms:** eGov APIs, GIS systems (Arc GIS), internal databases

- **Custom Connectors:** Custom connectors allow agencies to easily connect to REST APIs and external services that are not available through standard connectors. In other words, agencies can integrate both internal systems and public data sources by using built-in connectors or creating custom connectors specifically designed for their APIs.

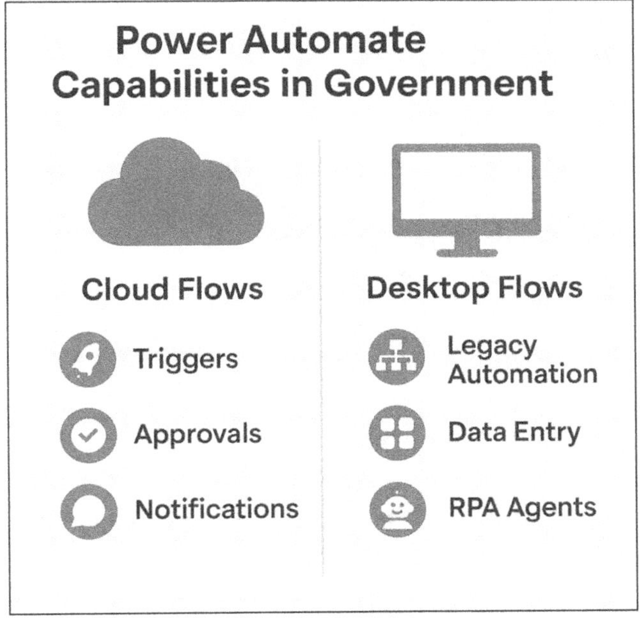

Figure 2-2. *Power Automate Capabilities in Government*

2.3 Power BI

Power BI is Microsoft's enterprise-grade business intelligence platform. It is designed to turn raw data into insightful/interactive dashboards and reports. In the public sector, Power BI helps decision-makers and frontline workers. They can make informed and data-driven decisions. This is essential in an era where transparency and agility are very important.

Dashboards for Leadership

Government leaders need timely and accurate insights. They use them to allocate resources, track progress, and respond to emerging challenges. Power BI enables executive dashboards that present real-time metrics with powerful visualizations.

Examples

- Budget utilization and variance tracking

- Emergency response readiness dashboards

- Tax collection and revenue analytics

- Workforce provision and staffing gaps

Departmental Insights

Each government department can create role-specific dashboards. They can be customized to their missions.

- **Health:** Outbreak heatmaps, facility occupancy

- **Education:** School enrollment trends, funding allocation

- **Public Safety:** Crime patterns, 911 call distribution, response time analysis

- **Transportation:** Traffic flow analysis, infrastructure project tracking

Case Illustration: The transportation department of a town applies Power BI for observing traffic and delays. It has the capability to alter bus routes and refresh electronic signages nearly instantaneously.

Embedded Analytics

Power BI reports are also embeddable directly in **Power Apps, Power Pages**, and even **Teams** or **SharePoint**. This embeds contextual insights directly into where the decision is being taken.

Use Cases

- Embedded public dashboards in citizen portals

- Inspection results entered into field apps

- Internal reports available in Microsoft Teams channels

Security and Compliance Features

- Row-level security to show only allowed data

- Auditing and activity logs

- Regulated datasets for reporting

- Integration of Azure Synapse, Purview, and Defender for Cloud

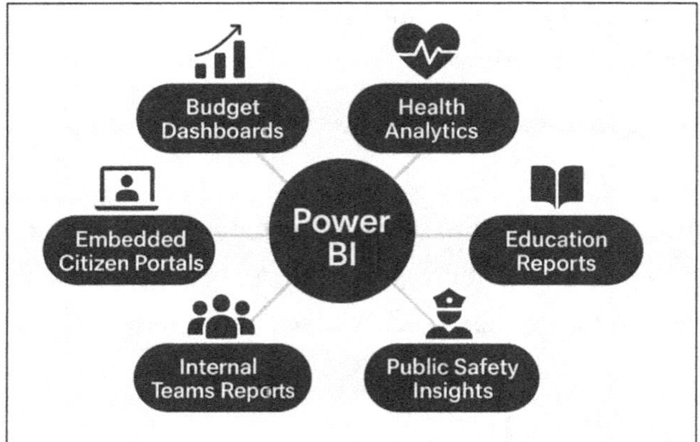

Figure 2-3. *Power BI Capabilities in Government*

2.4 Power Pages

Power Pages, formerly called Power Apps Portals, is Microsoft's low-code platform. It is for creating secure and externally facing websites. It enables government agencies to create digital front doors where citizens, businesses, and partner organizations can securely interact with public services.

Power Pages is particularly useful in offering services that require **authentication and data submission**. Also, **case tracking and public transparency**, all atop a secure, scalable foundation with Dataverse.

Key Capabilities

1. **Secure Citizen and Staff Portals**

   - Azure AD B2C/B2B or Microsoft Entra ID authentication

   - Role-based access and permissions for citizens, businesses, and internal staff

   - Seamless integration with other Power Platform tools

2. **Data-Driven Forms and Views**

- Embed Dataverse forms, views, and dashboards

- Display user-specific data (e.g., submitted applications, license status)

- Enable document uploads/file downloads and digital signatures

3. **Customizable UI and Branding**

- Templates and themes for consistent government branding

- Low-code tools for designers + pro-code extensions with HTML/CSS/JS

- Responsive layouts for mobile/tablet and desktop

4. **Integration with External Services**

- Power Automate to trigger workflows on portal submission

- External API calls (e.g., validate license number, load GIS data)

- Consolidated Power BI reports for public insights

Example Applications

- Renewal of business licenses and tax returns

- Applications for rental assistance and housing

- Permit and inspection scheduling

- Public grievance and case tracking portals

- Submissions under FOIA

Security and Compliance

- Data encrypted in transit and at rest

- Built-in support for WCAG 2.1 and Section 508 accessibility

- Role-based views, CAPTCHA, and IP restrictions

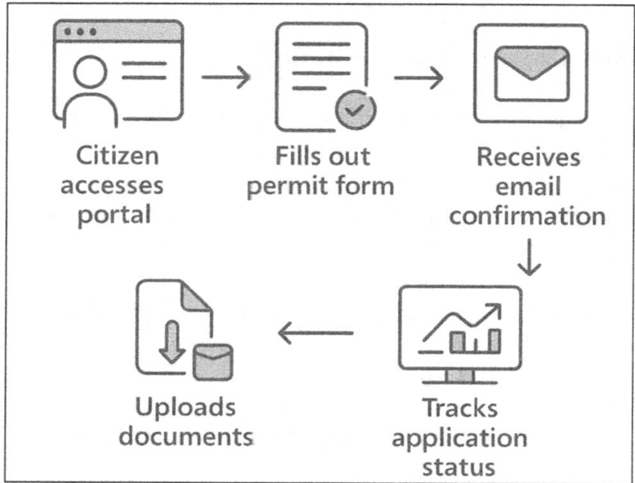

Figure 2-4. *Power Pages for Citizen Interaction Flow*

2.5 Dataverse

Microsoft Dataverse is the base data system for Power Platform. It gives a safe, expandable, and organized space for keeping and controlling data that are utilized in Power Apps, Power Automate, Power Pages, and also in Power BI.

With Dataverse, government agencies can center their information, make sure data is correct and complete, set controls based on roles for access to the system, and keep complete record-ability. All these are important for compliance/transparency and public trust.

Key Features of Dataverse

1. **Centralized and Secure Data Management**

   - **Table-based storage** for structured data with relationships

   - Data encrypted at rest and in transit

   - **Built-in RBAC** (role-based access control) and field-level security

   - Full audit history for accountability and traceability

2. **Business Rules and Logic**

   - Validation and logic enforced at the data layer

   - Reusable **business rules** to control field visibility and behavior

   - Support for **business process flows** and **workflow automations**

3. **Relationships and Lookups**

   - Create complex relationships: one-to-many, many-to-many

   - Lookup fields for connecting records (e.g., Citizen ➤ Permit ➤ Inspection)

   - Visual diagramming of data models

4. **Column Types and Calculations**

   - Rich column types: Choice, Currency, File, Image, Multiselect

   - **Calculated and rollup columns** for dynamic values (e.g., total permit fees, application aging)

5. **Compliance and Auditing**

- Native support for audit logs, field history tracking, and change detection

- Full integration with Microsoft Purview and Azure Synapse for governance and analytics

Use Cases in Government

- Citizen records and identity management

- Grant tracking and fund disbursement

- Asset and inventory registries

- Service requests, permits, and inspections

- Case and complaint tracking systems

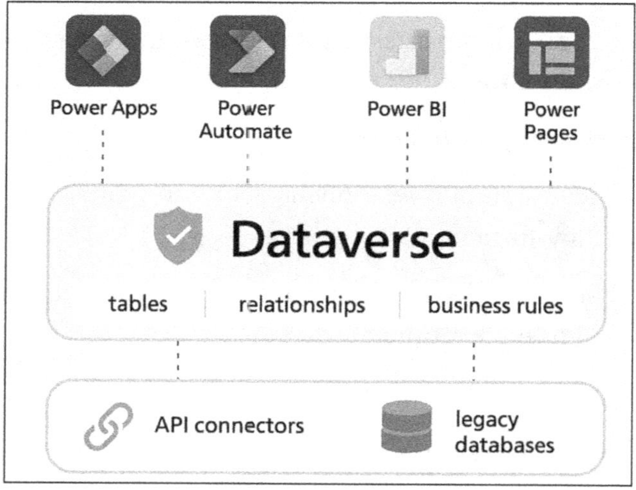

Figure 2-5. *Dataverse in Action*

2.6 AI Builder

AI Builder is Microsoft's low-code AI platform within the Power Platform. It gives government agencies direct access to powerful Azure AI capabilities including GPT-based text generation, document intelligence, form recognition, object detection, and predictive analytics—all without needing data science skills.

With AI Builder, agencies can easily integrate advanced AI into everyday workflows. Prebuilt models simplify tasks like extracting data from documents, analyzing sentiment in public feedback, or classifying case types. Agencies can also train custom AI models tailored to their unique data and use cases such as forecasting service demand or automating complex form processing.

By embedding AI across their Power Apps, Power Automate flows, Power Pages, and Power BI dashboards, government teams can significantly improve service accuracy, reduce manual workload, and enable faster, data-driven decision-making—driving smarter and more responsive public services.

The Core Capabilities of AI Builder

1. **Prebuilt AI Models**

    - **Form Processing:** Extract text and data from scanned government forms, handwritten applications, or tax documents.

    - **Object Detection:** Identify physical items like signage, equipment, or vehicles using mobile devices.

    - **Sentiment Analysis:** Classify citizen emails, feedback, or comments as Positive, Negative, Neutral, or Mixed—helping agencies quickly gauge overall public sentiment. (Note: This model is focused on general sentiment classification, not detailed emotion detection.)

- **Category Classification:** Incoming service requests are automatically categorized by urgency or department.

- **Entity Extraction:** Identify and retrieve key entities such as names, relevant dates, addresses, and reference numbers within documents or blocks of texts.

- **ID Reader:** Perform reading and extracting data from identity card documents including driver's licenses, passports, and other government-issued cards.

- **Language Detection and Translation:** Detect the language of incoming text and can provide automated translation, improving accessibility and service for multilingual citizens.

2. **Custom AI Models**

- You can train AI on your agency's data such as housing claims or disaster surveys.

- You are able to build predictive models, such as

  - Will a license be refused for lack of documentation?

  - Which cases are most likely to become intractable and need follow-up?

3. **Seamless Integration**

- Embed AI models into **Power Apps** (e.g., auto-fill fields using OCR).

- Trigger intelligent workflows in **Power Automate** (e.g., route complaints with negative sentiment to priority teams).

- Display outcomes in **Power BI** dashboards.

4. **Licensing and Capacity**

- AI Builder capacity is based on credits allocated per tenant.

- Consumption depends on model type (document vs. prediction vs. object detection).

Use Cases in Government

- **Compliance and Auditing:** Auto-scan procurement documents for missing clauses.

- **Procurement:** Categorize vendor applications and flag high-risk bids.

- **Citizen Engagement:** Triage public comments or social media input using sentiment and classification.

- **Legal:** Extract entities (names, dates, sections) from lengthy legislative or contract PDFs.

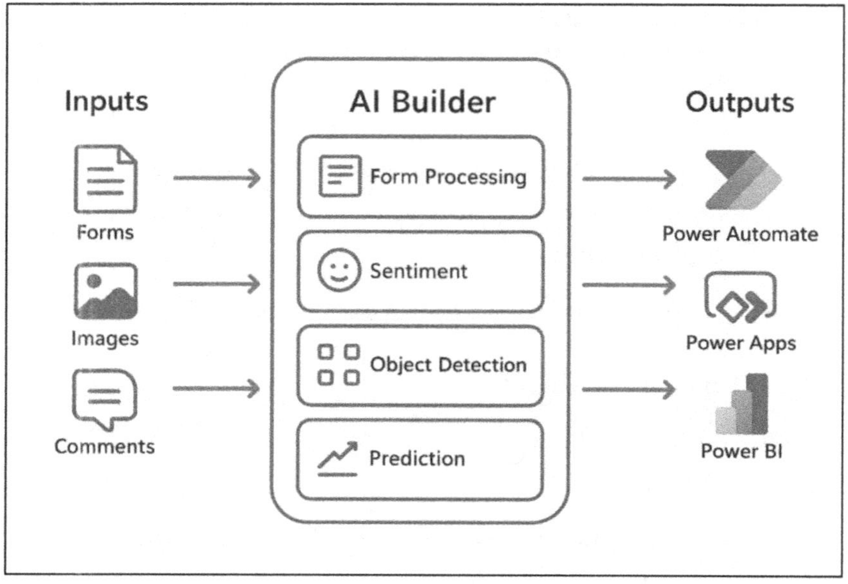

Figure 2-6. *How AI Builder Is Useful in Government System*

2.7 Copilot (Embedded in Power Platform)

Copilot is powered by generative AI and large language models (LLMs). It is revolutionizing how users interact with the Microsoft Power Platform. It enables users ranging from developers to frontline workers to build apps and create reports. They can also automate workflows using **natural language prompts** instead of traditional development tools.

Copilot functions as a digital assistant in government settings. It improves data interpretation and streamlines complexity. It also expedites the delivery of solutions.

Core Capabilities of Copilot in Power Platform

1. App and Flow Creation with Prompts

- Use natural language to describe what you want:

  - "Create a leave request form with approval routing."

  - "Automate an email when a safety violation is logged."

- Copilot translates your intent into a working app, flow, or data structure.

2. Dashboard Summaries and Report Insights

- Copilot in **Power BI** can generate summaries of charts and answer natural-language queries about data. It also explains trends (e.g., "Why did citizen complaints spike in Q3?").

3. Embedded Contextual Help

- Copilot makes context-based recommendations for formulas, field names, and next steps in Power Apps and Power Automate design environments.

- Reduces learning curve for new developers and supports continuous improvement.

Government-Specific Use Cases

- **Caseworkers** use Copilot to build intake apps without writing a single line of code.

- **Supervisors** ask Power BI, "Show me departments with overdue requests," and get instant, actionable visuals.

- Using natural queries, **policy teams** synthesize survey data or legislative sentiment.

Prompt Engineering Tips

- Be clear and specific about entities and actions (e.g., "Create a table called Emergency Requests with fields: Date, Location, Severity").

- Use follow-up questions to refine outputs (e.g., "Add a lookup to inspector profiles").

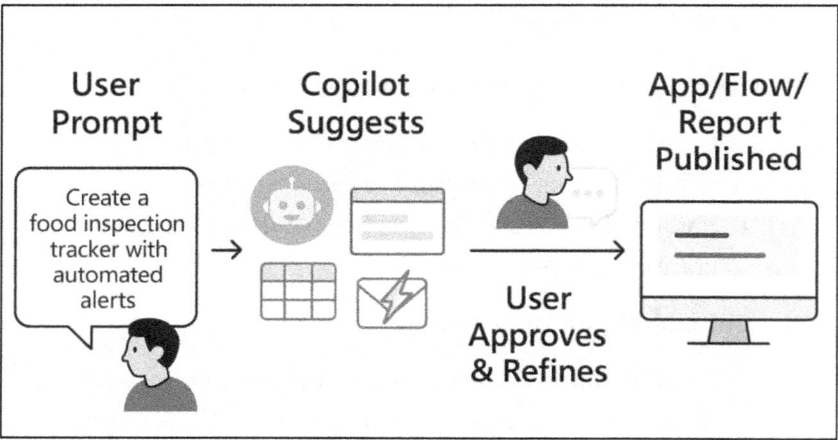

Figure 2-7. Using Copilot in Government Application

CHAPTER 3

Planning a Government Low-Code Strategy

3.1 Assessment for Readiness

Prior to diving into low-code implementation, government organizations need to assess their technical, organizational, and cultural readiness. A strategic groundwork guarantees that low-code efforts are sustainable, scalable, and support long-term objectives.

1. **Technology Inventory and System Audit**
   It involves a detailed auditing that eases the finding of

   - Existing applications, platforms, and databases already implemented

   - Retiring or automated legacy systems

© Sarat Piridi 2025
S. Piridi, *GovOps with Microsoft Power Platform and Copilot*, Inside Copilot,
https://doi.org/10.1007/979-8-8688-1796-0_3

- Licensing capability and integration that are currently offered (e.g., Microsoft 365, Azure, Dynamics 365)

Checklist:

☑ Inventory all important processes.

☑ Identify systems without APIs.

☑ Call out manual workflows and duplicate efforts.

2. **Stakeholder Mapping**

Success with low-code transformation is dependent on collaboration between IT, business units, and executive leadership.

- **IT Teams:** Focus on governance, integration, and architecture.

- **Business Users:** Identify bottlenecks and build prototypes.

- **Leadership:** Set KPIs and synchronize digital initiatives with agency priorities.

Tip   Organize workshops to gather input from all stakeholder groups early in planning.

---

3. **Cultural and Skill Readiness**

Low code is as much a mindset shift as it is a technology shift. Agencies must assess

- Readiness to implement new tools

- Capacity for departmental innovation

- Training needs of staff and learning paths (e.g., Power Platform Fundamentals)

Example: One government public health agency ran a 6-week Power Apps boot camp in order to shift analysts and break the outsourced development dependency.

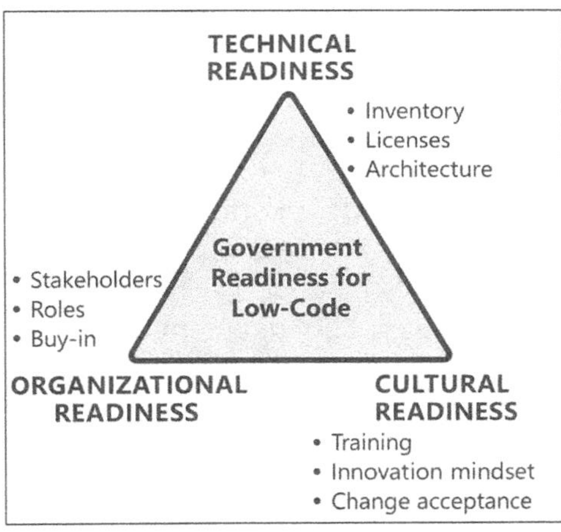

Figure 3-1. *Assessment for Readiness*

3.2 Use Case Identification

Identifying suitable use cases is the key to low-code success. Projects that need to be highlighted by the government are those finding a balance of impact, feasibility, and visibility to build traction and secure stakeholders' buy-ins.

1. **Prioritize High ROI, Low Complexity Projects**

   The best spot to concentrate initial adoption efforts is in activities that

   - Are currently paper-based, repetitive, or manual

   - Have well-defined stakeholders and business owners

   - Require minimal backend integration

   - Support large numbers of users or departments

   Examples

   - Permit and license requests

   - Field inspection checklists

   - Budget approval processes

   - IT service requests or tickets

   - Internal HR portals (e.g., onboarding, leave management)

   Quick Win: A municipality developed a Power App to manage lost-and-found items, replacing a shared spreadsheet with automated tracking and reporting.

2. **Map Use Cases to Citizen Services and Internal Operations**

   Use cases can be broadly categorized into

   Citizen-Facing

   - Complaint submissions

   - Benefit eligibility checkers

- Application status trackers

- Digital service requests

Internal Operations

- Document routing and approvals

- Compliance reporting

- Case assignment and escalation

- Asset inventory and lifecycle tracking

3. **Implement a Prioritization Framework**

   Use an **Impact vs. Effort** Matrix to objectively analyze and prioritize potential use cases. This prevents agencies from chasing shiny objects that are difficult to deliver or losing sight of fundamental improvements with measurable benefits.

   Axes Described

   - **Impact:** Citizen satisfaction, cost savings, time savings, service improvement

   - **Effort:** Development time, data availability, integration difficulty, regulatory burden

Figure 3-2. *Use Case Prioritization Framework Axis*

3.3 Governance Model

As government agencies scale low-code adoption, a strong model of governance is crucial. Governance ensures security, compliance, quality, and sustainability without impeding innovation.

1. **Environment Strategy: Dev, QA, Prod**

   A good environment strategy keeps development, testing, and production loads segregated in order to reduce risks and facilitate controlled releases.

   Best Practices

   - Create independent environments: Development, Quality Assurance (QA), and Production.

   - Use Power Platform Pipelines or Azure DevOps to deploy the solution.

   - Use environment variables to manage API key, endpoint, and secret.

2. **Solution Ownership: IT vs. Business**

Define who owns what:

- **IT Teams** will own security, integration, and life cycle.

- **Business Units** may own and support some apps and flows with the right governance.

- Use **Dataverse teams** and **security roles** for access and responsibilities.

Example: The leave approval app is managed by an HR team, and IT owns Dataverse schema, connectors, and governance policies.

3. **Application Life Cycle Management (ALM)**

Adopt a formal ALM process using

- Managed solutions for production

- Source control for versioning and rollback

- Automated testing and approval workflows

- Change tracking and rollback plan

4. **Center of Excellence (CoE) Considerations**

A Center of Excellence (CoE) provides standardized tools, templates, policies, and support. It facilitates adoption without compromising on control.

Core Components

- **App catalog** for reusable parts

- **Governance dashboards** (e.g., quantity of apps, flows, makers)

- **Citizen developer support** and training paths

- **DLP policies** for connector control

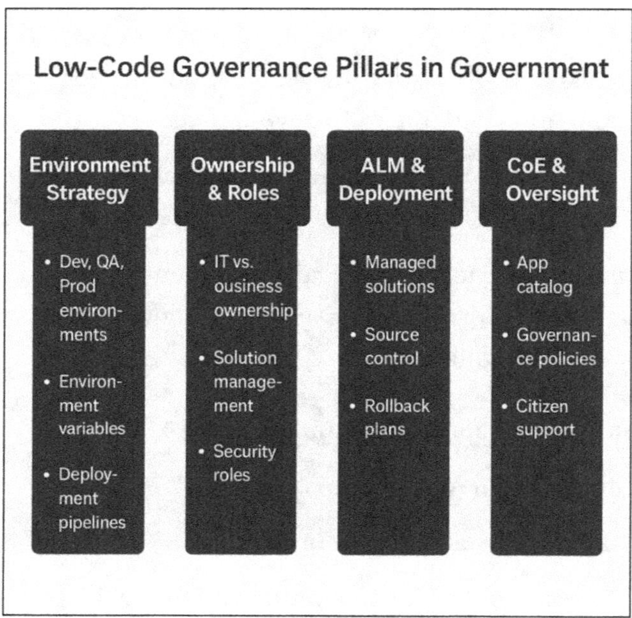

Figure 3-3. *Governance Pillars in Government*

3.4 Budgeting and ROI Planning

A considered low-code strategy is accompanied by good financial management. Budgeting involves more than the licensing cost of the platform—there's training, support, governance, and innovation to keep going on. At the same time, ROI monitoring will serve to justify expansion and future investment.

1. **Be Aware of the Cost Structure**

    Licensing

    - The cost structure for Microsoft Power Platform licensing depends on user types, apps, and capacity.

    - Government-specific plans (e.g., GSA pricing, nonprofits discounts) might be included.

    Infrastructure

    - Costs of environment provisioning, Azure capacity, Dataverse storage, and premium connectors.

    - Scaling might require additional optional tools like Azure API Management or Power BI Premium.

    Support and Training

    - Charge onboarding costs, workshops, certifications (e.g., PL-900), and internal documentation.

    - Include CoE setup costs, e.g., tooling, templates, and DLP policy enforcement.

2. **Estimate Time and Cost Savings**

    Low-code projects will typically reduce

    - Manual processing and data entry hours

    - Developer burden on custom applications

    - Inefficiencies in operations and turnaround time

Sample Metrics

- Time saved per process (e.g., saved form processing time from 2 hours to 15 minutes)

- Reclaimed staff hours translated into higher-value work

- Development cost savings vs. cost savings through outsourcing

3. **Create ROI Models**

   Create ROI projections based on

   - Cost of initial development vs. annual savings

   - Manual processing cost vs. cost of automation

   - Errors eliminated, resulting in lower compliance risk

   Example: A finance team builds a Power Automate flow to automate approval of invoices, removing 2 FTEs' worth of manual effort per year—$180K yearly in savings.

4. **Alignment with Strategic Result**

   Link ROI to measurable government goals:

   - More citizen satisfaction

   - Increased application throughput

   - Backlog or processing delay reduced

   - Better transparency and reporting

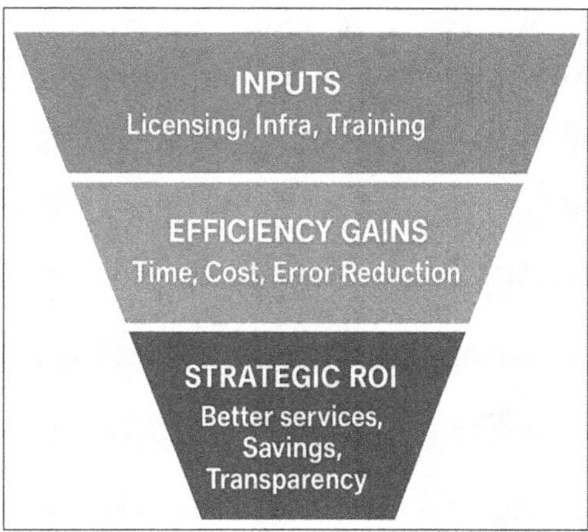

Figure 3-4. *ROI Planning Framework*

3.5 Compliance and Accessibility

Government agencies need to meet high levels of accessibility, security, and data handling. Any low-code solution will have to comply with regulatory and legislative regulations and also maintain inclusiveness and trust.

1. **Accessibility Standards**

   Ensuring all citizens, including disabled citizens, have the ability to use digital services is not only best practice but it's a legislation.

   Key Guidelines

   - WCAG 2.1 (Web Content Accessibility Guidelines) for visual, cognitive, and motor impairment

   - Section 508 (United States) requires that the federal digital content must be made available to individuals with disabilities

- Use **screen-reader-friendly labels**, keyboard navigation, and high-contrast color schemes

- **Power Pages** and **Power Apps** keyboard navigation and high contrast color schemes

---

Tool Tip   Run Microsoft's Accessibility Checker and Power Apps Accessibility Guide.

---

2. **Data Privacy and Residency**

Governments ought to manage where and how data will be stored, especially when dealing with sensitive or personal data.

Key Considerations

- **Data Residency:** Store within required geographic locations (e.g., US Government cloud, EU data centers).

- **Encryption:** Require encryption at rest and in transit with Azure Security Center.

- **Retention Policies:** Enforce policies for archiving, purging, and life cycle management.

- **Role-Based Access Control (RBAC):** Enforce least-privilege access via Dataverse roles and Azure AD groups.

3. **Regulatory Compliance**

Common Frameworks

- **NIST** (US security standards)

- **FedRAMP** for US federal cloud deployments

- **HIPAA** for health data

- **GDPR** for personal data protection (EU)

Power Platform complies with numerous frameworks, such as

- Microsoft's Government Cloud (GCC, GCC High)

- Azure compliance programs

Note   Use Microsoft Compliance Manager to assess and manage regulatory obligations.

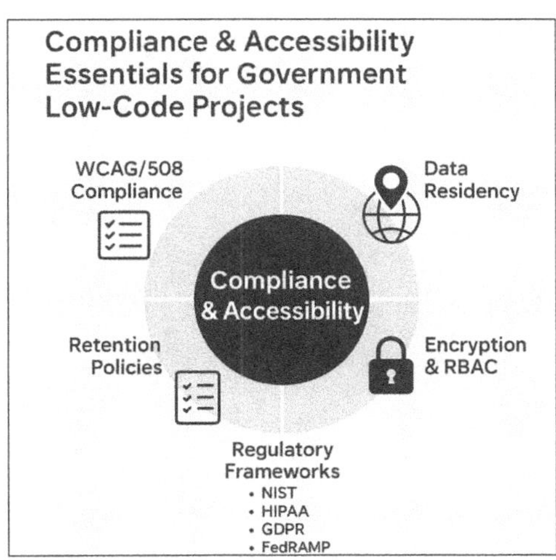

Figure 3-5. *Compliance and Accessibility Requirement*

CHAPTER 4

Building End-to-End Solutions

4.1 Solution Architecture Patterns

Building Power Platform-based secure, scalable, and sustainable government solutions involves having an architecture well thought out. Depending on the level of complexity of a solution and whether integration is required, a number of architecture patterns may be employed as needed to satisfy agency needs.

1. **Microservices Model with Dataverse at the Core**

   This pattern treats every solution as a collection of configurable services with Dataverse as the data central repository.

   Benefits of This Pattern

   - Clean separation of concerns (e.g., permit management vs. inspection vs. reporting)

   - Independent app and flow deployment and scalability

   - Central data auditing and data governance

© Sarat Piridi 2025

S. Piridi, *GovOps with Microsoft Power Platform and Copilot*, Inside Copilot,
https://doi.org/10.1007/979-8-8688-1796-0_4

Sample Use Case

- A department develops standalone apps for

- Citizen permit submission (Canvas App)

- Staff approvals (Model-Driven App)

- Inspection scheduling (Power Automate) Same Dataverse schema used by all apps

2. **Hybrid Integrations with Azure Services**

Power Platform can reach pro-code services through **Azure Functions, Logic Apps**, and **API Management**. This offers

- Custom business logic executed

- Integration with non-connector systems

- Data transformation or enrichment

Example: Azure Function verifies contractor licenses via third-party API prior to Power Apps consuming submission.

3. **Custom Connectors and API Gateways**

When there is no native connector, **custom connectors** enable you to invoke REST APIs securely in Power Apps or Power Automate.

Best Practices

- Secure APIs via API keys or OAuth 2.0

- Throttle or cache remote API calls.

- Centralize and monitor with Azure API Management.

4. **Event-Driven Patterns**

Invoke actions based on events using **Power Automate, Azure Event Grid**, or **Service Bus** (e.g., application submitted, inspection scheduled).

Advantages

- Response in real time

- Loosely coupled

- Better performance when loaded

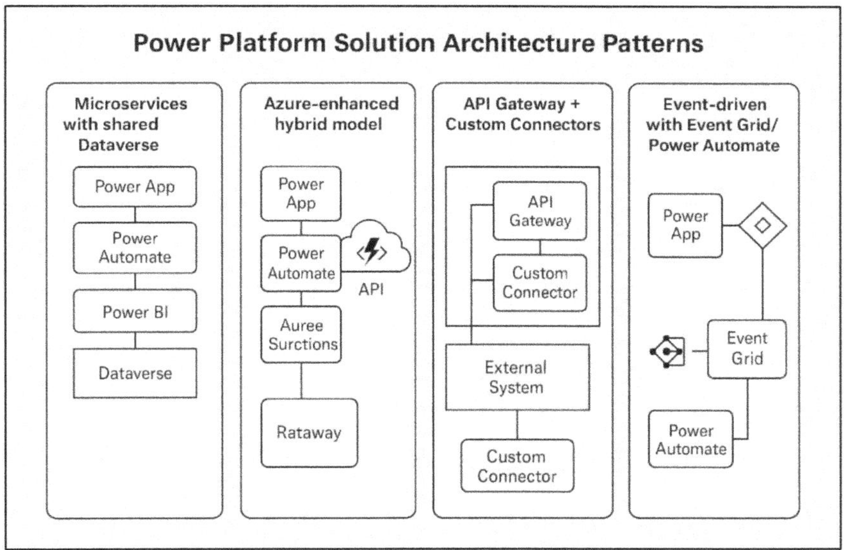

Figure 4-1. *Power Platform Solution Architecture Platform*

4.2 Agency Building Using Power Apps

Power Apps empowers agencies to develop responsive, secure, and accessible apps that conform to government workflows. Canvas Apps or Model-Driven Apps are leveraged by the platform for handling internal users, field agents, and citizen interactions with agility and velocity.

1. **Role-Based Navigation and UI**

   Build apps that customize the experience for different roles of users.

   Methods

   - Leverage Power Fx logic to display/hide screens and components.

   - Use Dataverse roles and Azure AD groups to manage the visibility.

   - Offer customized dashboards for every user type (e.g., Clerk, Supervisor, Field Inspector).

   Example: A field inspector logs in to the app and only views assigned cases and nearby appointments.

2. **Responsive UI for Field Agents**

   Field agents are likely working on different screen sizes and network conditions. Apps must fit nicely.

   Key Features

   - **Flexible layout containers** for adaptive design

   - GPS and camera functionality for photos and location

   - Quick capture of data through touch interfaces

   Case: An inspector takes code infractions with a tablet and imports them directly into the inspection report.

3. **Offline Functionality**

   Power Apps supports **offline mode** through **local collections** and **LoadData/SaveData** support. This is required for use in low-connectivity areas.

   Use Case

   - Site inspectors go to sites, record notes/pictures offline, and sync to Dataverse when online.

Tip   Test heavy test offline scenarios and include sync status indicators.

---

4. **Performance and Accessibility**

   - Optimize formulas and minimize delegation issues.

   - Paginate huge datasets or use gallery filters.

   - Comply with accessibility guidelines (high contrast, screen readers, logical order tabs).

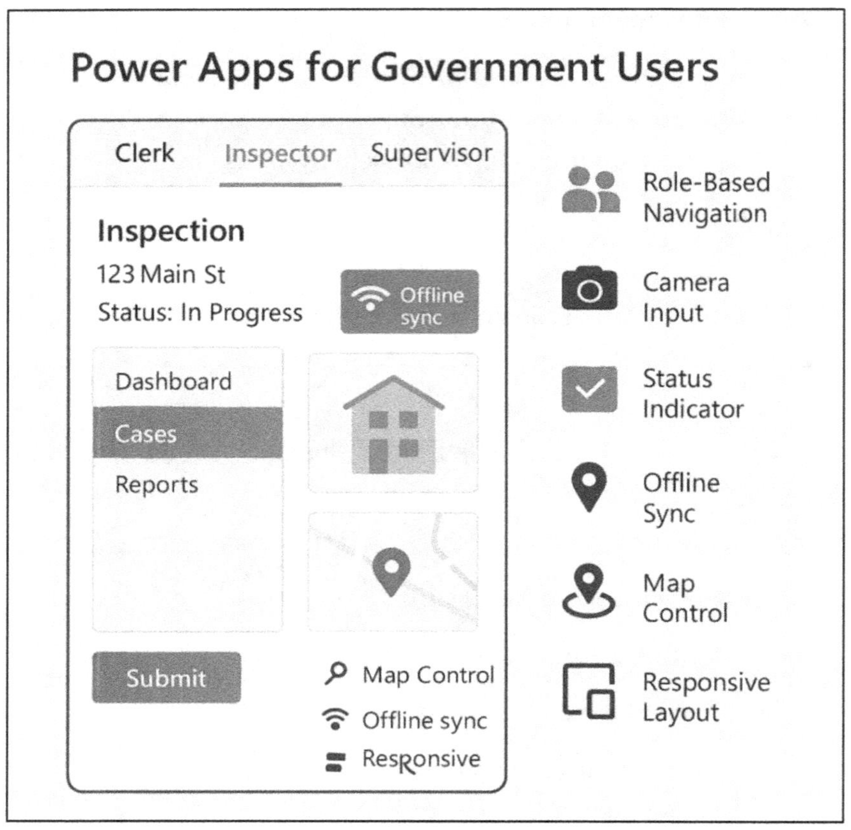

Figure 4-2. Power Apps for Government Users

4.3 Power Automate Automation

Power Automate facilitates agencies to automate menial tasks, minimize human error, and consolidate disparate systems—streamlining service delivery without compromising control or compliance.

1. **Sequential and Parallel Flows**

   Sequential Flows

   - Steps are carried out one after the other.

   - Best applied to automate workflows, process documents, or work orders.

   Parallel Flows

   - Perform multiple actions at the same time.

   - It is a good practice to warn multiple teams, trigger simultaneous reviews, or warn multiple systems.

   Example: Receipt of a citizen complaint initiates a concurrent flow to notify the local office, update the central CRM, and respond with an acknowledgment to the citizen.

2. **Retry Policies and Error Handling**

   Government workflows have to be fault-tolerant.

   Techniques

   - Support retry policies on connectors for transient faults.

   - Utilize scope blocks with run after to manage errors tailored by users.

   - Notify support teams or users via email/Teams in case of fail.

Tip   Log all failed runs to a Dataverse table for single-pane-of-glass monitoring.

---

3. **Auditing and Tracking**

   Have an end-to-end audit trail for compliance and transparency.

   Best Practices

   - Log-dated key events (e.g., request received, approval approved).

   - Use **Power BI dashboards** to monitor usage and exceptions.

   - Save important outputs and decisions to Dataverse for reporting.

4. **Reusability and Optimization of Flows**

   - Distribute large flows into reusable **child flows**.

   - Use **solution-aware flows** to improve ALM.

   - Prevent redundant API calls and take advantage of **trigger conditions**.

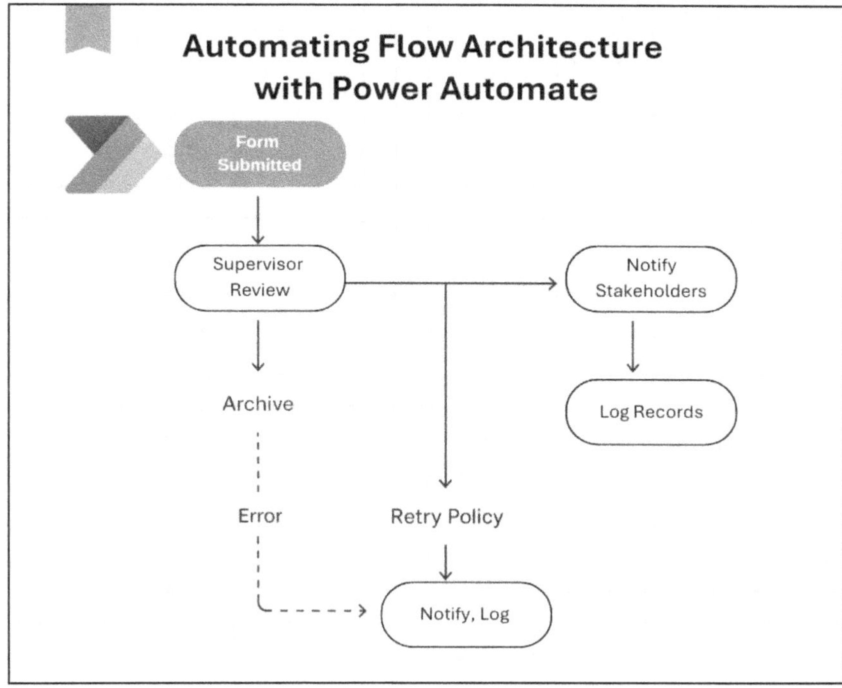

Figure 4-3. *Power Automate for Flow Architecture*

4.4 Power BI Visualization

Power BI allows government agencies to monetize operational, financial, and citizen data in interactive dashboards and reports to support informed decision-making and transparency.

1. **Taking Advantage of Bookmarks and Drill-Through**

   Bookmarks and drill-through pages are more interactive and user-friendly on dashboards.

Bookmarks

- Save individual views or filters of a report.

- Create guided stories or "report tours" for managers.

- Enable switching between filtered and all data views.

Drill-Through

- Enable clicking on a data point to display a detailed page.

- Use case: Click a district on a map to view detailed case reports or appropriations.

Tip   Combine slicers and bookmarks for dynamic navigation.

---

2. **Paginated Reports for Compliance**

    Some reports require a consistent, print-ready format to audit or submit officially. Power BI Paginated Reports (reporting on behalf of **Report Builder**) are particularly suited for

- Legislative reporting

- Justification reports about the budget

- Citizen feedback digest

- PDFs in export-friendly format with page numbers, footers, and headers

3. **KPI Dashboards**

   Track against agency goals using Key Performance Indicators (KPIs) like

   - Permit processing time

   - Budget spend compared to allocation

   - Service-level agreement (SLA) compliance

   - Citizen satisfaction scores

   Example: A transit agency monitors county-to-county project completion timelines using KPIs.

4. **Embed and Share**

   - Embed into **Power Apps, Power Pages,** or **Microsoft Teams**.

   - Use **row-level security (RLS)** to see data by role only.

   - Schedule refreshing of reports to real-time or daily status.

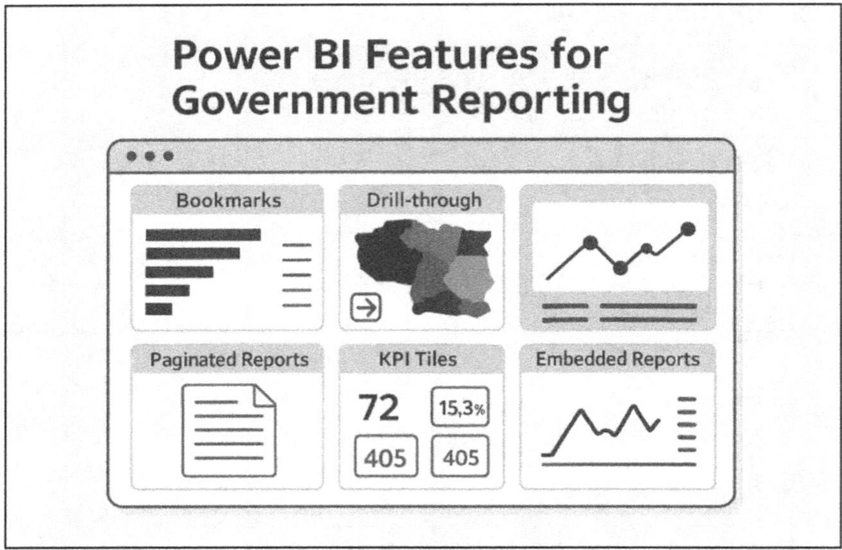

Figure 4-4. Power BI Features

4.5 Secure Portals with Power Pages

Power Pages provides government ministries the ability to build secure, accessible, and informative websites for consumption by citizens as well as staff members. Power Pages enables services such as permits, license applications, and complaints to be computerized without compromising user responsibility and data confidentiality.

1. **Web Roles and Permissions**

   Control users access using a combination of

   - **Web Roles** in Power Pages

   - **Microsoft Entra ID for internal users** and **Microsoft Entra External ID** for citizen or partner access (formerly known as **Azure AD B2C/B2B**).

   - Human **dataverse security roles** with column-, form-, and table-level, fine-grained access

Example: Citizens can view submitted requests, and employees can view and modify all pending requests.

2. **Integrating Forms and Views**

   Portals can present interactive content straight from Dataverse:

   - **Basic Forms:** Send data (e.g., requests, complaints)

   - **Advanced Forms:** Multistep business workflows (e.g., grant requests)

   - **Lists/Views:** Present data filtered by status or user (e.g., application status, inspection results)

3. **CMS-Style Content Management**

   Utilize **the Design Studio** or **VS Code integration** to control portal content:

   - Pages, navigation, header/footer structure

   - Content snippets, reusable pieces

   - Styling with Bootstrap and custom CSS

4. **Automation and Integrations**

   - Run flows on form submission with Power Automate.

   - Use external API integrations with JavaScript and custom connectors.

   - Embed Power BI reports for citizen-facing transparency.

Use Case: A housing portal enables applicants to verify eligibility, apply for aid, and monitor approval status with real-time notification.

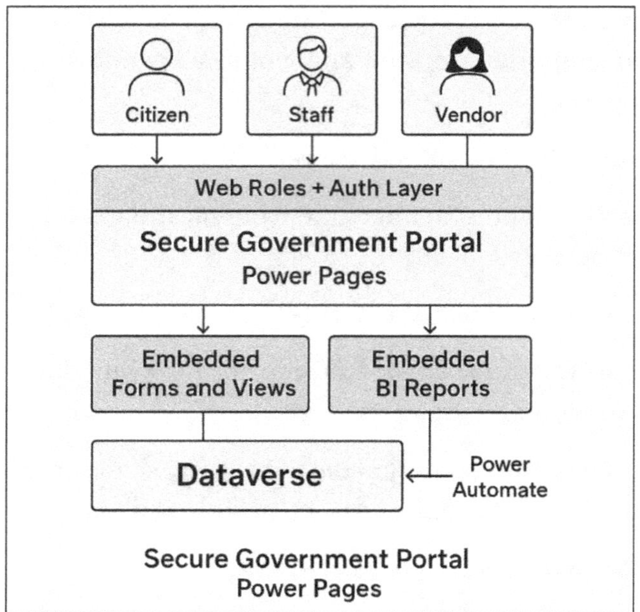

Figure 4-5. *Power Pages for Secure Government Portal*

4.6 Dataverse Best Practices

Dataverse is the data backbone of Power Platform solutions. Adhering to best practices keeps your government apps responsive, secure, and manageable—particularly when dealing with complex workflows and sensitive information.

1. **Naming Conventions**

   Utilize consistent, readable names for

   - **Tables:** Plural nouns (e.g., "Permits," "Inspections")

   - **Columns:** Lowercase with underscores or PascalCase (e.g., permit type, approval_status)

   - **Relationships:** Name lookup fields explicitly (e.g., citizen_id instead of simply contact)

Tip   Prefix custom columns and tables with department or agency codes (*hr_leave_request, for example*).

---

2. **Types of Column Data and Optimization**

   Use suitable column types:

   - Use **Choice fields** for fixed fields

   - **Lookup fields** for relationships

   - Shun image or large text columns unless essential

   - **Calculated** and **rollup columns** rather than workflows if appropriate

   - **Performance Tip**

   - Utilize **Views and FetchXML filter**s for large-volume sets

   - Index heavily used columns (status, region, etc.)

3. **Business Process Flows (BPFs)**

   Utilize BPFs to direct users through multiple-step processes like

   - Complaint intake

   - Permit approval

   - Inspection cycles

   Example: A license application has a BPF with the following steps: "Submitted ➤ Under Review ➤ Approved/Rejected."

4. **Security and Audit Settings**

- Implement **row-level and field-level security** to secure confidential data.

- Implement **auditing** on mission-critical tables and columns (financial, private data).

- Map **Azure AD groups to Dataverse teams** for highly scalable access management.

5. **Solution Structuring**

- Use **unmanaged solutions** in Dev and **managed solutions** in QA/Prod.

- Organize by domain: e.g., HR Solutions, Public Safety Apps.

- Group app flow, tables, and dashboards into modular, reusable packages.

Figure 4-6. *Dataverse Best Practices*

CHAPTER 5

Integrating AI and Copilot

5.1 What Is AI Builder?

AI Builder is the no-code artificial intelligence engine of Microsoft Power Platform. AI Builder allows government agencies to implement artificial intelligence into their workflows and apps without having to rely on an internal data science team. AI Builder enables users to automate document processing, forecast outcomes, identify sentiment, and classify data—all by making easy-to-make models.

Core Components of AI Builder

1. **Prebuilt Models**

   - Pre-trained models with matching standard government requirements:

     o **Document Processing:** Reads permit, applications, or claims forms to text

     o **Sentiment Analysis:** Reads public comment reply or survey

© Sarat Piridi 2025
S. Piridi, *GovOps with Microsoft Power Platform and Copilot*, Inside Copilot,
https://doi.org/10.1007/979-8-8688-1796-0_5

- o **Category Classification:** Routes complaint or service request to the relevant department

- o **Object Detection:** Detects physical objects (e.g., road signs, building equipment)

Use Case: Auto-fill Dataverse with form processing to read hand-written disaster relief forms.

2. **Custom Models**

- Trained on your agency's data to address particular problems.

    - o **Prediction Models:** Automatically predict resource demand, case backlogs, or application chances of approval.

    - o **Text Classification Models:** Automatically tag case priority levels or legal tags.

Example: An agency of public safety allows it to predict which reported incidents need escalation.

3. **Integration**

- Automatically connect with Power Apps for real-time forecast or pre-filled fields.

- Trigger power automation (e.g., direct flagged responses to managers).

- Present model results in Power BI.

Licensing and Capacity Management

AI Builder takes the credit-based approach, with capacity reserved per tenant.

Key Notes

- Various models have varying credit charges.

- AI capacity can be shared and combined across environments.

- Use watch via Power Platform Admin Center.

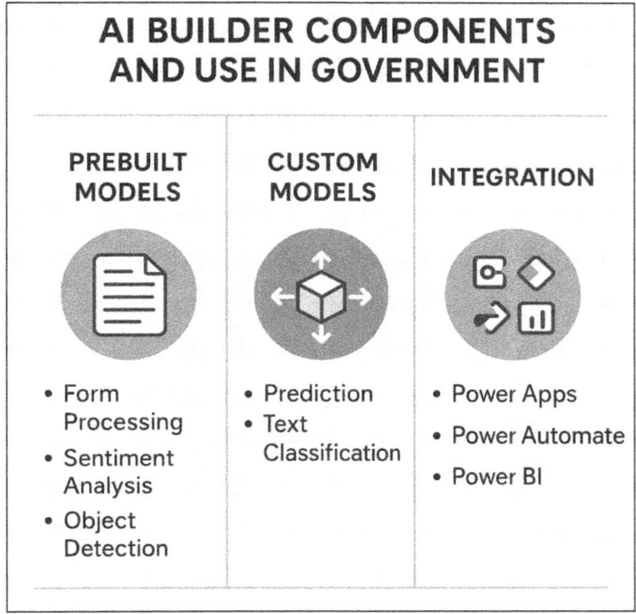

Figure 5-1. *AI Builder Use Case in Government*

5.2 Use Case Deep Dive

AI Builder works much better when applied to real government use cases. It is a comprehensive, industry-focused use case wherein pre-trained and customized AI models can be employed in order to automate, make it efficient, and gain insights.

1. **Legal and Contracts Document Understanding Challenge**

   Government institutions handle thousands of legal documents, contracts, and laws—scanned or otherwise for the majority.

   Solution

   - Use Form Processing to extract vendor names, dates, and contract terms.

   - Use Custom Document Models to categorize clauses (e.g., termination, indemnity).

   - Use Power Automate to route incomplete or marked-up contracts to legal subject-matter experts for approval.

   Example: 500 monthly contractor contracts handled by a municipal purchasing department—AI Builder reduces 60% of the processing labor.

2. **Routing of Help Desk and Citizen Requests with AI**

   Problem

   Manual sorting of tickets is time-consuming, unpredictable, and error-prone.

   Solution

   - Apply Text Classification to classify the text of incoming requests.

   - Automatically assign category and priority (e.g., "Technical Issue," "Account Locked").

   - Routing with Power Automate to impacted teams.

Case Study: An education ministry employs AI Builder to automatically classify 2,000+ IT help desk tickets monthly at a confidence rate of more than 90%.

3. **Public Comment Sentiment Analysis**

Challenge

Citizen feedback and public sentiment are unstructured and subjective.

Solution

- Execute Sentiment Analysis to measure tone (positive, neutral, negative).

- Graph shifts in public opinion over time or by the department in Power BI.

- Forward negative sentiment posts to managers for follow-up.

Example: A housing agency applies AI Builder to monitor complaints and reveal recurring frustration motifs by ZIP code.

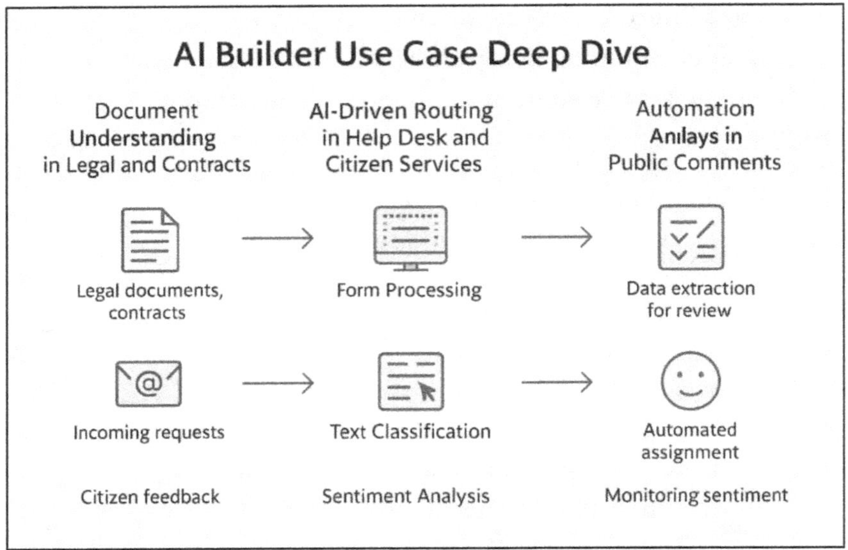

Figure 5-2. *AI Builder Use Case Deep Dive*

5.3 Copilot in Action

Copilot applies generative AI to bring natural language skills to Power Platform. Copilot allows government employees to define what they want to build, and Copilot constructs the code, logic, or report—time and technical barriers avoided.

1. **Writing Flows with Natural Language**

   Power Automate Copilot helps construct flows from simple text descriptions.

   Example Prompts

   - "Send an alert to the applicant on Teams when a new permit is approved in Dataverse."

   - "Send a due tickets summary to the department head on Mondays."

Copilot automatically offers suggestions for triggers, actions, and phrases.

2. **Power BI Summarization**

Copilot in Power BI can

- Employ natural language dashboard summaries.

- Respond to questions like

- "Why did permit approvals in Q2 reduce?"

"Show the top-performing ZIP codes for last month's service requests."

- Provide suggestions based on the dataset.

3. **Power Apps enhancement**

Copilot helps

- Write Power Fx formulas from your intention

- Auto-complete field values or lookups

- Suggest a table schema and data sample

Use Case: A business analyst builds an app to resolve complaints within 30 minutes using Copilot's form design and logic suggestion.

4. **Prompt Engineering Tips**
Best Practices

- Plain, easy-English commands (e.g., "Create a table with columns Name, Address, and Status.").

- Use follow-ups to make it more precise ("Add a default value of Pending' to the Status column.").

- Experiment with phrasing for better results.

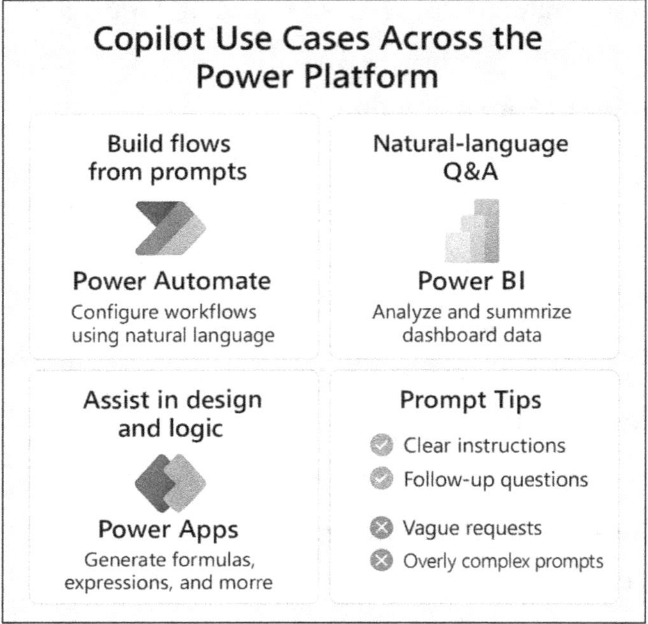

Figure 5-3. *Copilot in Action*

5.4 Training Custom Models

Custom AI Builder machine learning models allow agencies to apply machine learning to data and processes. It is particularly valuable where there isn't a pre-configured standard model available that fits perfectly into the working environment.

1. **Image Classification for Inspections**
   Utilize image classification to enable field officers and inspection crews to identify

   - Property violations

   - Equipment defects

   - Infrastructure damage (e.g., cracked roads, damaged signs)

Steps

- Import tagged images into AI Builder.

- Train the model to recognize special kinds.

- Make predictions to be used within a Power App for testing in the field.

Example: A public works organization applies image classification to tag potholes, broken signs, or litter infractions from pictures taken.

2. **Prediction for Resource Planning**
   Train predictive models against the history data to

   - Predict demand for service (e.g., emergency calls).

   - Predict the possibility of grant application approval.

   - Guesstimate case time of resolution by patterns.

   Steps

   - Choose a history dataset from Dataverse.

   - Choose the outcome field (e.g., "Approved" or "Escalated").

   - Train and validate the model on test data.

   - Publish output to apps or flows.

   Use Case: A relief agency employs prediction models for pre-staging assets in high-risk regions.

3. **Form Processing Model Setup**
   Extract valuable information from scanned paper or electronic forms (e.g., licenses, expense reports).

Steps

- Import test documents with labels (e.g., Amount, Date, Name).

- Train the model to recognize and pull out fields.

- Publish the output to Power Automate or Power Apps to process.

Tip   Use Form Processing for paper forms or scanned PDFs that aren't natively digital.

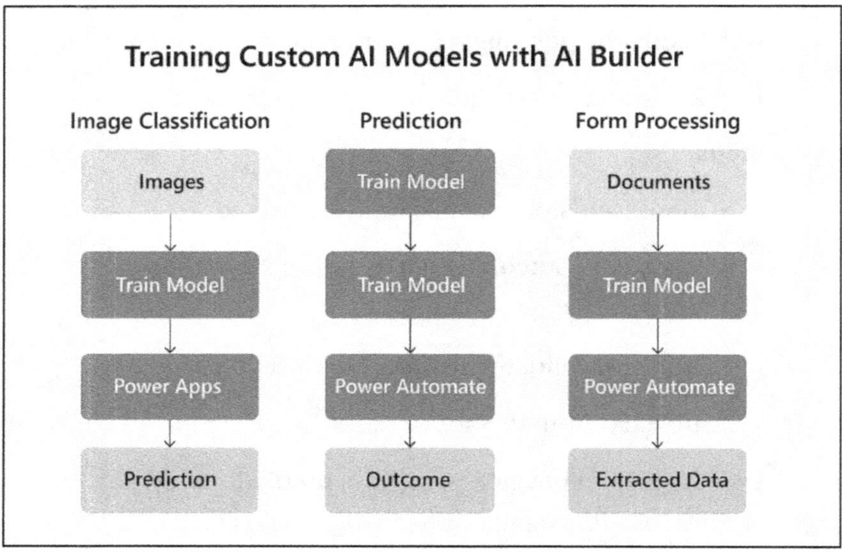

Figure 5-4. *Training Custom Models with AI Builder*

5.5 Responsible AI in Government

Since AI is increasingly being used in government business processes, it should be ensured that its use is ethical, transparent, and accountable. Public agencies must strike a balance between innovation and accountability, especially where the decisions affect citizens' lives, benefits, or rights.

1. **Ethics and Prevention of Bias**

   AI models may unintentionally inherit historic biases in training data.

   Best Practices

   - Regularly review training data for gaps in representation.

   - Use inclusive, diverse datasets.

   - Monitor biased outcomes by demographic subgroup.

   Example: A housing benefit model needs to be audited so that it will not unfairly favor specific ZIP codes or incomes.

2. **Explainability and Transparency**

   Government agencies must be capable of explaining why an AI model came to a specific decision.

   Methods

   - Employ model cards or abstracts to document

     o   Data sources

     o   Training procedures

     o   Levels of confidence

- Clearly state that AI is augmenting—not replacing—decision-making

---

Tip   Always have human-readable machine output audit logs.

---

3. **Human-in-the-Loop Designs**

   Have human validation for high-risk decisions:

   - AI classifies or scores a case ➤ A human validates the recommendation.

   - Ultimate approval rests with the authorized employee.

   This makes AI accountable and gives the people who trust AI services peace of mind.

4. **Regulatory Alignment**

   Adhere to international and national AI ethics standards:

   - US Executive Orders on AI and digital equity

   - EU AI Act principles (i.e., risk-based approach, human oversight)

   - Microsoft's Responsible AI Standard (for government cloud partners)

   Tool: Use Microsoft's Responsible AI Dashboard to measure and monitor model fairness, performance, and error rates.

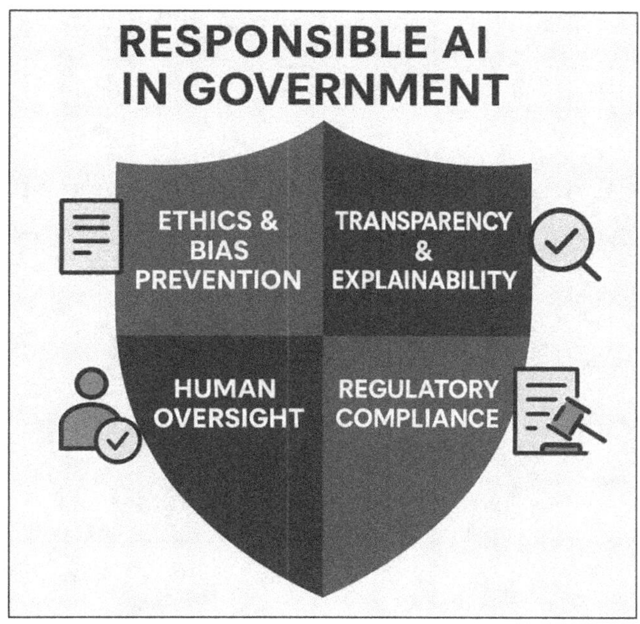

Figure 5-5. *Responsible AI*

CHAPTER 6

Deployment and Governance

6.1 ALM with Power Platform Pipelines

Application Life Cycle Management (ALM) requires low-code solutions to be written, tested, and released reproducibly, securely, and under control. Security and compliance, no less important in the governmental space as elsewhere, the protocols for solid ALM processes are imperative there.

Power Platform Pipelines are a **low-code-native Application Life Cycle Management (ALM) experience** that makes deployment to environments such as Dev, QA, and Production straightforward.

1. **Solution Packaging**

   Integrate all the elements (apps, flows, tables, dashboards, environment variables) into Power Platform solutions.

© Sarat Piridi 2025

S. Piridi, *GovOps with Microsoft Power Platform and Copilot*, Inside Copilot,

https://doi.org/10.1007/979-8-8688-1796-0_6

Best Practices

- Build using unmanaged solutions.

- Export as managed solutions for production and QA.

- Split big solutions into modular packages (e.g., "Permit Core," "Notification Logic").

2. **Deployment Pipelines**

Power Platform Pipelines deploy automatically with **click-based configuration**; no DevOps is needed.

Key Features

- Push solutions between environments with approval gates.

- Rollback broken deployments.

- Track deployment history for compliance.

Example: A public works team uses the latest inspection logic from Dev to QA and Production with testing checkpoints as part of the build.

3. **Automated Triggers and Integration**

Integrate with GitHub or Azure DevOps to automatically trigger deployments for

- A new version has been checked in

- Test coverage succeeded

- Approval is granted

This hybrid mix enables both pro-devs and low-code teams to collaborate effectively.

4. **Version Control and Rollback**

- Tag solution versions prior to every release.

- Utilize **restore points** to roll back in case of errors in Production.

- Maintain **release notes** for change control and audit trails.

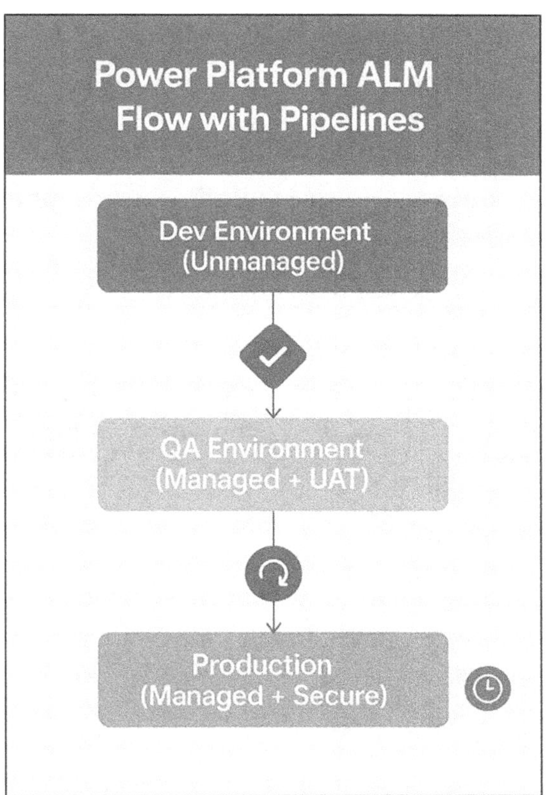

Figure 6-1. *Power Platform ALM Flow*

6.2 Environment Management

Good environment management provides stability, security, and scalability to Power Platform solutions—particularly in large government agencies with multiple teams and departments.

1. **Capacity Planning**

   - **Monitor and Manage**

   - **Dataverse storage** (database, file, and log)

   - **API call limits** per user/environment

   - **AI Builder credit consumption**

   Use the **Power Platform Admin Center** to monitor usage and get alerts.

Tip   Allocations should be capacity-based on criticality, for example, production first and then sandbox environments.

---

2. **Naming and Segregation**

   Global standard naming across environments makes it easy to track life cycle, train teams, and govern.

   Best Practices

   - Use prefixes (e.g., Gov-Dev, Gov-QA, Gov-Prod).

   - Separate environments by

     o **Life cycle stage** (Dev, QA, Prod)

- **Department/Business Unit** (e.g., Public Works, HR)

- **Solution domain** (e.g., Permit Systems, Financials)

Example: HR-LeaveMgmt-Dev, Finance-Grants-Prod

3. **Environment Variables and Secrets**

Don't embed URLs, IDs, or credentials into flows and apps.

Use

- **Environment Variables** to store dynamic values (API base URLs, email addresses, IDs)

- **Azure Key Vault or DLP-compliant storage** for sensitive secrets

- **Solution-aware flows** so that variables update automatically at deployment

---

Tip   Limit environment variables with limited permissions.

---

4. **Managed Environments**

For greater control, assign **Managed Environments** to

- Enable sophisticated governance features

- Initiate approval flows for sharing apps or adding connections

- Track usage, maker activity, and solution health

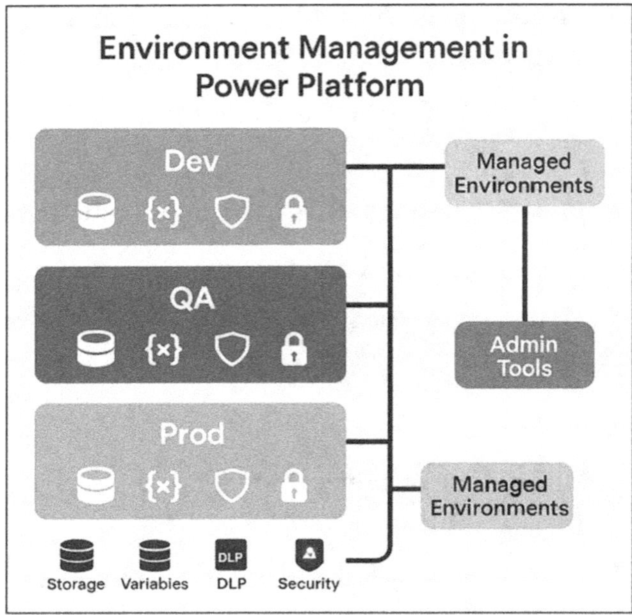

Figure 6-2. *Managing Environment in Power Platform*

6.3 Security

Security is a foundation block of government-level applications. Power Platform has several layers of protection—anything from identity access controls to encryption and policy enforcement—to safeguard sensitive data.

1. **Role-Based Access Control (RBAC)**

    RBAC gives users access to view data and functions that are associated with their role.

    Implementation

    - Establish **security roles** in Dataverse (e.g., Viewer, Editor, Admin).

- Assign roles to **Azure AD security groups**.

- Utilize **teams** for shared access (e.g., Housing Review Team).

  Example: A "Permit Clerk" can submit and update requests, whereas a "Supervisor" can approve or deny them.

2. **Field-Level and Record-Level Security**

   Limit access to certain fields or rows according to the user profile.

   Field-Level Security

   - Suppress sensitive fields (e.g., SSN, income) from unauthorized users.

   Record-Level Security

   - Employ owner-based or team-based sharing.

   - Employ row filters using Power Apps, Power BI, and Power Automate.

3. **Integration with Azure AD and Conditional Access**

   Deploy enterprise-class identity management with Microsoft Entra ID (formerly Azure AD).

   Security Features

   - Single sign-on (SSO)

   - Multifactor authentication (MFA)

   - Conditional access policies (e.g., block from unknown IPs or outside working hours)

4. **Data Loss Prevention (DLP)**

Stop unauthorized data transfer between services.

Best Practices

- Setup **DLP policies** by environment.

- Limit the use of high-risk connectors (e.g., Twitter, Dropbox).

- Monitor for misuse of connectors or shadow IT.

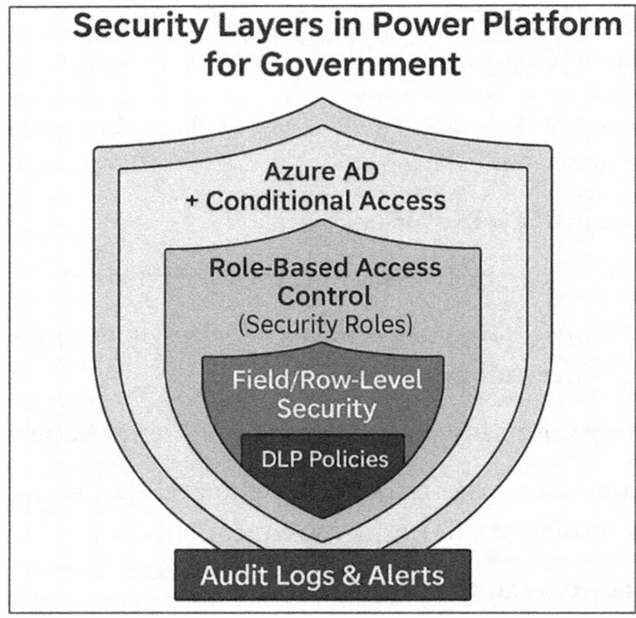

Figure 6-3. *Security Layers in Power Platform for Government*

6.4 Policies and Monitoring

Continuous management is critical to the success of compliant and secure low-code platforms. Microsoft Power Platform offers guardrails and monitoring capabilities for all environments, applications, flows, and connectors.

1. **Data Loss Prevention (DLP) Policies**

   DLP policies define which connectors are to be used together to avoid inadvertently or maliciously exposing data.

   Key Practices

   - Categorize connectors into **Business** and **Non-Business** types.

   - Block high-risk connectors such as Dropbox and Gmail in Production.

   - Enforce independent policies for Dev vs. Prod environments.

Tip   Use environment-level DLP policies for fine-grained control.

---

2. **Audit Log Analysis**

   Monitor platform activity to identify anomalies, confirm compliance, and react to incidents.

   Features

   - Turn on auditing in the Power Platform Admin Center.

- Export logs to Azure Monitor or SIEM tools for analysis.

- Monitor

  o App and flow creation

  o Sharing changes

  o Data export events

3. **Alerts and Anomaly Detection**

   Configure proactive notification to identify and act on risk.

   Examples

   - Alert when a new connector is being used.

   - Alert on large volumes of export data.

   - Highlight failing flows recursively.

   Enable **Power Automate** and **Microsoft Purview** to provide real-time alerts and policy compliance.

4. **Admin Dashboards and CoE Toolkit**

   Center of Excellence (CoE) Starter Kit delivers Power BI dashboards and platform-level tools for visibility.

   Includes

   - App and flow inventory

   - Reports on maker activity

   - Unused or orphaned resources

   - Connector usage breakdown

Tip Execute CoE reports on a weekly basis for IT governance teams to review.

Figure 6-4. *Monitoring Governance in Power Platform*

Facilitating Government Modernization Through Use Cases

Government agencies in the current digital age are increasingly pressured to deliver better services, become more transparent, and answer citizens' calls at once—all in a compliant condition with limited resources. Chapter 7 offers a carefully selected collection of **50 detailed use cases** illustrating how Microsoft Power Platform can assist agencies in modernizing, saving costs, and revolutionizing the citizen experience.

They cover **10 of the most important state departments**, from Health to Education, to Transportation, Emergency Services, Labor, and Human Services. Each use case is rolled out to address actual issues with low-code solutions—such as **Power Apps, Power Automate, Power Pages, Power BI, and Dataverse**—without depending on traditional software development schedules or sophisticated infrastructure redesigns.

© Sarat Piridi 2025

S. Piridi, *GovOps with Microsoft Power Platform and Copilot*, Inside Copilot, https://doi.org/10.1007/979-8-8688-1796-0_7

It is what makes these use cases so potent they're **modular, reusable architecture**. They are not experiments in thought. They are **practical blueprints** built out of actual implementation patterns existing in local, state, and federal agencies. Each use case contains

- **Who It Benefits**: Concise table of beneficiaries and how each stakeholder is being helped

- **Problem Statement and Modernization Drivers**: Directly speaking to inefficiencies, silos, and manual processes

- **Power Platform Architecture**: How Microsoft low-code solutions integrate into current systems to provide scalable solutions

- **End-to-End Workflow Diagrams**: Visual explanations of how each process functions

- **Performance Dashboards**: Power BI dashboards to monitor outcomes and measure success

Quantified Results: Crisp before-and-after impact statements with measurable results.

By embracing these patterns, IT leaders and government CIOs will be able to drive their own modernization projects, expedite digital transformation initiatives, and hasten innovation in their agencies. Whether you are building a new intake portal, automating workflows for emergency services, or developing case management dashboards, this chapter gives you a solid ground to build from.

Strategic Benefits of These Use Cases

These solutions in action will enable agencies to

☑ **Automate Manual Processes**: Replace paperwork with digital forms and flows.

☑ **Improve Cross-Agency Collaboration**: Modeling data to automation and standard referral.

☑ **Deliver Citizen-Centric Services**: Creating consumer-centric portals and dynamic status.

☑ **Achieve Faster Compliance**: Document combining, supporting audit trails, minimizing review cycles.

☑ **Drive Results with Data**: Leveraging dashboards for driving policy, risk reduction, and accountability maximization.

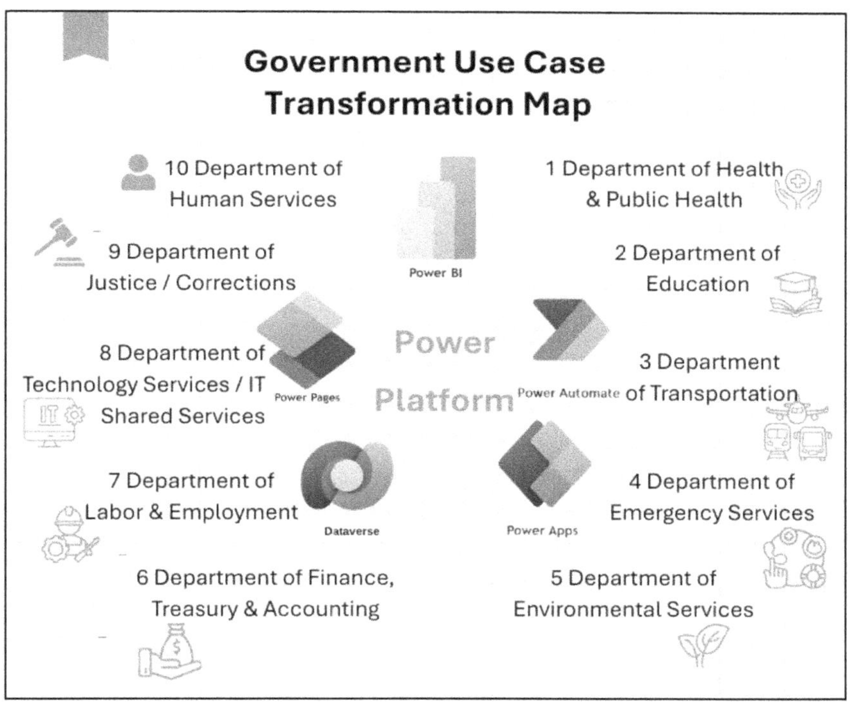

Figure 7-1. *Transformation Map for Government Use Cases*

7.1 Department of Health and Public Health

Use Case 1: Real-Time Reporting System and Disease Surveillance

Overview and Context

Public health agencies are usually the first line of defense in monitoring, responding to, and mitigating infectious disease pandemics. Be it flu, COVID-19, foodborne disease, or upsurge vector-borne diseases, the capability to gather, analyze, and respond to healthcare data in real time can transform public safety results.

However, most local and state health agencies still depend on outdated systems—manual Excel logs, email reports from laboratories, and delayed communication with clinics or hospitals. These reporting and response lags can lead to unchecked spread, inadequate preparation, and unaccountability.

This solution demonstrates an end-to-end **low-code Disease Surveillance System** on Microsoft Power Platform to transform the way health departments track, report, and act on public health threats.

Who It Benefits

Stakeholder	Benefit
Epidemiologists	Receive real-time outbreak trend dashboards, test positivity rates, and geographic clusters
Public Health Nurses and Field Agents	Utilize mobile-optimized Power Apps to track field visits, suspect cases, and vaccination campaigns
Clinics, Labs, and Hospitals	Report test results and alerts through secure portals, reducing dependence on fax and email
Agency Leadership and Policy Makers	Get visual response measures and severity of outbreak to better allocate resources
Citizens	Experience quicker interventions, alerts, and access to testing in times of health crises

Key Drivers for Modernization

- **Lagging Detection**: Excessive lag times in case identification with manual typing of lab tests and fax/email-based reporting.

- **Siloed Data**: Surveillance data resides in scattered systems without one point to analyze.

- **Lack of Real-Time Actionability**: Reports are typically received days after the closure of exposure windows.

- **No Mobile Accessibility**: Field workers are unable to log findings or suspected exposures in the field.

- **Compliance Risks**: Failing to meet CDC and state reporting deadlines on time, with auditability.

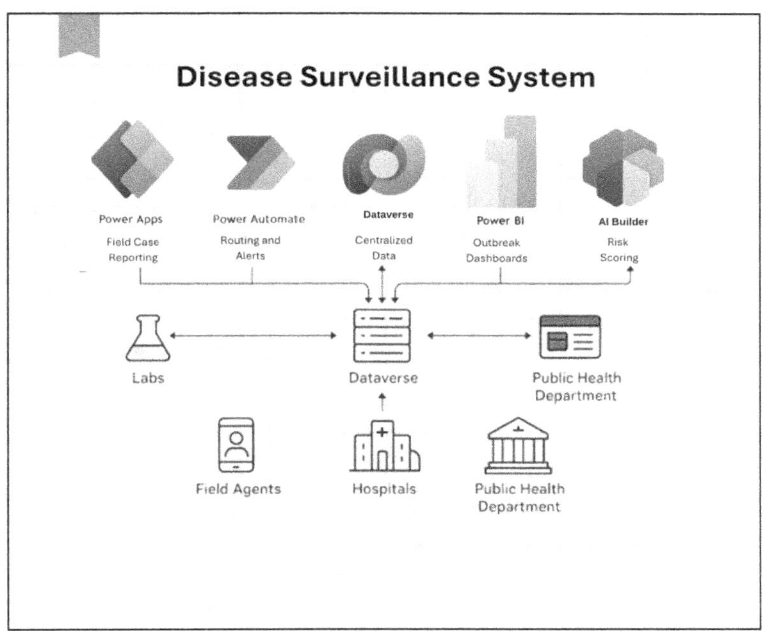

Figure 7-2. *Architecture Diagram—Disease Surveillance and Reporting System*

Technical Solution Architecture

Power Platform components are utilized in this solution to enable real-time public health dashboards, smart triage, and centralized reporting.

Component	Purpose
Power Apps (Canvas)	Used by field agents for reporting suspected/confirmed cases while on-site visits (schools, clinics, long-term care facilities)
Power Pages	Portal for secure submission of lab test results with attachments by hospitals, labs, and clinics
Dataverse	Core data platform storing case metadata, test results, exposure chains, patient demographics, and timestamps
Power Automate	Triggers workflows for exposure alert, regional health officer alert, triage queue, and SLA tracking
AI Builder	Performs risk scoring (e.g., likely superspreader event, exposure severity index) and recommends intervention urgency
Power BI	Geographic overlay visual dashboards, trend charts, test turnaround times, and real-time infection rate heatmaps

Workflow Overview

1. **Case Detection**

   - Lab reports result through the Power Pages portal.

   - The field agent reports a suspected case on Power Apps at the on-site visit.

2. **Validation and Routing**

- Power Automate verifies completeness and authenticates the source.

- Automatically directs to the proper local health office.

3. **Risk Scoring and Alerting**

- AI Builder analyzes patient attributes (age, location, setting).

- High-risk cases auto-trigger Teams or SMS alerts to supervisors.

4. **Contact Tracing and Monitoring**

- Dataverse related contacts.

- Follow-up activities created for outreach staff.

5. **Visualization and Response**

- Power BI heatmaps and outbreak charts are updated in real time.

- Management dashboards show resource needs and SLA metrics.

Dashboards and Reporting Views

- **Hotspot Heatmaps**: Reveal clusters of infection by counties.

- **Test Result SLA Tracker**: Display turnaround time by lab or clinic.

- **Age and Risk Distribution Charts**: Illustrate groups at risk.

- **Intervention Coverage KPIs**: Monitor cases with follow-up within 24 hours.

Use Case 2: Immunization Compliance and Outreach Platform

Overview and Context

State and local health departments are tasked with monitoring immunization compliance in schools, child care facilities, elder care facilities, and poor communities. Current vaccination records, exemption tracking, and notification outreach campaigns are essential to community immunity and outbreak prevention.

Unfortunately, too many jurisdictions are still using stand-alone databases, manual parent notifications, and limited reporting. This means incomplete records, late deadlines, and inadequate outreach—particularly in times of public health emergencies or back-to-school time.

This use case sets up an **Immunization Compliance and Outreach Platform** on the Microsoft Power Platform that streamlines immunization tracking, reminds parents, and facilitates proactive community outreach.

Who It Benefits

Stakeholder	Benefit
Public Health Immunization Officers	Central dashboard with rates of compliance by region, school, and age group
School Nurses and Admin Staff	Simple app to input student immunization records and check for compliance
Parents/Guardians	Personalized reminders for past-due vaccinations and upload new records via the portal
Field Outreach Teams	Utilize the mobile app to plan community events and track on-site vaccinations
Leadership	Track trends and gaps in coverage to plan resource deployment and campaign launches

Key Drivers for Modernization

- **Incomplete Data**: Manual entry and paper records cause compliance reporting errors.

- **Inefficient Reminders**: Telephone or mailer reminders—slow and usually ineffective.

- **Siloed Systems**: Immunization data is not communicated to clinics, field programs, or schools.

- **No Community Visibility**: The noncompliance zones cannot simply be seen by agencies.

- **Limited Campaign Management**: Follow-up and outreach are not quantified or coordinated.

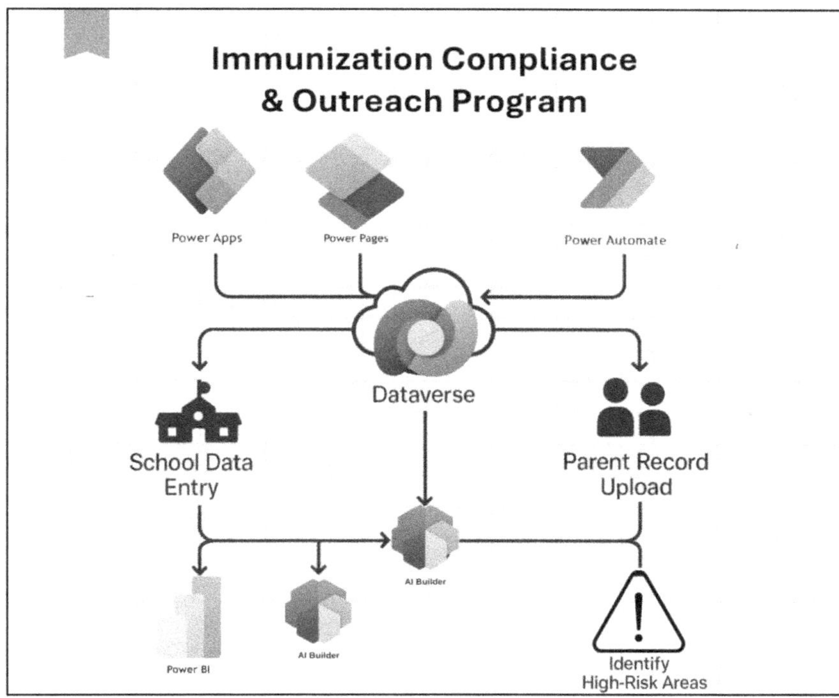

Figure 7-3. *Architecture Diagram—Immunization Compliance and Outreach*

Technical Solution Architecture

Component	Role
Power Apps (Canvas App)	Used by school nurses, field staff, and clinic personnel to log immunizations, file documents, and access student records
Power Pages	Secure parent portal to submit vaccination reports, download immunization schedules, and get status notices
Dataverse	Stores immunization data, exemption status, deadlines, school and student profiles, and community event logs
Power Automate	Automatic reminders (email/SMS) sent, outreach events scheduled, past due vaccinations tracked, and escalations sent
AI Builder	Examines trends in identifying high-risk groups and predicting trends of noncompliance
Power BI	Tracking compliance by region, school, age group, and exemption status in interactive dashboards

Workflow Overview

1. **Data Collection and Intake**

   - Immunization history is entered by school administrators or parents through Power Apps or Power Pages.

   - AI Builder processes documents and detects incomplete or expired records.

2. **Validation and Notification**

   - Power Automate sends reminders for missed vaccinations or pending exemptions to parents.

   - Triggers priority student school compliance officer notifications.

3. **Outreach Planning**

   - Areas of low compliance are identified by AI Builder.

   - Outreach coordinators plan vaccination drives through Power Apps calendar view.

4. **Field Event Execution**

   - Field teams use mobile apps to capture on-site vaccinations, ID scans, and sync with Dataverse.

5. **Reporting and Dashboards**

   - Power BI depicts coverage by counties, schools, and demographics.

   - Tracks campaign performance, missed deadlines, and follow-ups.

Dashboards and Reporting Views

- **School-Level Compliance Reports**: Highlight districts or schools falling short of thresholds.

- **Exemption Monitoring**: Illustrates distribution and medical/religious exemption types.

- **Outreach Effectiveness Metrics**: Event attendance, follow-up completion, time-to-compliance.

- **Demographic Breakdown**: Age-specific vaccination rates, ZIP code-specific vaccination rates, socioeconomic group-specific vaccination rates.

Results and Measurable Impact

Metric	Before	After
Compliance visibility across districts	Manual audit	Real time via dashboards
Reminder coverage	30–40%	90%+
Parent record submission rate	50% by deadline	85%+ within deadline
Outreach targeting accuracy	General	AI-driven precision by ZIP and risk score

- **Outcome**: Enhanced vaccination coverage, fewer school outbreaks, and better inter-departmental coordination

Use Case 3: Telehealth Service Scheduling and Compliance Tracking

Overview and Context

Telehealth is now a central platform for the delivery of healthcare services—particularly for rural communities, geriatric patients, and in public health crises. Yet, numerous government-funded telehealth initiatives are faced with disjointed scheduling, poor patient engagement, and difficulty in monitoring follow-up care adherence or documentation.

Agencies typically lack the ability to schedule appointments, automate reminders, track utilization, and report on outreach performance. Lost appointments, inefficient scheduling, and low rates of service use thus decrease the impact of these highly valuable programs.

This use case demonstrates a **Telehealth Scheduling and Compliance Platform** developed with Microsoft Power Platform for rethinking access to care, streamlining processes, and having accountability in telehealth delivery.

Who It Helps

Telehealth Coordinators	Manage bookings and monitor, manage time slots, and assign patients to clinicians
Patients	Arrange telemedicine appointments through web or mobile portal and send reminders or follow-ups automatically
Public Health Clinicians	Monitor case summaries and observe and impose adherence to beneficial apps
Program Managers	View real-time coverage rates and performance measures to inform the optimization of service coverage
Leadership	Analyzes geographic and demographic group reach, equity, and compliance

Key Drivers for Modernization

- **Manual Scheduling**: Schedules coordinated over email or phone, error- and overlap-filled.

- **Missed Visits**: No automated reminders result in no-shows and lost slots.

- **No Central Dashboard**: Providers' availability cannot easily be viewed or appointment frequency.

- **Compliance Risk**: No charts, incomplete follow-up charts, and lack of treatment outcomes.

- **Limited Analytics**: No data is available on areas that have underserved populations or patients.

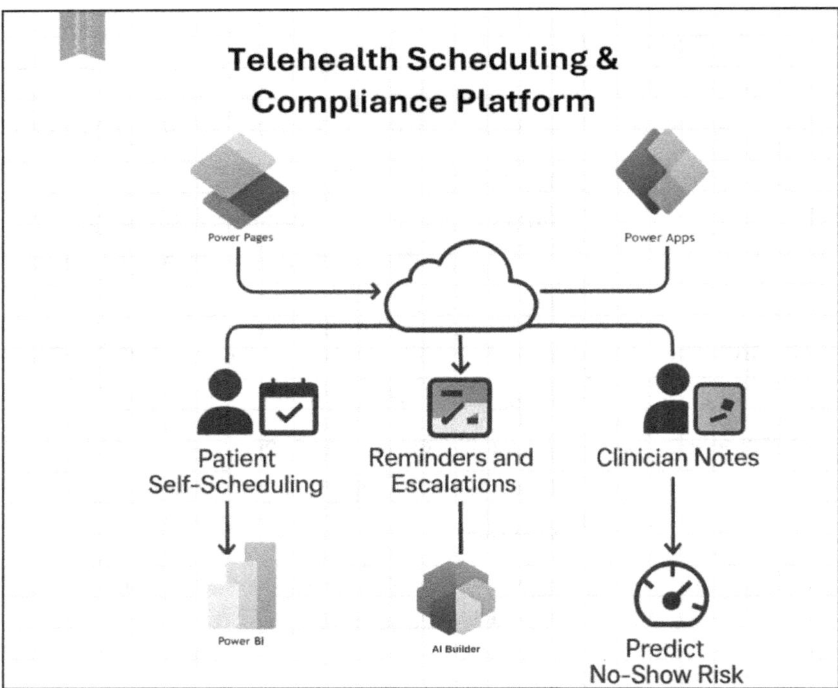

Figure 7-4. *Architecture Diagram—Telehealth Scheduling and Tracking*

Technical Solution Architecture

Component	Role
Power Pages	Patient-facing portal for scheduling telehealth visits, selecting available time slots, and submitting intake forms
Power Apps (Model-Driven App)	Used by health staff and providers to manage appointment queues, access patient history, and log consultations
Dataverse	Stores appointment data, patient profiles, provider availability, visit outcomes, and consent forms
Power Automate	Sends automated reminders, escalates no-shows, and logs feedback surveys post-visit
AI Builder	Predicts high-risk no-show patients based on history, demographics, and time of day
Power BI	Dashboards for program reach, appointment trends, wait time averages, and compliance by region

Workflow Overview

1. **Patient Schedules Visit**

   - Uses Power Pages to select time slots and submit pre-visit info.

   - The consent form is digitally signed and archived in Dataverse.

2. **Reminder and Confirmation**

- Power Automate provides email/SMS reminders 24 hours prior to the visit.

- Follow-up reminders are sent if not confirmed.

3. **Visit Execution**

- Provider logs into Power Apps, looks at scheduled cases, opens patient profile, and takes notes during/after session.

4. **Post-visit Follow-Up**

- AI Builder marks patients who need extra follow-up or behavioral health referrals.

- Surveys and resource links auto-sent through Power Automate.

5. **Dashboards and Oversight**

- Power BI reports provider utilization, no-shows, outcome monitoring, and equity coverage (rural/ urban, age, income).

Dashboards and Reporting Views

- **Appointment Completion Rate**: Reports no-show numbers and trends.

- **Utilization by Provider**: Tracks how many patients each provider sees.

- **Demographic Outreach**: Equity dashboard illustrating telehealth access by ZIP, race, and language.

- **Compliance Charts**: Display completion of follow-up visits and no-show case flags.

Results and Measurable Impact

Metric	Before	After
No-show rate	28%	< 8%
Appointment scheduling time	2–3 days by phone	< 5 minutes self-service
Collection of patient feedback	~10%	70%+ post-visit
Tracking equity	Manual audits	Real time through the dashboard

- **Outcome**: Greater reach, fewer no-shows, and improved care continuity—most notably for underserved patients

Use Case 4: Mobile Field Health Inspections and Licensing Tracker

Overview and Context

Public health inspectors have a vital role in ensuring that hospitals, nursing homes, restaurants, and public facilities are at health standards. These inspections include comprehensive checklists, documentation, license verification, photo evidence, and follow-up inspections.

Historically, inspection has been done either on paper or on old systems with no offline, no single record, and no tardy. Feedback to business owners. Not only does this put an administrative burden, but it also restricts transparency and holds back enforcement compliance.

It is here that the need for a Microsoft Power Platform-based **Mobile Field Inspection and Licensing Tracker** becomes important in automating compliance tracking, digitizing inspections, and providing real-time visibility to inspectors and agency management.

Who It Helps

Stakeholder	Benefit
Health Inspectors	Use a field mobile app to record infractions, send images, and synchronize with the central records even without internet connectivity
Licensing Officers	Monitor renewal status, view reports, and approve/revoke licenses
Business Owners	Receive mailed automated renewal notices, view reports, and infraction updates via email or portal
Compliance Managers	View the history of violations, frequency of inspections, and audit trails for all facilities
Public	Benefit through the optional publication of inspection grade or admonishment on Power Pages

Modernization Drivers

- **Paper-Based Field Notes**: Data is typed manually after site visits.

- **Slow License Updates**: Late issuance or revocation of licenses because of system out-of-sync.

- **No Offline Access**: Inspectors have to work harder, keying in data where internet connections are weak.

- **Disjointed Photos and Notes**: Data kept in emails, phones, or paper folders with no central linkage.

- **Limited Transparency**: No public dashboard or single platform to follow inspection history.

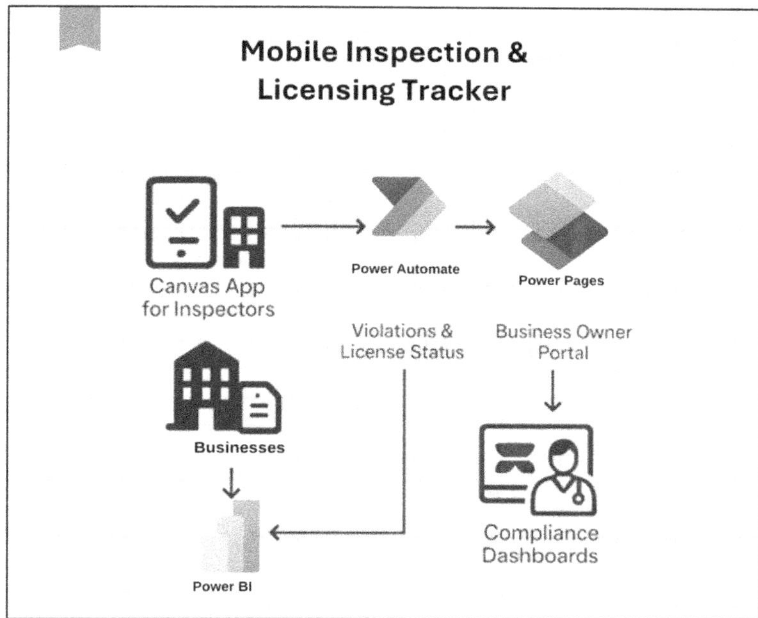

Figure 7-5. *Architecture Diagram—Mobile Health Inspection System*

Technical Solution Architecture

Power Apps (Canvas App)	Mobile app for inspectors to enter violation data, capture images, and generate reports (even offline)
Dataverse	Stores business profiles, licenses, inspection histories, types of violations, compliance scores, and attachments
Power Automate	Reminds for future inspections, license renewals, and repeat violations escalation
Power BI	Inspection volume dashboards, pass/fail rates, productivity of inspectors, and high-risk locations
Power Pages	Optional portal for public display of public health scores or to give business owners an option to download their reports

Workflow Overview

1. **Pre-visit Setup**

   - Inspectors see inspections assigned to the day in Power Apps.

   - Download records for an establishment offline.

2. **On-Site Inspection**

   - Complete the checklist within the mobile app.

   - Snap photos, GPS, and comments within the app.

   - Report outcomes immediately or sync when reconnecting.

3. **Violation Escalation**

   - Follow-up inspection task assignments or suspension workflows are triggered in Power Automate by violation type/severity.

4. **License Management**

   - Licensing officers review the history of inspections and mark license status in Dataverse.

5. **Compliance Dashboards**

   - Category, region, or inspector-level Power BI reports by violation.

   - Optional public results are published on Power Pages for transparency.

Dashboards and Reporting Views

- **Inspection Heatmap**: Most frequent-violating areas or overdue inspections.

- **Violation Trend Reports**: Industry-leading most frequent health code violations.

- **Inspector Productivity Dashboards**: Inspection time per inspection, findings captured, follow-up work.

- **Compliance Scorecards**: Pass/fail, re-inspection cycle, license status summary.

Results and Measurable Impact

Metric	Before	After
Paper-based data entry	100%	0% (fully digital)
Inspection report sync time	1–2 days	Instant or on reconnect
Missed license renewal alerts	Frequent	Automated through flows
Public access to inspection history	Manual FOIA	Portal-based (optional)

- **Outcome**: Safer venues, improved workflows, less lost renewals, and openness to the public

Use Case 5: Community Health Event Planning and Impact Reporting

Overview and Context

Community health events—such as vaccination clinics, health screenings, wellness fairs, mobile health clinics, and public awareness activities—are critical for reaching underserved populations and aiding overall public health outcomes. However, planning, execution, and monitoring the effect of these activities is normally in disarray and unplanned.

Typically, agencies rely on spreadsheets, email, and phone trees to manage logistics, scheduling staff, outreach, and reporting. This does not allow for managing inventories, targeting high-need communities, tracking attendance, and connecting health outcomes to program investments.

This solution suggests a **Community Health Event Management Platform** on Microsoft Power Platform to plan, execute, and analyze public health events with accuracy, clarity, and speed.

Who It Helps

Stakeholder	Benefit
Public Health Outreach Coordinators	Coordinate and schedule events, locations, personnel, and supplies in one app
Field Teams and Nurses	Leverage mobile apps for participant check-in, services rendered tracking, and outcome synchronization
Community Members	View future events, preregister, and provide post-event feedback via portals
Health Directors and Grant Managers	Monitor participation, reach, and ROI on outreach from real-time dashboards
Partner Organizations (NGOs, Clinics)	Have a shared calendar, upload participant data, and make optimal use of resources

Key Drivers for Modernization

- **Disjointed Planning Tools**: Logistics are coordinated through emails, phone calls, and separate tracking sheets.

- **No Central Registry**: Attendee information, services provided, and referrals are not centralized.

- **Difficult Reporting**: Grant compliance, reports on attendance, and cost monitoring are done by hand.

- **Outreach Blind Spots**: There is no convenient way to specify underserved ZIP codes or unseen demographic segments.

- **Limited Community Engagement**: Public may not be aware of the events or may not be able to preregister.

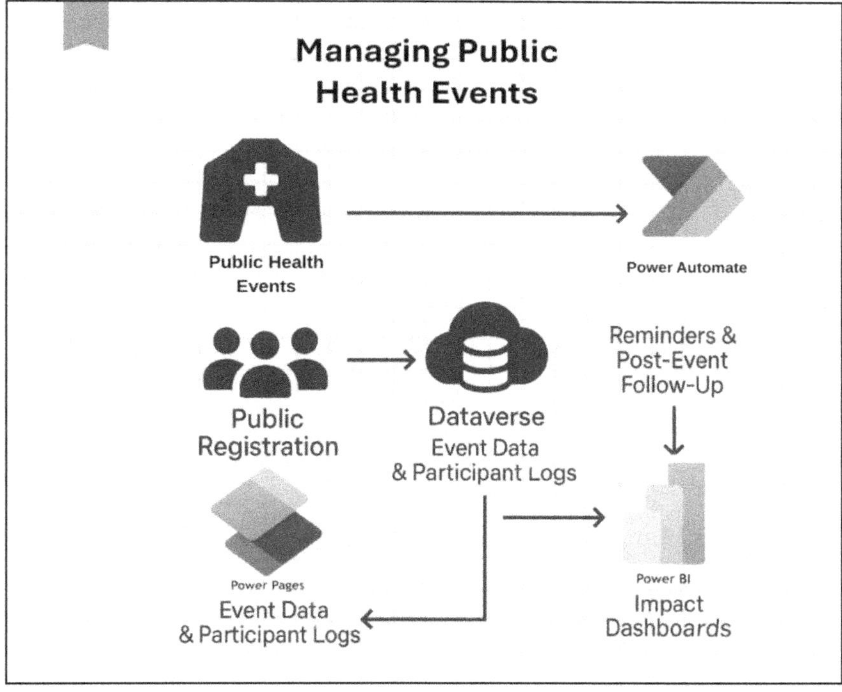

Figure 7-6. *Architecture Diagram—Community Health Event Platform*

Technical Solution Architecture

Power Apps (Canvas App)	Utilized by event organizers to organize events and utilized by field staff for mobile check-in of visitors and service tracking
Power Pages	Public-facing portal to see upcoming health events, sign up, and provide feedback after the event
Dataverse	Stores event metadata, attendance, services provided, community metrics, partner information, and outreach materials
Power Automate	Reminds registrants, sends reminders to follow-up surveys, and low attendance or supply alerts
AI Builder	Identifies underserved areas by health markers and historical event data for improved planning
Power BI	Provides attendance trends, service delivery statistics, regional coverage, and program impact overviews

Workflow Overview

1. **Event Planning**

   - Event planners schedule events, delegate roles, and track logistics with Power Apps.

   - AI Builder Provides sites based on community demand and past gaps in coverage.

2. **Public Engagement**

   - Citizens register on Power Pages, are confirmed, and view event FAQs or pre-screening forms.

3. **Event Day Execution**

   - Staff sign patients in, capture services (e.g., flu shot, diabetes screen), and obtain consent.

4. **Post-Event Follow-Up**

   - Surveys and care referrals are sent using Power Automate.

   - Staff scan incomplete paper logs or upload them.

5. **Dashboards and Reporting**

   - Power BI dashboards present turnout, outcome, and effect by geography.

   - Exported reports for federal grants or internal auditing.

Dashboards and Reporting Views

- **Event Attendance Breakdown**: Age, gender, ethnicity, return attendees

- **Service Delivered Totals**: Vaccines given, screenings, referrals

- **ZIP Code Coverage**: ZIP code coverage density maps and coverage gap maps

- **Impact Summary Program:** Percentage accomplishment through follow-up, per-participant cost, and grant KPIs

Results and Measurable Impact

Metric	Before	After
Attendee data collection method	Paper sign-in	Mobile digital entry
Public event awareness	Low, untracked	Portal with 5,000+ visits/month
Underserved area coverage	Anecdotal	AI-predicted and mapped
Time to generate impact report	2–3 weeks	Real time with Power BI

- **Outcome**: Greater reach, improved resource allocation, and increased compliance with federal and state health grant reporting

7.2 Department of Education

Use Case 1: Student Enrollment and Registration Portal with Eligibility Checks

Overview and Context

Registration of students is the most important and time-consuming procedure for schools and school districts. From kindergarten enrollments to transfers, each action—collection of forms, document verification, checking eligibility, zoning school, and program assignment—is coordinated among parents, administrative staff, and district IT.

The legacy process is typically worked through using PDF forms, email, and face-to-face office appointments, causing data inaccuracies, slow student onboarding, and family transparency issues. Minimal verification of eligibility (age, location, program capacity) is also done at the point of intake.

This use case deploys a **Self-Service Enrollment and Registration Platform** on Microsoft Power Platform to support secure, guided, and data-validated student enrollment, reducing staff workload and turnaround time.

Who It Helps

Stakeholder	Benefit
School Administrators	Streamline verification of eligibility, view all your applications at one time, and simply assign students to programs or schools
Parents and Guardians	Self-register students online, track application status, and receive updates through a mobile-friendly portal
District Enrollment Officers	Get real-time monitoring of enrollment trends, program capacity, and local demand through live dashboards
Compliance Staff	Verify all documents required to be submitted and authenticated upfront for regulatory or funding purposes

Key Drivers for Modernization

- **Paper-Based Submissions**: Forms printed, scanned, or emailed—error-prone with missing fields.

- **Manual Document Review**: Employees are required to manually verify age, residency, immunization, and IEP/504 plans.

- **No Real-Time Status Updates**: Parents are required to call or email to get updates; the status is not transparent.

- **Lack of Electronic Records:** Admission records are frequently missing or segmented across systems.

- **Limited Capacity Checks:** No automation exists to verify if the chosen school or program has available space for admission.

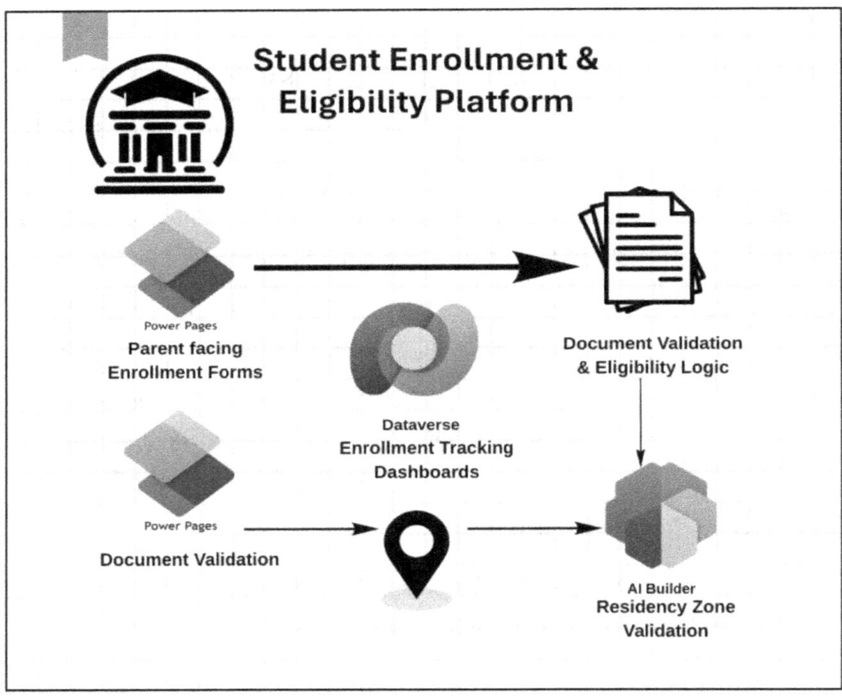

Figure 7-7. Architecture Diagram—Student Enrollment Portal

Technical Solution Architecture

Component	Role
Power Pages	Public-facing portal for parents to register students, upload documents, and track status
Power Apps (Model-Driven)	Staff administrative dashboard for viewing, validating, and approving/routing applications
Dataverse	Student profiles, guardian information, eligibility documents, residency zones, and school/program mappings are stored here
Power Automate	Age and address validation, routing applications by school capacity and geography, and reminder sending
AI Builder (Optional)	Utility bill scan or document upload to automatically validate proof of residency and determine school zones
Power BI	Visual dashboards showing enrollment pipeline, capacity trends, frequent application mistakes, and geographic breakdowns

Workflow Overview

1. **Application Intake**

   - The parent registers on Power Pages and completes the guided registration form.

   - Required documents (i.e., proof of address, birth certificate, immunization) are uploaded.

2. **Eligibility Validation**

- Power Automate checks age cut-offs, residency zoning, and completeness of documentation.

- AI Builder extracts address information from uploaded documents and checks school zone qualification.

3. **Staff Review and Assignment**

- Enrollment staff uses Power Apps to access triggered records, sign-off applications, and school/program assignments.

4. **Notification and Tracking**

- Power Automate notifies parents (waitlisted, more info needed, accepted).

- Parents may access the portal to view updates or schedule onboarding appointments.

5. **Reporting and Oversight**

- Power BI plots various pending vs. enrolled, demographic profiles, common issues, and staff workload.

Dashboards and Reporting Views

- **Live Enrollment Pipeline**: Waitlisted, approved, pending, rejected

- **School Capacity Heatmap**: Available Seats by School/Program

- **Enrollment Error Tracking**: Default document errors or missing fields

- **Demographic Overview**: Age, grade, ethnicity, and school district breakdown

Results and Measurable Impact

Metric	Before	After
Application review time	5–7 days	< 48 hours
Parent support requests	High (calls/emails)	Low (self-service portal)
Rate of document errors	~40%	< 10% with validation
Redundancy of data entry	Frequent	Removed (automated capture)

- **Outcome**: More rapid, more transparent enrolling; reduced workload for staff; and more fairness in school/program placement

Use Case 2: Digital Student Attendance and Absence Management System

Overview and Context

Student attendance recording accurately is crucial not just for academic success but also for state reporting, funding qualification, truancy prevention, and early recognition of struggling students. Many schools continue to use attendance sheets by hand, spreadsheets, or stand-alone SIS (Student Information Systems) that slow data collection and constrain actionable data.

This creates an administrative burden for teachers, heightens errors, and makes it challenging to intervene early when students exhibit signs of chronic absenteeism.

119

This use case shows a **Digital Attendance and Absence Management System** on the Microsoft Power Platform to automate attendance capture, alert stakeholders, and visualize trends that guide interventions.

Who It Helps

Stakeholder	Benefit
Teachers	Record attendance through a straightforward mobile or desktop app and auto-submit to the district
Attendance Clerks	See real-time absence information, verify records, and mark for chronic absenteeism
Parents/Guardians	Receive absence alerts and input excuse notes online
School Administrators	See school-wide trends and target students requiring early intervention
District/State Auditors	See auditable attendance records and compliance reports to aid funding

Key Drivers for Modernization

- **Manual Logs**: Teachers complete paper rosters or simple spreadsheets—error-inducing and time-consuming.

- **Delayed Visibility**: Schools are unable to track trends or alert parents until end-of-day or later.

- **No Central Dashboard**: Isolated tracking across classes, schools, and programs.

- **Limited Parent Engagement**: Absences are unexcused because of insufficient timely communication.

- **Compliance Risk**: Challenge in creating defensible logs during audits or investigations.

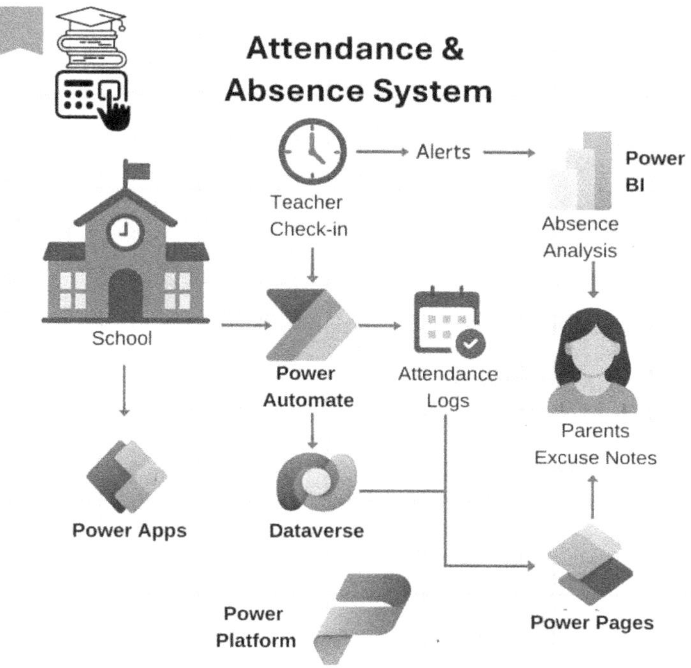

Figure 7-8. *Architecture Diagram—Attendance and Absence System*

Technical Solution Architecture

Component	Role
Power Apps (Canvas App)	Used by teachers to record attendance by period or day; mobile/tablet-friendly
Dataverse	Unified attendance table of student ID, timestamp, course information, and reason codes (unexcused, medical, etc.)
Power Automate	Reports absence to admin, sends reminders for an unexcused absence, escalates after repeat absence days

(continued)

Component	Role
Power Pages	Parent portal for entry of electronic absence notes or for confirming sent reminders
Power BI	Dashboards showing up-to-date attendance trends by grade, class, school, or student

Workflow Overview

1. **Daily Attendance Capture**

   - Teachers log into Power Apps, choose class, and then click present/absent for every student.

   - Syncs automatically with Dataverse and records timestamp, teacher ID, and period.

2. **Parent Notification**

   - Power Automate sends a message to parents if the student is recorded as absent, and there is no note in their file.

3. **Absence Justification**

   - The parent signs into Power Pages to post a doctor's note or justify the absence.

4. **Clerk Review**

   - Attendance staff utilize a Power Apps dashboard to examine highlighted absences and validate excuse notes.

5. **Escalation**

   - When there has been a configurable number of unexcused days (e.g., five), a follow-up case is opened by the counselor.

6. **Insights and Reporting**

   - Power BI graphs attendance rates, chronic absenteeism flags, and state reporting compliance.

Dashboards and Reporting Views

- **Attendance Rate Dashboard**: Class/school daily, weekly, and monthly trends

- **Chronic Absenteeism Flags**: Students with a few unexcused absences

- **Demographic Analysis**: Contrast absenteeism by grade level, ethnicity, and socioeconomic status

- **Compliance Summary**: What percentage of records contain proper excuse documentation to validate audit

Results and Measurable Impact

Metric	Before	After
Teacher time to submit daily attendance	15+ minutes	< 5 minutes
Parental notification delay	Same or next day	Immediate
Chronic absence identification	Reactive (post-report card)	Proactive, near real time
Audit readiness	Collation of manual logs	Real-time access to dashboards

- **Outcome**: Active student support, minimized chronic absenteeism, increased parental engagement, and audit-ready reporting

Use Case 3: Individualized Education Plan (IEP) Management and Tracking System

Overview and Background

Individualized Education Plan (IEP) management for special needs students is a multifaceted, legally required process involving several interested parties—teachers, special education personnel, parents, psychologists, therapists, and school officials. It encompasses the development and revision of comprehensive learning plans, progress reporting, setting review dates, and maintaining IDEA (Individuals with Disabilities Education Act) and Section 504 compliance.

The majority of school districts employ antiquated systems or siloed workflows for IEP management, resulting in missed deadlines, inaccessible documents, inconsistent tracking, and excessive administrative burdens.

This use case presents a **Low-Code IEP Management and Tracking System** on the Microsoft Power Platform that brings transparency, automation, and secure collaboration into each phase of the special education process.

Who It Helps

Stakeholder	Benefit
Special Education Coordinators	Monitor upcoming IEP review cycles, coordinate student plans, and maintain compliance using one dashboard
Teachers and Case Managers	Access student goals, make updates in progress, and share information with specialists
Parents/Guardians	Join in on IEP meetings, electronically sign documents, and review updates in progress

(continued)

Stakeholder	Benefit
Therapists (OT/PT/SLP)	Upload session notes, progress measures, and proposed adjustments to goals securely
District Leadership	Keep up with compliance levels and document appropriate support services to show audits or for purposes of funding justification

Key Drivers for Modernization

- **Paper-Based Plans**: Most IEPs are still written and managed through Word documents, PDFs, and email threads.

- **Overdue Milestones:** Milestone due dates and annual reviews can be forgotten without reminders.

- **Fragmented Records**: All accommodations, goals, and progress notes can be generated in separate systems or folders.

- **Limited Parent Access**: Parents feel ignored or placed on hold in obtaining up-to-date plans or comments.

- **Audit Risk**: Absence of a centralized system would put the district at risk for legal compliance problems.

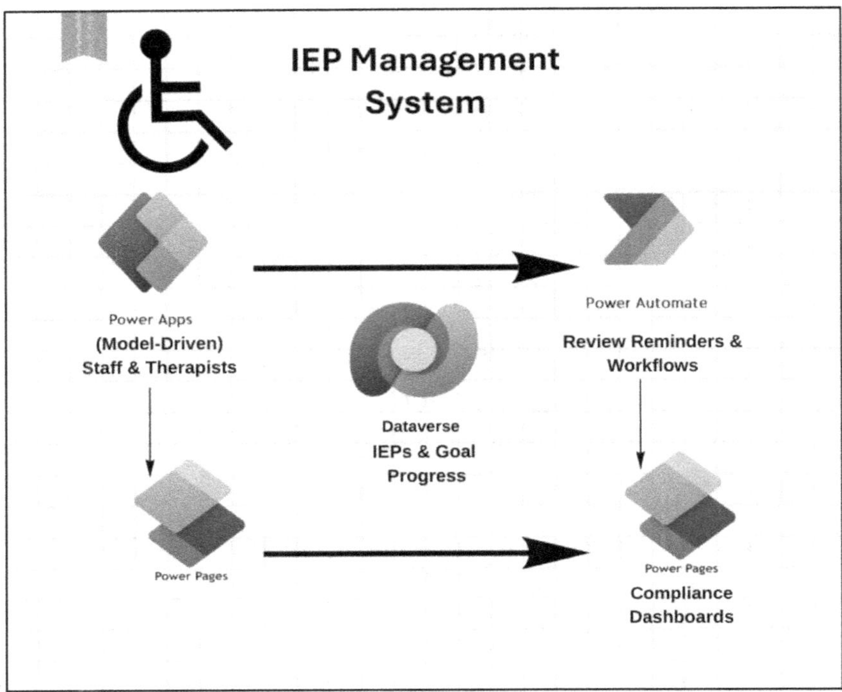

Figure 7-9. IEP Management Platform Architecture Diagram

Technical Solution Architecture

Component	Role
Power Apps (Model-Driven App)	Common interface for therapists, case managers, and teachers to track and enter updates for IEPs
Dataverse	Stores student records, IEP documentation, milestone dates, goal progress, accommodations, and services

(continued)

Component	Role
Power Automate	Automates reminders for annual reviews, overdue updates, meeting scheduling, and signature tracking
Power Pages	Optional parent portal to view IEPs, receive reminders, submit consent forms, or ask for services
Power BI	Compliance calendars, caseloads, snapshots of student progress, and zones of documentation are needed

Workflow Overview

1. **Plan Creation**

   - The case manager has a new IEP record created in Power Apps that is associated with the student profile.

   - Staff and specialists input services, goals, accommodations, and schedules.

2. **Progress Monitoring**

   - Teachers and therapists log goal status by reporting period.

   - Notes and session logs are secure in Dataverse.

3. **Meeting and Signature Tracking**

   - Upcoming reviews and route plans for parent digital signatures are alerted through Power Pages by Power Automate.

4. **Parent Access**

   - Parents also have access to approved IEPs and minutes of meetings and may submit questions via a secure Power Pages portal.

5. **Oversight and Compliance**

   - The coordinator or the school can view how strictly schedules are being adhered to, how far behind schedule reviews are, and completion rates within Power BI.

Dashboards and Reporting Views

- **Compliance Calendar**: Future review dates, outstanding assignments, and a year-cycle status

- **Caseload Summary**: The number of students assigned to each case manager and the percentage of targets met

- **Parent Engagement Tracking**: Communications history and signature return rates

- **Funding/Service Audit Logs**: Sessions for rendered services

Results and Measurable Impact

Metric	Before	After
Missed review deadlines	High	< 5%
Parent access to IEPs	Limited	24/7 via secure portal
Duration to finish documentation audit	Manual, 2–3 weeks	Dashboards in real time
Progress reporting on goal	Ad hoc	Standardized, visualized

- **Outcome**: Legally sound, transparent, and student-focused IEP processes with improved coordination and parent trust

Use Case 4: Digital Counseling and Student Support Case Management

Overview and Context

With increased student concern over mental health, academic stress, bullying, behavior problems, and personal trauma, school counseling services are more important than ever before. Caseload management, recording of interventions, confidentiality, and follow-up, however, may result in disparate systems or paper-based logs.

This limits counselors from directly manipulating students' needs, on-time replies, and sending outcomes for grants, compliance, or intervention programs.

This use case captures a **Digital Counseling and Student Support Case Management System** on the Microsoft Power Platform that assists schools in creating, monitoring, and responding to counseling referrals, behavior plans, wellness programs, and follow-up care in a secure, collaborative environment.

Who It Helps

Stakeholder	Benefit
School Counselors	Monitor student sessions, track support plans, and notify on high-priority follow-ups
Teachers and Staff	Securely and efficiently refer students with guided digital forms
Parents	Be kept in the know (as appropriate) and work together on behavior or emotional support plans
District Behavioral Health Coordinators	Manage trends, refer to cases, and manage counselor workloads
Grant Managers	View mental health funding applications and compliance audit data

Key Drivers for Modernization

- **Informal Referrals**: Unsecured, unstandardized paper notes or emails.

- **No Central Log:** Interventions by students are dispersed in notes, spreadsheets, and calendars.

- **Missed Follow-Ups:** Poor task management tools cause missed or delayed follow-ups.

- **No Analytics**: Districts cannot report on the success of wellness programs or the impact of caseload.

- **Privacy Concerns**: Confidential records are even kept regularly in unsafe formats or audited without suitable RBAC.

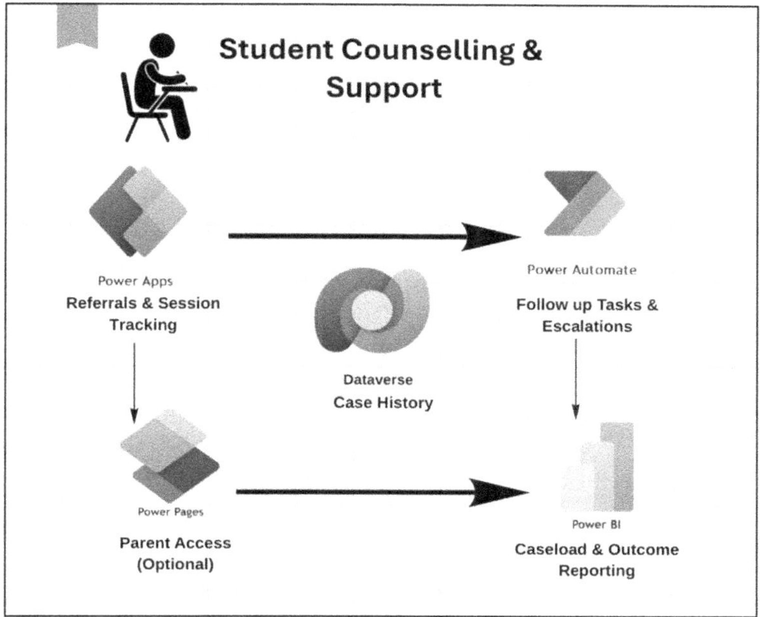

Figure 7-10. *Architecture Diagram—Counseling Case Management*

Technical Solution Architecture

Component	Role
Power Apps (Model-Driven)	Case initiation, referral tracking, session notes, follow-up logs, and counselor progress dashboards
Power Automate	Raises priority cases, assigns counselors, and automatic check-in reminders
Dataverse	Stores securely student cases, action plans, referral history, meeting logs, and service notes
Power Pages (Optional)	Facilitates family engagement when necessary (FERPA and consent basis)
Power BI	Service delivery dashboards, incident types, repeat referrals, and counselor workload

Workflow Overview

1. **Referral Submission**

   - The teacher, nurse, or staff submits a digital referral in Power Apps.

   - Anonymous, general, or priority-marked options.

2. **Case Assignment and Review**

   - School/site counselors receive reminder emails sent by Power Automate.

   - The case manager documents the first contact and schedules follow-up reminders.

3. **Support Sessions**

   - Secure forms in Power Apps document sessions.

   - Notes, interventions, and goals are dated and monitored.

4. **Parent Collaboration**

   - (Where applicable) Parents can view reports or approve action plans via Power Pages.

5. **Monitoring and Reporting**

   - Power BI monitors intervention outcomes, frequency of service, and escalation trends.

   - Facilitates reporting to the funding agencies or health departments.

Dashboards and Reporting Views

- **Caseload by Counselor**: Number of open, closed, and escalated cases

- **Intervention Types**: Academic, emotional, behavior, peer conflict, family trauma

- **Repeat Referral Flags**: Flag students requiring intensive intervention

- **Intervention Impact Summary**: Monitor outcome effectiveness and follow-up success

Results and Measurable Impact

Metric	Before	After
Referral to first contact time	3–5 days	Same day or next
Missed follow-ups	Common	Tracked with alerts
Case documentation compliance	Inconsistent	100% in centralized system
District understanding of student	Anecdotal	Real-time dashboards

- **Outcome**: Efficient, student-focused mental health and support services with quantifiable impact and counselor overload avoidance

Use Case 5: Digital Course Scheduling, Capacity Management, and Resource Allocation

Overview and Context

Course scheduling is a vital process implemented in schools, colleges, and vocational schools. Scheduling the course offerings, teachers, rooms, and registrations of students using optimal resource usage and satisfying the student-teacher ratios is an issue of logistics.

The old-fashioned scheduling mechanisms are rigidity-based, non-real-time, coupled with available capacity, and provide little insight into constraints and wasted resources. Due to this, students may have course conflicts, over-booked courses, or random cancellations.

This use case introduces a **Low-Code Course Scheduling and Capacity Management Platform** on Microsoft Power Platform to transform and automate course scheduling, optimize resource utilization, and enhance student and faculty experience.

Who It Helps

Stakeholder	Benefit
Academic Planners	Publish and create course schedules, assign instructors, and allocate classroom availability
Students	See course offerings, register online, and get conflict notifications or availability alerts in real time
Instructors	See assigned courses, handle capacity requests, and see schedules through the mobile dashboard
Admin Staff	Track over/under-enrolled courses, highlight schedule gaps, and reassign rooms or staff
District/College Leadership	See patterns of usage and enrollments and maximize use of budget

Main Drivers to Modernize

- **Static Schedules**: Paper-based/Excel Schedules: It lacks flexibility and update visibility.

- **Manual Registration**: Staff have to enter by hand or settle student choices and clashes.

- **No Real-Time Capacity View**: This means it leads to over-subscribed or under-loaded classes.

- **Limited Reporting**: Unable to determine classroom utilization, teacher workloads, or cost-effectiveness.

- **Lack of Student Visibility**: Students do not know class capacity or current status.

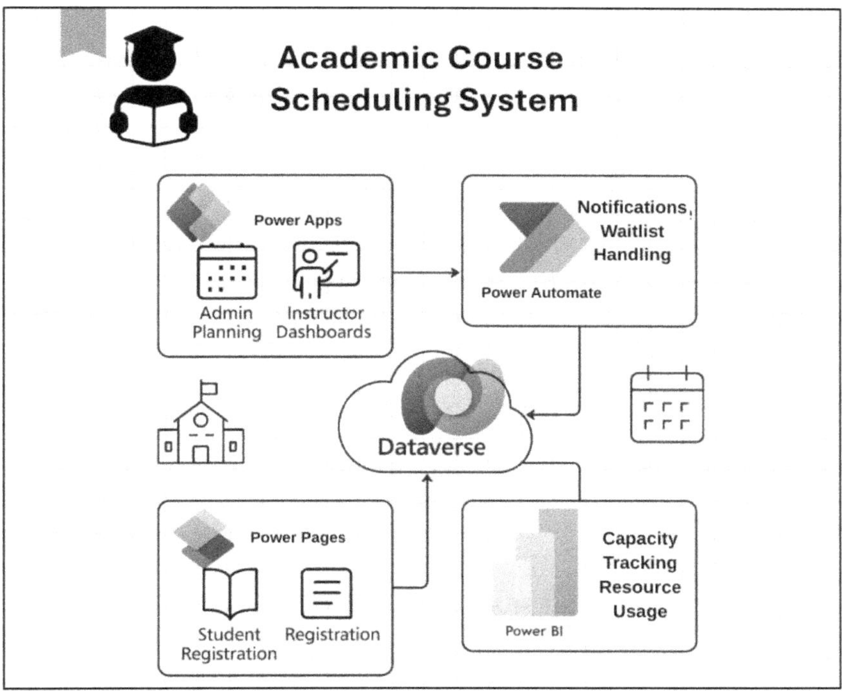

Figure 7-11. *Architecture Diagram—Course Scheduling System*

Technical Solution Architecture

Component	Role
Power Apps (Model-Driven App)	Plan and teach with, used by planners and teachers to create schedules, monitor capacity, and see resource allocation
Power Pages	Student browser for viewing course catalog, enrollments, and waitlist status
Dataverse	Central repository for courses, instructors, classrooms, capacity, time slots, and enrollments
Power Automate	Handles live class update notifications, capacity alerts, waitlist promotion, and room reassignment
Power BI	Enrollment statistics dashboards, room usage, overbooked classes, and instructor assignments

Workflow Overview

1. **Schedule Creation**

   - Academic planners in Power Apps create semester schedules from preloaded course templates and instructor preferences.

   - Capacity, time slots, and room assignments are maintained in Dataverse.

2. **Student Registration**

   - Students search and enroll using Power Pages.

   - Power Automate checks for scheduling conflicts and class space and adds or enrolls students to a waitlist.

3. **Instructor Management**

   - Instructors see teaching schedules in Power
     Apps, ask to make changes, and collect resource
     requirements (lab, AV, etc.).

4. **Capacity Monitoring**

   - When capacity thresholds are reached, Power
     Automate executes waitlist promotion or suggests
     room/class section addition.

5. **Reporting and Optimization**

   - Power BI monitors class usage, registration trends,
     in-demand courses, and instructor workload
     allocation.

Dashboards and Reporting Views

- **Classroom Utilization Heatmap**: Monitor space
  utilization by campus.

- **Instructor Load Tracker**: Measure available vs.
  assigned instructional hours.

- **Course Enrollment Trends**: Mark high-/low-demand
  courses by semester.

- **Budget Efficiency Metrics**: Cost per enrolled student
  per department or class.

Results and Measurable Impact

Metric	Before	After
Manual scheduling errors	Frequent	< 2%
Over-enrolled courses per term	High	Reduced by 80%
Classroom utilization	< 60%	> 85%
Student registration conflict rate	Common	Flagged and resolved automatically

- **Outcome**: Smarter scheduling, balanced instructor workloads, increased student satisfaction, and improved resource optimization

7.3 Department of Transportation

Use Case 1: Road Maintenance and Pothole Reporting Automation System

Overview and Context

Road infrastructure maintenance, especially pothole detection, rehabilitation, and tracking, is the most common but manpower-bloated transportation department task. Manually automated hotlining or mail reporting, nonfunctional inspection log maintenance, and undue repair delays force residents to send complaints, ensure public safety risk, and additionally incur additional motor claims of damages.

Agencies often have standalone reporting mechanisms, unclear repair tracking, and insufficient real-time dashboards to be able to prioritize and dispatch repair crews.

The use case uses a **Power Platform-based Road Maintenance and Pothole Reporting System** to computerize the entire life cycle—all the way from citizen reports to allocating repair crews, confirming repairs, and real-time dashboards.

Who It Helps

Stakeholder	Benefit
Citizens	Report potholes or road defects easily in a public portal with status notifications
Field Inspectors and Repair Crews	Get work orders via GPS-tagged photo-reporting-capable mobile apps that track completion
Maintenance Supervisors	Construct, monitor, and build up repairs geographically and by teams
Transportation Planners	Monitor repeat hot spots and conduct proactive maintenance through dashboards
Executive Leadership	Monitors real-time service-level agreements (SLAs), public satisfaction, and elimination of backlogs

Key Drivers for Modernization

- **Manual Intake Processes**: Phone calls, emails, or walk-in-reported hazards—inefficient and unstructured.

- **No Public Visibility**: Residents don't know if/when a problem is fixed.

- **Disjointed Field Operations**: No mobile equipment for assignment or verification.

- **No SLA Tracking**: Slowness is not seen, putting liability at risk.

- **Lack of Trend Analysis**: Not able to see areas of shared problems.

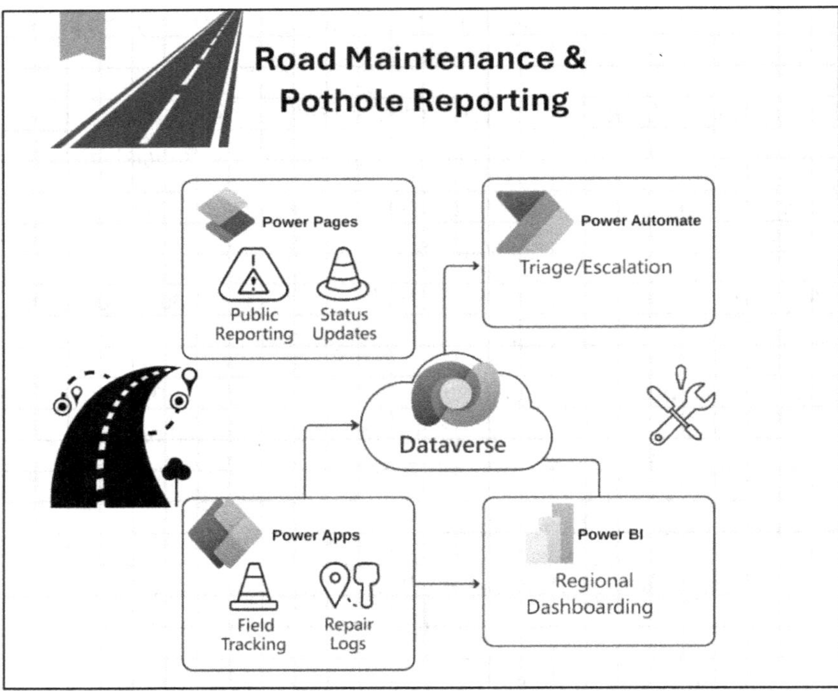

Figure 7-12. *Architecture Diagram—Road Maintenance Reporting*

Technical Solution Architecture

Component	Role
Power Pages	Citizen's pothole or road hazard reporting portal with photos, descriptions, and coordinates
Power Apps (Canvas App)	Mobile app to receive assignments, mark as fixed, photograph, and verify GPS location
Dataverse	Central data store for reported defects, inspection reports, repair history, SLA timestamps, and region mappings
Power Automate	Sends new reports to respective zone managers, reminds outstanding repairs, and notifies citizens of progress
Power BI	Operational tracking dashboards, SLA compliance dashboards, regional trends dashboards, and repair effectiveness analysis dashboards

Workflow Overview

1. **Report Submission**

   - Citizens report issues on Power Pages with optional images and real-time GPS capture.

   - Case created in Dataverse with priority level and date/time.

2. **Assignment and Inspection**

   - New work orders are reviewed by the supervisor on Power Apps and allocated inspectors or crews based on region and load.

3. **Repair Execution**

- The crew utilizes Power Apps to report arrival, capture repair information, capture before/after photos, and report progress.

4. **Notifications**

- Power Automate notifies citizens by email/SMS on repair initiation and completion.

5. **Dashboards and Insights**

- Power BI shows open/closed reports by status, response time, high-activity areas, and crew effectiveness.

Dashboards and Reporting Views

- **SLA Compliance Tracker**: Report to fix time vs. SLA target.

- **Repair Volume by Region**: Highlight high-activity areas and backlogged areas.

- **Public Engagement Metrics**: Open reports received, closed reports received, and customer satisfaction ratings.

- **Crew Performance Analytics**: Repairs per technician per week/month.

Results and Measurable Impact

Metric	Before	After
Average response time to citizen report	5–7 days	< 48 hours
Repair crew visibility into tasks	Limited	real time with mobile updates
Public communication of issue status	None	Transparent via portal notifications
Issue resolution audit trail	Manual	Automated and timestamped in Dataverse

- **Outcome**: Increased citizen confidence, decreased delay in repair, improved resource planning, and measurable improvement in maintenance of infrastructure

Use Case 2: Smart Traffic Signal Monitoring and Incident Response Automation

Overview and Context

Traffic signal failures, synchronization faults, and congestion incidents affect road safety, travel times, and emergency response efficiency. Departments predominantly depend on manual status checks or public reports to identify signal faults, delaying incident response and lowering operational effectiveness.

This solution brings a **Smart Traffic Signal Monitoring and Incident Automation System** based on Microsoft Power Platform to consolidate sensor notifications, automate crew dispatch, and offer real-time visibility into signal status and traffic flow anomalies.

Who It Helps

Stakeholder	Benefit
Traffic Operations Centers (TOC)	Monitor signal outages or irregularities in real time and assign crews instantly
Field Technicians	Receive signal maintenance tasks through a mobile app with location, instructions, and severity level
City Engineers	Examine timing problems, congestion trends, and infrastructure performance over time
Emergency Dispatch	Have faster access to real-time signal status for emergency rerouting of vehicles
Commuters	Enjoy shorter wait times and better traffic signal coordination

Key Drivers for Modernization

- **Reactive Detection**: Failures are mostly detected after complaints by citizens or after manual inspection with a lag.

- **Lack of Automation**: Dispatching and status reporting are done through phone calls and spreadsheets.

- **Disconnected Systems**: Traffic signal sensors are not linked to work orders or reporting systems.

- **No Trend Analysis**: It is not easy to identify which intersections have recurring failures.

- **Manual Reporting**: Laborious documentation processes slow response and auditing.

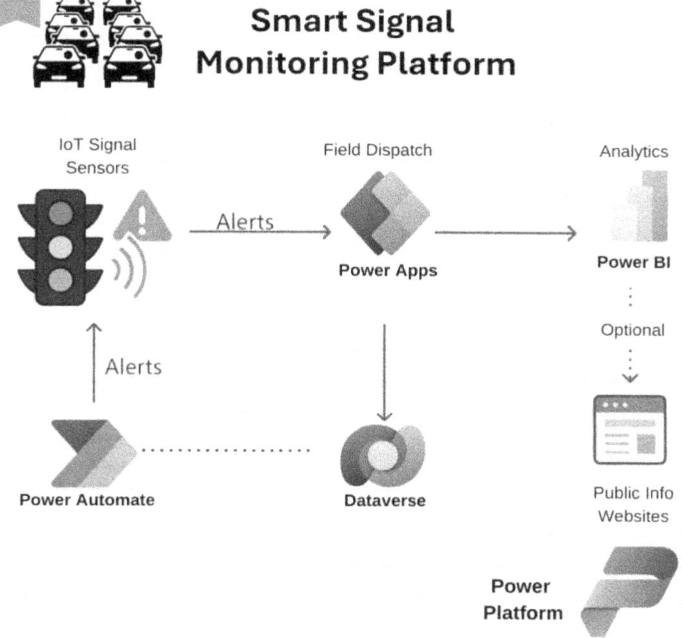

Figure 7-13. *Architecture Diagram—Smart Signal Monitoring Platform*

Technical Solution Architecture

Component	Role
IoT Sensor Feed (External Integration)	Sends status updates for traffic signals (e.g., power outage, sync failure) via Azure IoT Hub or custom API
Power Automate	Listens for alerts and directs to traffic ops dashboard or field technician depending on location/severity
Power Apps (Canvas App)	Utilized by field staff to accept alerts, record repairs, and mark signal status with photos

(continued)

145

Component	Role
Dataverse	Repository for incident logs, repair history, assignments of technicians, timestamps, and SLA metrics
Power BI	Real-time dashboards for outages by zone, signal health status, repeating issues, and team productivity

Workflow Overview

1. **Alert Triggered**

   - IoT traffic signal sensor connected to IoT sends outage or anomaly notifications to Azure.

   - Power Automate captures and logs incidents in Dataverse with timestamp and severity.

2. **Assignment and Response**

   - The supervisor looks at the dashboard and delegates repair jobs using Power Apps.

   - Field tech is tasked with intersection data, GPS, and issue description.

3. **On-Site Action**

   - Tech updates status, adds repair notes and photos, and marks job done in the mobile app.

4. **Notifications and Escalation**

   - Unless resolved within SLA, Power Automate escalates to the regional ops manager.

   - Optional notification to emergency responders or public info dashboards.

5. **Analytics and Reporting**

- Power BI tracks issue frequency, crew productivity, repair categories, and risk-incident intersections.

Dashboards and Reporting Views

- **Signal Health Map**: Real-time status of all intersections on an interactive GIS map

- **Response Time Analytics**: Region, technician, or issue-type time-to-resolution

- **Failure Frequency Heatmap**: Find where infrastructure is aging or repeated problem areas

- **Technician Performance Dashboard**: Percentage of job completion, workload balance, SLA compliance

Results and Measurable Impact

Metric	Before	After
Time to detect signal outage	> 6 hours (avg.)	< 10 minutes via sensor
Field crew dispatch time	Manual, 2+ hours	Automated in 15 minutes
Backlog of failures reported	High	Zero (auto-recorded in Dataverse)
Overseeing SLA adherence	Spreadsheet-based	Real-time dashboard

- **Outcome**: Safer roads, quicker response to traffic failure, less congestion, and greater audit/compliance visibility

Use Case 3: Fleet and Fuel Management Dashboard for Government Vehicles

Overview and Context

State and local transportation agencies maintain fleets of trucks for road maintenance, inspections, snow removal, field operations, and emergency services. Accurate monitoring of usage, fuel cost, maintenance schedules, and allocations for these fleets is essential to cost savings, serviceability, and sustainability objectives.

The majority of agencies retain discrete systems, fuel card reports, or paper records, leading to reporting errors, timing for maintenance issues, and extra fuel costs or assets idle.

This is an example of a **Power Platform-Based Fleet and Fuel Management Dashboard**, where transport departments can optimize vehicle utilization, automate reminders, and monitor fuel usage through linked dashboards.

Who It Helps

Stakeholder	Benefit
Fleet Managers	Real-time viewing of vehicle utilization, fuel consumption, and maintenance status
Drivers and Field Staff	Capture trips, issues, and refueling via mobile app interface
Maintenance Teams	Scheduled reminders for pending service schedules or reported issues
Finance Officers	Track fuel costs, detect abuse, and predict operational costs
Executive Leadership	Treats KPIs as emissions, usage, idle time, and cost savings

Key Drivers for Modernization

- **Paper-Based Logs**: Maintenance, fuel, and mileage logs are handwritten or even turned in after the fact.

- **No Central Dashboard**: Fleet usage by groups or geographies is not visible.

- **Inefficient Scheduling**: Some trucks are overused, while others are underused.

- **Fuel Leakage**: Refueling vs. mileage tracking has zero real-time visibility, and hence, untracked losses happen.

- **Missed Service Intervals**: Breakdowns, downtime, and safety problems occur due to manual tracking.

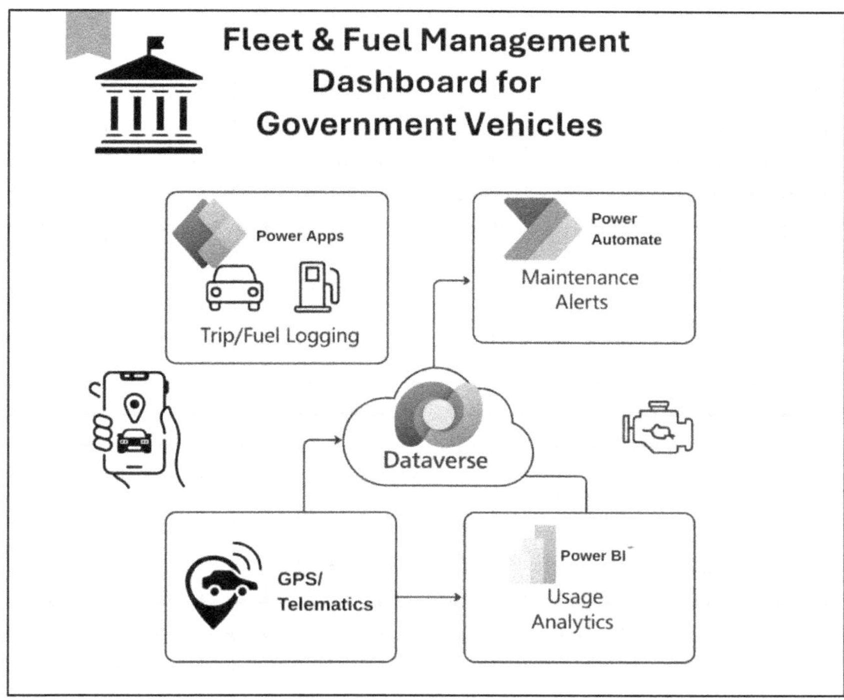

Figure 7-14. *Architecture Diagram—Fleet Management Dashboard*

Technical Solution Architecture

Component	Role
Power Apps (Canvas App)	Drivers capture mileage, refueling, vehicle condition, and trip information
Dataverse	Saves all vehicle records, usage history, service intervals, fuel transactions, and driver comments
Power Automate	Triggers maintenance alerts, overdue inspections, and fuel efficiency anomaly indicators
Power BI	Fuel expenditure dashboards, mileage trends, service forecasts, vehicle usage, and idle time
External APIs (optional)	Imports GPS/telematics data or fuel card vendor data into Dataverse

Workflow Overview

1. **Trip and Fuel Logging**

   - Drivers use Power Apps to record trip purpose, miles, and fuel transactions at the end of every shift.

2. **Maintenance Monitoring**

   - Power Automate monitors mileage cycles, and time-sensitive maintenance triggers to alert maintenance staff.

3. **Usage and Fuel Analytics**

   - Power BI dashboards show vehicle usage patterns, detect fuel inefficiencies, and detect idle fleets.

4. **Cost Tracking and Compliance**

   - Finance can monitor fuel costs by department or asset using trip logs.

5. **Strategic Planning**

   - Managers use data to maximize fleet size, minimize carbon footprint, and schedule replacements.

Dashboards and Reporting Views

- **Fuel Spend Analysis**: Costs per vehicle, per team, or per mile

- **Vehicle Utilization Report**: Active vs. idle days, average daily miles

- **Service Tracker**: Reminder of scheduled service, past-due, and history

- **Environmental Impact**: Approximate emissions, electric vehicle comparisons

Results and Measurable Impact

Metric	Before	After
Manual trip logs	100%	0% (fully digitized)
Missed maintenance	Frequent	Reduced by 90%
Fuel tracking errors	Common	Tracked in real time
Underutilized vehicles	Difficult to detect	Visualized and reduced

- **Outcome**: Efficient processes, reduced fuel expenses, longer vehicle life, and extremely high compliance rate with asset tracking requirements

Use Case 4: Road Construction Project Monitoring and Milestone Tracking

Overview and Context

Transportation departments oversee large, complex infrastructure projects such as road widening, bridge maintenance, and freeway replacement. These capital projects have several stakeholders, contractors, funding parties, timelines, environmental permits, and public postings.

Conventional project management approaches—scattered across spreadsheets, Gantt charts, unconnected systems, and email chains—introduce inefficiencies, delays, lack of accountability, and a lack of transparency.

This use case brings in a **Power Platform-Based Project Oversight and Milestone Tracking System** to consolidate project planning, automate progress reporting, and provide real-time insights to stakeholders and leadership.

Who It Helps

Stakeholder	Benefit
Project Managers	Track construction timelines, resource allocation, and contractor deliverables in a single dashboard
Field Engineers	Log site updates, inspections, and safety reports with photos and locations using mobile apps
Finance Teams	Track budget vs. actuals by milestone and funding stream
Leadership	Sees overall portfolio health, red-flagged delays, and high-risk items in real time
Public Relations and Citizens	(Optional) Get traffic impact, lane closure, and estimated project completion updates through Power Pages

Key Drivers for Modernization

- **Fragmented Planning Tools**: Timelines, budgets, and contractor notes are stored separately.

- **Manual Progress Reporting**: Status reports are collected via email and re-typed into reports.

- **Delayed Risk Detection**: No timely notifications when a milestone is in danger of slipping.

- **No Field-to-Office Sync**: Field crews are unable to post real-time updates from the field.

- **Dashboards Not Available**: Management is forced to wait for manual rollups to view progress.

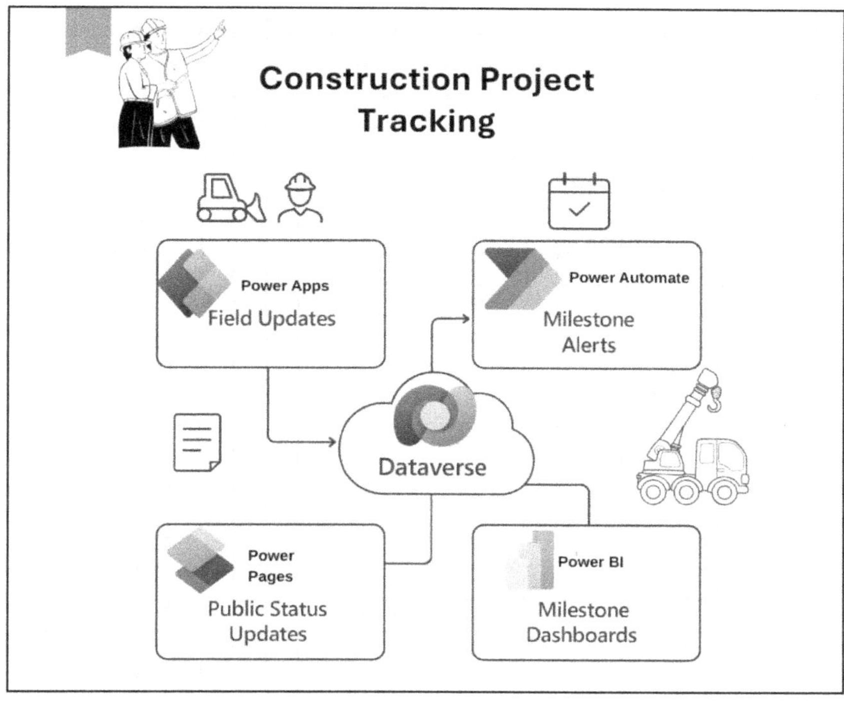

Figure 7-15. *Architecture Diagram—Project Milestone Tracker*

Technical Solution Architecture

Component	Figure out the role
Power Apps (Canvas App)	Utilized by engineers and supervisors in the field to report project status, take pictures, and alert delays
Dataverse	Saves project plans, milestones, funding information, contractor logs, and inspection reports
Power Automate	Sends reminders for missed milestones, budget excess, or change orders that need approval
Power BI	Project initialization, budget tracking dashboards, region-wise portfolio health dashboards, and critical path delay dashboards
Power Pages	(Public facing optional) Public-facing interface for key projects—share progress diagrams, timelines, and lane closure notices

Workflow Overview

1. **Project Initialization**

   - PM initializes projects in Power Apps or Dataverse template with phases, tasks, budgets, and dependencies.

2. **Field Progress Updates**

   - Engineers record updates on milestones, inspection findings, or problems using Power Apps on site (GPS/pictures).

3. **Alerting and Escalation**

   - Power Automate triggers on behind-schedule tasks, over-budgeting limits, or recorded safety reports.

4. **Leadership Oversight**

- Power BI dashboards present earned value, Gantt schedules, and risk overviews by region/project.

5. **Public Transparency (Optional)**

- Power Pages indicate project status, on-time anticipated, and diversion paths for public awareness.

Dashboards and Reporting Views

- **Project Portfolio Health Dashboard**: Reports status of all active projects, by funding source or by region.

- **Gantt View of Milestones**: Graphical view showing status-coded color (on track, at risk, delayed).

- **Budget vs. Actual Tracker**: Show cost spent against forecast at each milestone.

- **Field Activity Summary**: Reports submitted, issues assigned, and work completed.

Results and Measurable Impact

Metric	Before	After
Time to detect milestone slippage	Weeks	Real-time alerts
% of overdue milestones detected late	60%	< 10%
Field report turnaround	2–3 days	Instant sync
Visibility of budget deviation	Delayed to the end of the month	Dashboards

- **Outcome**: Increased transparency, quicker risk elimination, better coordination with subcontractors, and tighter budget management

Use Case 5: Permit and Lane Closure Coordination with Utility Partners

Overview and Context

Telecom, electric, water, and gas utility operators often have to perform work that requires road closure either partially or entirely. Permit coordination, schedule management, safety compliance, and traffic disruption avoidance involve the transportation department, public works, and external contractors collaborating.

Traditionally, this process entails forms sent via email, printed permits, last-minute approval, and out-of-phase closing dates—frustrating commuters, creating public safety hazards, and harming the reputations of city agencies.

This solution leverages a **Permit and Lane Closure Coordination Platform** developed on Microsoft Power Platform to streamline permit workflows, facilitate communication with utility partners, and offer real-time visibility into all active closures by jurisdiction.

Who It Helps

Stakeholder	Benefit
Transportation Permit Officers	Process review, approval, and schedule closure allow a simplified way through automated routing and conflict detection
Utility and Construction Companies	Submit requests, view status, and upload compliance documents in a self-service portal
Traffic Operations	See planned closures to improve signage, signal timing, and detour plans
Public Safety	Route closure notifications to fire, EMS, and police agencies for emergency planning
Citizens	See live roadwork status through public-facing portals or GIS dashboards

Principal Drivers of Modernization

- **Manual Permit Submission**: Applications are submitted through emails or PDFs, which is time-consuming.

- **Schedule Conflicts**: Overlap of closures produces traffic and penalties to the contractors.

- **No Field Validation**: No evidence that safety flagging or safety signage procedures were properly followed.

- **Disjointed Communication**: City and utility partners have different timelines and processes.

- **No Public Transparency**: There will be no public announcement to the customers in the future about disruptions and detours.

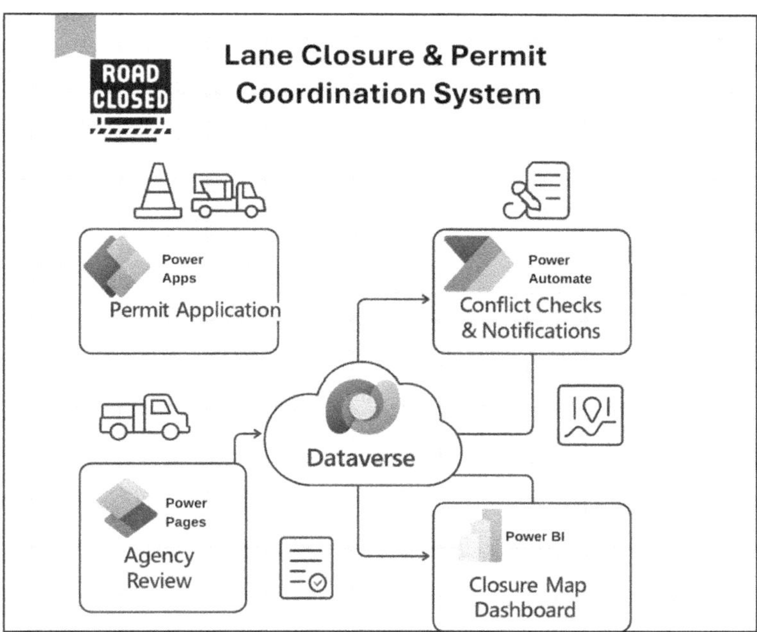

Figure 7-16. Lane Closure and Permit Coordination System Architecture Diagram

Technical Solution Architecture

Component	Role
Power Pages	Outside portal for utility partners and contractors to file closure permits, upload safety plans, and check application status
Power Apps (Model-Driven App)	Permit officers' internal application for viewing submissions, allocating inspectors, and approving/rejecting requests
Power Automate	Coordinates allows routing processes, conflict detection with other projects, automatic notice of approval or rejection, and emergency notices
Dataverse	Allows permit details, location information, start/end dates, documents, and compliance comments
Power BI	Dashboards of all planned closures by region, type of closure, risk of conflict, and status of compliance

Workflow Overview

1. **Permit Submission**

   - The utility company logs in to Power Pages and requests closure with scheduled dates, impacted lanes, and safety documents.

2. **Automated Review Routing**

   - Power Automate directs the request to the proper district/agency team based on location and impact type.

3. **Conflict Detection**

   - The system checks for duplicate closures, special events, or already permitted construction work.

4. **Approval and Notification**

   - Upon approval, notifications to the utility companies, traffic teams, and emergency services are sent.

   - Power Automate performs inspections or compliance checks when required.

5. **Closure Monitoring and Reporting**

   - Compliance data is tracked by field personnel, photo proof, or signage status using Power Apps.

   - Future closures, compliance trends, and issue logs are graphed using Power BI.

Dashboards and Reporting Views

- **Upcoming Closure Map**: Interactive GIS display of all approved lane closures with filtering.

- **Permit Volume by Type**: Utility, resurfacing, special event, etc.

- **Conflict Risk Heatmap**: Allow overlap zones or low detour capacity zones.

- **Compliance Tracker**: Percentage of permits with safety plan received, signage verified, or passed final inspection.

Results and Measurable Impact

Metric	Before	After
Average permit approval time	7–10 days	< 48 hours
Closure conflicts per month	10–12 issues	< 2 (with real-time detection)
Public access to closure info	Limited	Real time via portal/dashboard
Missed safety compliance	Common	Tracked and auditable

- **Outcome**: Shorter approval times, decreased conflict closures, improved safety work environment, and improved transparency with utility partners and the public

7.4 Department of Environmental Services
Use Case 1: Environmental Hazard Reporting and Field Response Automation

Overview and Context

Environmental officials need to respond to hazardous events like chemical spills, dumping, air pollution alerts, and water contamination. These are usually reported by staff or members of the community and need to be rapidly triaged, fielded, and required to report for regulatory purposes.

Legacy process—hotline calls, email, paper forms, and manual dispatch—has responses behind, documentation minimal, and tracking resolution times or environmental footprint challenging.

This use case demonstrates a **Power Platform-Based Environmental Hazard Reporting and Response System** that enables agencies to automate hazard intake, streamline response processes, and monitor field investigations in real time.

Who It Helps

Stakeholder	Benefit
Citizens	Report environmental hazards quickly through a photo-capable, mobile-capable portal with descriptions and locations
Field Inspectors	Auto-assigned and recorded observations in a field application by GPS-geotagged images and comments
Environmental Response Managers	Directly received reports, dispatched field investigators, monitored response time, and referred to serious incidents
Compliance Officers	Close cases in times mandated by regulation and ensure documentation completeness for audits
Policy and Leadership Teams	View data on environmental hazards, geospatial patterns, and response performance

Drivers for Modernization

- **Unstructured Reporting**: Incidents arrive by calls, faxes, or unstructured emails.

- **No Dispatch Logic**: Delayed manually, triaged, and field-assigned.

- **Disjointed Field Reports**: Field inspection pictures and comments are archived elsewhere or are lost.

- **Lack of Audit Trail**: Verification of meeting EPA or state deadlines is challenging.

- **No Environmental Analytics**: Agencies find it hard to track repeat offenders or hotspots of pollution.

Figure 7-17. *Architecture Diagram—Environmental Hazard Reporting System*

Technical Solution Architecture

Component	Role
Power Pages	Portal for public use to report environmental risk on behalf of a company or public, optionally with photo and location
Power Apps (Canvas App)	Field responders employ them to enter cases, visit sites, take photos, and post results in real time
Dataverse	Removes case information, location, time stamps, field comments, photos, status posting, and resolution results securely
Power Automate	Routing sets direction by type of risk; geography zone sets due date to engaged departments; flags late reply informing concerned department
Power BI	The trend of the incidents as they occur, geographic locations where incidents have taken place, achievement of SLA, and rate of violation boards

Workflow Overview

1. **Hazard Submission**

   - Submission by staff or citizen using Power Pages, nature of the report (air, water, unauthorized dump, etc.), explanation, and any secondary additional pictures, if chosen.

2. **Automated Triage and Assignment**

   - Severity and location are determined by Power Automate, flows to a relevant regional team, and assigns new inspection tasks.

3. **On-Site Investigation**

   - The investigator conducts the investigation via Power Apps on a mobile device, posts photos, and documents findings.

4. **Case Closure and Compliance**

   - At closeout, the investigator inputs and updates corrective action taken: Power Automate tracks closeout time and also compliance status.

5. **Analytics and Oversight**

   - Power BI allows for displaying case volumes, response times, geographic trends, and agency performance vs. EPA/state SLAs on dashboards.

Dashboards and Reporting Views

- **Incident Heatmap**: High-risk repeat offense hotspots or sources of pollution

- **Resolution SLA Dashboard**: Time to close by violation type (e.g., illegal dumping, air complaint, water spill)

- **Inspector Activity Summary**: Assigned, closed, late, and escalated cases

- **Compliance Reports**: Timely closing of cases by federal and state reporting

Results and Measurable Impact

Metric	Before	After
Average response time	5–7 days	< 48 hours
Overdue EPA/state resolution timelines	Common	Cut by 80%
Consistency in inspector reports	Inconsistent	Real time with picture reporting
Trend visibility into incidents	Manual reports	Power BI dynamic dashboards

- **Outcome**: Responsive incident response, public confidence gain, better regulatory compliance, and environmental data-driven planning

Use Case 2: Water Quality Monitoring and Lab Result Integration Platform

Overview and Context

Water quality monitoring is an essential function of state and local environmental agencies to provide the safety of public drinking water supplies, surface water bodies, and industrial discharge locations. Testing generally includes more than one sample point, laboratory result uploading, regulatory requirements, and public transparency.

But current systems aren't working: field crews manually gather samples, laboratory results are reported by PDF or email, and compliance tracking is kept in spreadsheets—both creating silos of data, lagging reporting, and regulatory risk.

This use case illustrates a **Water Quality Monitoring Platform** on Microsoft Power Platform with automated lab ingestion of data, real-time compliance alerting, and centralized health, utility, and regulatory coordination dashboards.

Who It Helps

Stakeholder	Benefit
Field Monitoring Teams	Monitor water sample collection and site calendars in the field on mobile apps
Laboratory Technicians	Publish results directly to a secure portal and get an alert for reported results
Environmental Analysts	See lab data as images, cross-reference against regulatory limits, and detect contamination trends
Regulatory Compliance Officers	Get an automatic notification on threshold violations and create audit-ready reports
Public Stakeholders (Optional)	See sanitized dashboards of local water safety status and recent test events

Key Drivers for Modernization

- **Manual Result Entry**: Lab reports arrive as PDFs or spreadsheets with no data format.

- **Delayed Threshold Alerts**: Employees only realize contaminations once standard reading of reports is undertaken.

- **Disjointed Logs**: Sample gathering, test outcomes, and location metadata are not linked.

- **No Historical Trend Analysis**: Difficult to recognize long-term environmental trends or contamination hotspots.

- **Limited Public Transparency**: Citizens have no easily obtainable data regarding nearby water-quality status.

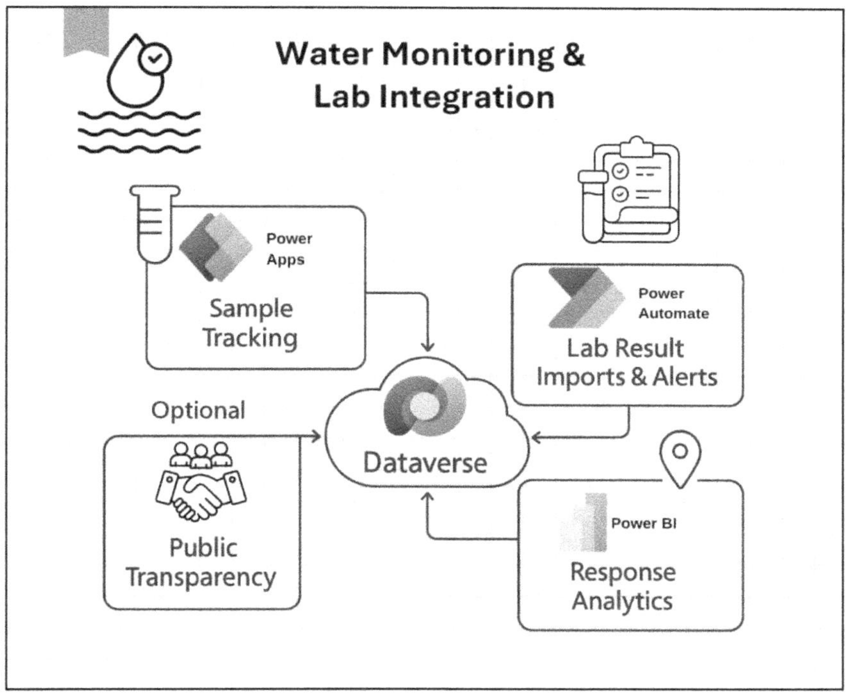

Figure 7-18. *Architecture Diagram—Water Monitoring and Lab Integration*

Technical Solution Architecture

Component	Role
Power Apps (Canvas App)	Used by field staff to record sampling activity and GPS-mark locations, record turbidity/temperature, and set follow-ups
Power Automate	Processes structured lab result files by email/API and sends alerts if contamination is found or parameters are breached
Dataverse	Structured, centralized data model with sampling location metadata, lab results, thresholds, timestamps, and follow-up actions
Power BI	Dashboards for monitoring compliance with safety, water health metrics by location, and trends by sampling types (potable, industrial, natural)
Power Pages	Optional public portal to view simplified dashboards and region-based news on water quality

Workflow Overview

1. **Sample Collection**

   - Field staff input sample collected, date/time, GPS location, and sample type in Power Apps.

   - Barcode or sample ID auto-generated.

2. **Lab Result Intake**

   - Lab input test results via secure email/API.

   - Power Automate reads and imports structured data into Dataverse.

3. **Compliance Alerting**

   - Notifying is facilitated where EPA/state threshold violations take place by Teams/email to environmental officers and compliance managers.

4. **Analysis and Oversight**

   - Power BI accumulates over time, captures trends, and notifies ongoing exceedances and test frequency monitoring.

5. **Public Transparency**

   - Power Pages (if enabled) post dashboards of current test results for a water body or each of the service districts.

Dashboards and Reporting Views

- **Compliance Scorecard**: Pass/fail rate by location, test type, and parameter (e.g., nitrates, bacteria, lead).

- **Contamination Heatmaps**: Show exceedances over time by area.

- **Sampling Frequency Tracker**: Highlight when each location was last sampled and future windows for sampling.

- **Historical Trends Dashboard**: Trends over long terms to see chronic issues or seasonality drivers.

Results and Measurable Impact

Metric	Before	After
Threshold violation detection time	2–5 days	Real time with Power Automate
Lab data entry manual	High	Eliminated (auto-ingestion)
Historical trend visibility	Minimal	Multiyear interactive reports
Public transparency	Static PDFs	Live portal or exportable dashboard

- **Outcome:** Enhanced water safety compliance, quicker contamination response, and enhanced coordination of field, lab, and oversight staff

Use Case 3: Air Quality Sensor Data Aggregation and Community Exposure Alerts

Overview and Context

Public health can be safeguarded through monitoring the air quality, particularly in industrialized areas plagued by industrial operations, wildfires, traffic, or climate-related pollution episodes. Despite this, the sensor data usually comes from a disjointed collection of networks, and poor air-quality alerts are sporadic or out of sync for agencies.

This solution involves an **Air Quality Monitoring and Exposure Alert System** on Microsoft Power Platform that consolidates real-time information from IoT sensors, assesses exposure thresholds, and sends targeted alerts to environmental teams and the public.

Who It Helps

Stakeholder	Benefit
Environmental Analysts	Aggregate live sensor data, identify threshold violations, and view regional air quality in real time
Emergency Managers	Get early notice of pollution surges or wildfire smoke events to activate contingency procedures
Public Health Agencies	Monitor exposure risk for at-risk populations, schools, and senior centers
Citizens	Receive local alerts via SMS or email when air quality reaches dangerous levels
Policy Makers	Gain data visualizations to inform regulations, emission limits, and long-term planning

Major Drivers for Modernization

- **Disparate Sensor Networks:** Information is dispersed between vendor platforms or stand-alone municipal systems.

- **No Single Alerting Mechanism:** Exposure risks are not alerted to the affected populations in a timely fashion.

- **Delayed Reporting**: Acute pollution incidents or wildfire smoke require daily reports fast.

- **Limited Public Access**: Citizens do not have easy-to-understand information for their immediate ZIP code or region.

- **No Predictive Insights**: Agencies cannot monitor long-term air-quality patterns or compare exposure incidents.

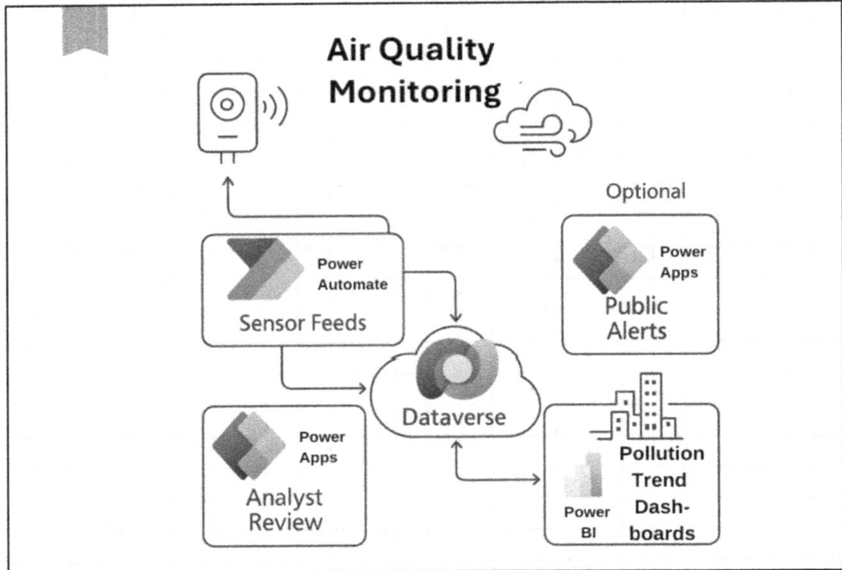

Figure 7-19. *Architecture Diagram—Air-Quality Aggregation and Alerting System*

Technical Solution Architecture

Component	Role
IoT Sensor Integration (via Azure)	Aggregates PM2.5, ozone, NO_2, CO, VOC, and temperature/humidity from city or regional monitors
Power Automate	Processes sensor readings in real time and compares to predefined health thresholds (e.g., AQI values)
Dataverse	Holds hourly readings, sensor metadata, thresholds, event history, and alert delivery logs

(continued)

Component	Role
Power Apps (Model-Driven)	Enables environmental officers to view flagged data, mark pollution events, and control alerting rules
Power BI	Dashboards of AQI maps, exposure hours, most polluted ZIP codes, and day-over-day breakdowns
Power Pages/SMS Connector	(Optional) Delivers targeted notifications to citizens on subscribed ZIP codes or groups (e.g., schools and elder care facilities)

Workflow Overview

1. **Sensor Data Ingestion**

   - An hourly real-time feed from Azure IoT Hub or APIs feeds air-quality metrics into Power Automate and Dataverse.

2. **Threshold Assessment**

   - Power Automate cross-references AQI values with EPA and state standards and raises alerts in the event of exceedance.

3. **Targeted Notification**

   - Environmental health teams receive alerts and, as an option, public subscribers by email/SMS or Power Pages.

4. **Data Review and Annotation**

- Forestation officers employ Power Apps to verify spikes, add notes (i.e., the location of wild-fire start), and indicate exposure incidents.

5. **Public Reporting and Trends**

- Power BI displays historical trends, repeat hotspots, day-to-day comparisons, and health risk scores.

Dashboards and Reporting Views

- **Live AQI Map:** Displays sensor-based AQI values by location in color-coded form.

- **Top Contaminated ZIP Codes:** Ordered by daily or weekly exposure means.

- **Health Risk Timeline:** Summary of red/orange AQI events by hour by community.

- **Long-Term Trend Viewer:** Compare monthly/seasonal trends between years or regions.

Results and Measurable Impact

Metric	Before	After
Time to alert on AQI exceedance	2–4 hours	< 5 minutes
Public awareness of exposure	Low	Region-based real-time alerts
Data integration challenges	High	Unified via Dataverse
Trend analysis capability	Minimal	Full Power BI analytics with annotation history

- **Outcome**: Quicker emergency response, enhanced public health safety, and more informed environmental policies through real-time and predictive air-quality intelligence

Use Case 4: Environmental Permit Workflow and Compliance Dashboard

Overview and Context

The issuing and management of environmental permits for construction, emissions, solid waste management, stormwater runoff, and land development are important functions of environmental agencies. The permits are regulated by the EPA and states, often involve multi-agency authorization, and necessitate ongoing monitoring of compliance.

The existing permit issuance and monitoring process is paper-heavy or email-centric, with routing lag, status opaqueness, and weak tracking of enforcement. This leads to missed deadlines for compliance, legal exposure, and restricted performance reporting.

This use case deploys an **Environmental Permit Workflow and Compliance Dashboard** based on Microsoft Power Platform, simplifying end-to-end permit processing, incorporating task automation, and facilitating real-time monitoring of permit status, conditions, and infractions.

Who It Helps

Stakeholder	Benefit
Allow Permit Process	Permit Coordinators allow Permit Process applications, forward them to reviewers, track deadlines, and approve/reject with comments
Applicants (Developers/Businesses)	Apply online for permits, submit supporting documents, and track approval status
Regulatory Analysts	Guarantee conformity with permit conditions, schedules, and inspection intervals
Legal and Enforcement Teams	View violations, missed milestones, and documentation deficiencies for legal follow-up
Executive Oversight	View dashboards of backlog, turnaround time, and high-risk activities or geographic locations

Drivers for Modernization

- **Manual Routing**: Permit allowances are passed around via email or printed folders, generating delays and errors.

- **Not Transparent**: Candidates have to call/email in order to obtain status information.

- **No Automated Deadlines**: There is no automatic monitoring of renewal and compliance activities.

- **Disconnected Compliance Checks**: Inspections and documentation are typically not attached to the initial permit.

- **Poor Performance Insights**: Monitoring the volume of permit issuances, timelines, and average delays is challenging.

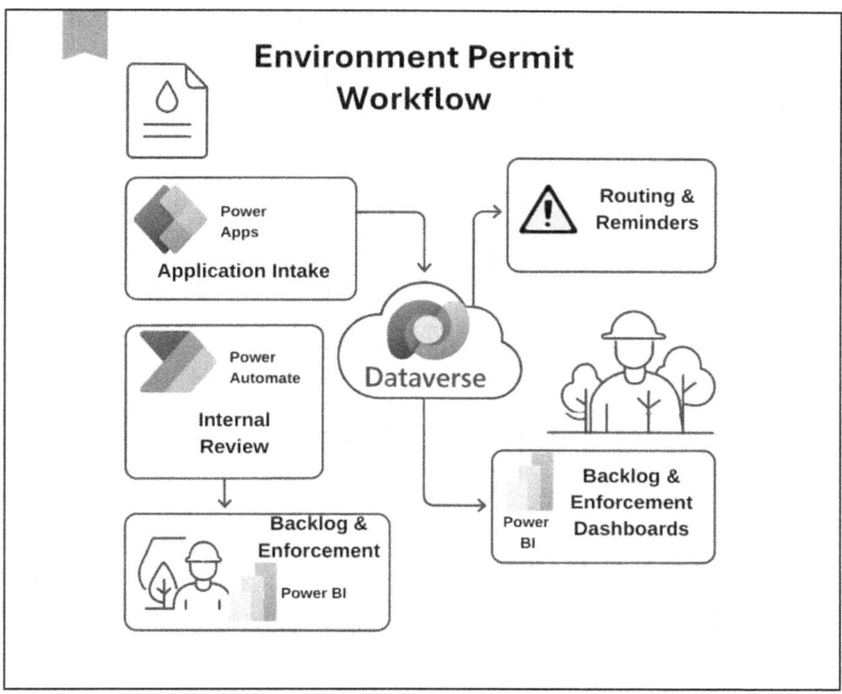

Figure 7-20. *Architecture Diagram—Environmental Permit and Compliance System*

Technical Solution Architecture

Component	Role
Power Pages	Applicants (e.g., developers, industrial plants) use to submit permit forms, upload documents, and view approval status
Power Apps (Model-Driven App)	Agency personnel process applications, assign reviewers, record decisions, track conditions, and schedule inspections
Dataverse	Central database for permit metadata, conditions present, renewal due dates, and historical information
Power Automate	Automatically sends to reviewers, reminders for inspection or filing of documents, and marks as overdue
Power BI	Allows volume dashboards, cycle time, condition status, and compliance patterns by region and industry

Workflow Overview

1. **Permit Application Intake**

   - Provide files in Power Pages with all required fields, uploads, and statements.

2. **Automated Routing and Review**

   - Power Automate sends to respective internal teams (e.g., air, water, land) based on activity type and location.

3. **Review, Comments, and Approval**

   - Staff record the results, append advice, and forward for ultimate sign-off in Power Apps.

4. **Permit Issuance and Compliance Setup**

- A permit is issued with conditions and deadlines (e.g., 90-day inspections and quarterly discharge reports).

5. **Compliance Monitoring**

- Power Automate reminds before condition deadlines; inspectors record findings through Power Apps.

6. **Analytics and Escalation**

- Power BI shows open work, allows backlogs and impending expirations, and notes compliance risk.

Dashboards and Reporting Views

- **Permit Processing Timelines**: Average number of days to approval, behind-schedule permits, near expirations

- **Condition Fulfillment Tracker**: Percentage of permits with unfulfilled or past-due conditions

- **Reviewer Workload Dashboard**: Approval awaiting reviewer or team feedback

- **Violation Risk Heatmap**: Facility type or region with the highest compliance problems

Results and Measurable Impact

Metric	Before	After
Time to process permit	15–30 days	< 7 days (automated routing)
Condition tracking	Manual via spreadsheets	Real time via Dataverse and dashboards
Public access to permit status	None or phone/email	Live portal with tracking
Missed compliance tasks	Frequent	Reduced by 85% with alerts and automation

- **Outcome**: Quicker approvals, increased applicant satisfaction, enhanced compliance monitoring, and audit trails that can be defended in regulatory enforcement

Use Case 5: Sustainability Program Management and Environmental Impact Dashboard

Overview and Context

Numerous government environmental agencies oversee sustainability programs in the air, water, energy, and waste sectors. These can be programs like recycling incentives, urban tree planting, emissions reduction, green building certification, energy conservation tracking, and public awareness campaigns.

Yet, program information is dispersed across spreadsheets, third-party portals, and grant-tracking platforms—hindering the ability to assess success, report on KPIs, or inform policy decisions.

This use case introduces a **Sustainability Program Management Platform** constructed using Microsoft Power Platform to centralize program tracking, monitor environmental KPIs, automate reporting, and aid decision-making through transparent dashboards and visualizations.

Who It Helps

Stakeholder	Benefit
Program Managers	Track projects, goals, timelines, and funding milestones in a centralized system
Environmental Analysts	Track impact metrics (e.g., CO_2 savings, waste diversion) and compare by districts
Grant Administrators	Align funded projects with sustainability objectives and auto-generate impact reports
Public Policy Teams	Access real-time data to inform new green policies and justify program growth
Citizens (Optional)	Interact with dashboards that display how their region is doing on sustainability objectives

Key Drivers for Modernization

- **Fragmented Program Data**: Goals, results, and reports are scattered across many systems with no central view.

- **Manual Impact Reporting**: KPIs are manually tabulated at year-end, resulting in reporting delays and inaccuracy.

- **No Standardized Metrics**: Varying teams measure impact in different ways (e.g., GHG savings).

- **Challenging Linking Actions to Results**: It is difficult to relate a project (e.g., deployment of EV chargers) to environmental impacts.

- **Limited Public Engagement**: Sustainability progress isn't clearly communicated to constituents.

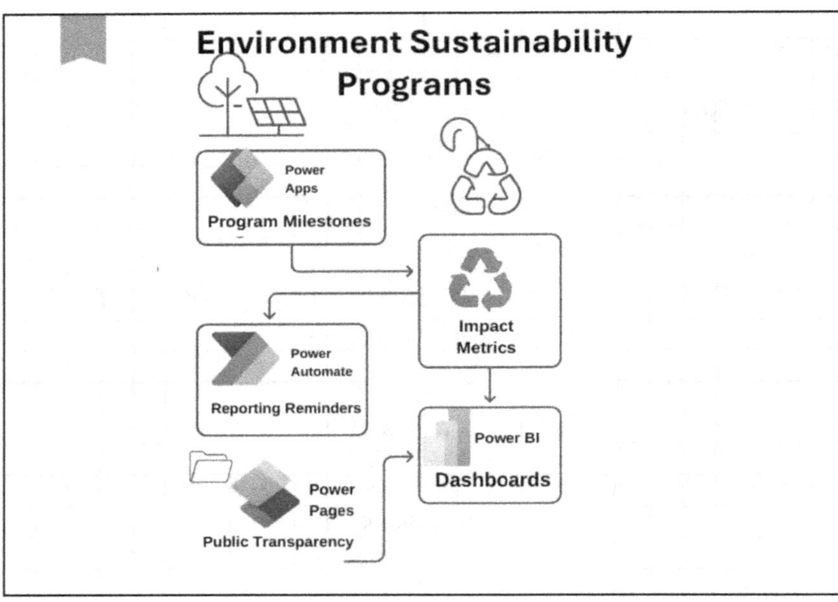

Figure 7-21. Architecture Diagram—Sustainability Program Tracker

Technical Solution Architecture

Component	Role
Power Apps (Model-Driven App)	Access for program managers to input project milestones, monitor environmental KPIs, and timeline and fund management
Dataverse	Serves as the centralized hub for all the program's data, including emissions savings by locations, project data, emission savings, energy metrics, and volumes of waste
Power Automate	Reminders for report deadlines, review goals, or close-out milestones on grants
Power BI	Progress dashboards toward sustainability targets, regional metrics, and policy impact
Power Pages	(Optional) Public-facing dashboards to showcase carbon savings, clean energy milestones, and citizen engagement metrics

Workflow Overview

1. **Program Setup**

   - The sustainability program is set up in Power Apps, like goals (e.g., 30% CO_2 reduction), deadlines, and funding sources.

2. **Data Entry and Updates**

   - Teams update project progress (e.g., # trees planted, kWh saved) in Power Apps, either manually or via integrations.

3. **Reporting and Review**

- Reminders for quarterly or yearly updates are sent by Power Automate and escalate if past due.

4. **Dashboards and Analytics**

- Power BI displays influence by program (e.g., emissions, energy, waste), compares districts, and displays leading initiatives.

5. **Public Engagement**

- Optional Power Pages allow citizens to view sustainability achievements by ZIP code, participate in campaigns, or download infographics.

Dashboards and Reporting Views

- **Program Progress Scorecard**: Current completion % by project or goal

- **CO$_2$ Reduction Tracker**: Prevention by sector (transport, energy, buildings)

- **Resource Impact Summary**: Water conserved, waste diverted, energy saved

- **Funding Utilization Report**: Actual vs. budget for grant-funded sustainability initiatives

- **Public Dashboard** *(optional)*: Region-based scorecards, green community challenges, project maps

Results and Measurable Impact
Metric Before After

Metric	Before	After
Preparing impact reports	4–6 weeks	Instant, dynamic dashboards
Tracking project milestones	Inconsistent	Structured, automated in Power Apps
Citizen awareness of green initiatives	Low	Improved via transparent dashboards
Grant reporting compliance	Manual and delayed	Timely with workflow automation

- **Outcome**: Centralized sustainability management, better program management, greater public engagement, and faster access to impact-driven decision-making

7.5 Department of Emergency Services

Use Case 1: Emergency Incident Intake, Dispatch, and Resource Tracking System

Overview and Context

Emergency organizations such as fire departments, emergency medical services (EMS), and disaster response units need a real-time facility for incident intake, dispatching field personnel, vehicle and material tracking, and coordinating response activities efficiently. Existing dispatch and tracking systems, in many cases, are legacy-based, standalone, or rely on radio communication and hand-updating.

This use case implements a **Power Platform-Driven Emergency Incident Intake, Dispatch, and Resource Tracking System** to upgrade field coordination, reduce incident response time, and increase visibility across agencies in emergencies.

Who It Helps

Stakeholder	Benefit
Dispatch Officers	Record new incidents, severity rank, and send teams with GPS-based coordination
Field Responders (EMS, Fire, Hazmat)	Assignments, status update of response and reporting incident information using mobile apps
Emergency Management Officers	Monitor incidents by location/type, asset management available (supplies, equipment, vehicles), and redirect based on current demand
City/County Leadership	Oversee response effectiveness, view live incident maps, and receive incident analytics for planning and budgeting

Key Drivers Toward Modernization

- **Manual Intake**: Calls and paper forms enter incidents, thus slowing down dispatch and leaving room for human error.

- **No Real-Time Tracking**: Response teams lack mobile connectivity for updates, leading to delays in coordinating.

- **Disjointed Asset Oversight**: Motor vehicles, medical equipment, rescue gear, and supplies are monitored on standalone systems or spreadsheets.

- **Behind Schedule Reporting**: Incident reports and logs are recorded in days, limiting readiness for the next incident.

- **No Central Analytics**: There is no central dashboard where the leadership can surf through to analyze patterns of incident density, response time, or resource deployment.

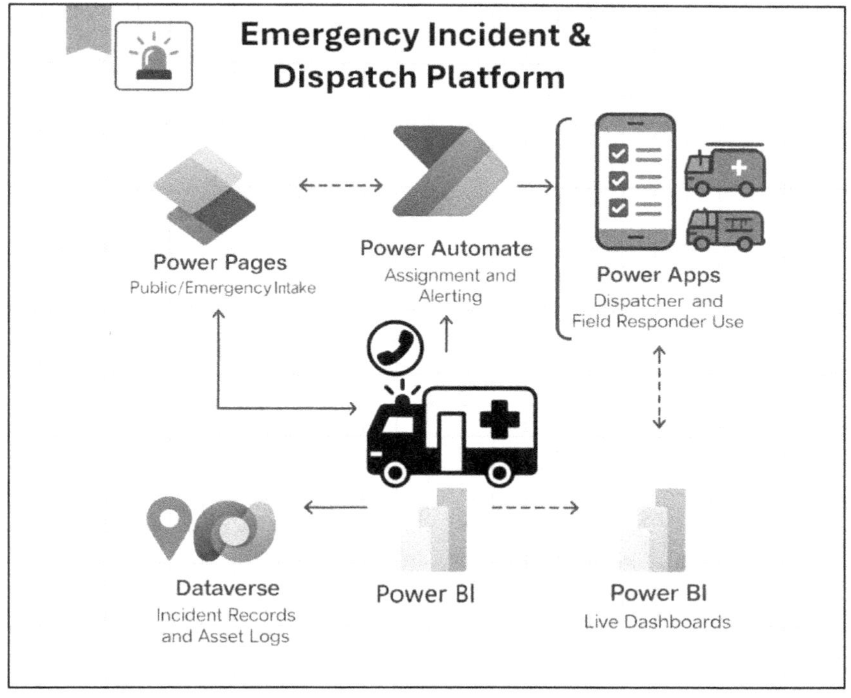

Figure 7-22. *Architecture Diagram—Emergency Incident and Dispatch Platform*

Technical Solution Architecture

Component	Role
Power Pages	Incident intake portal for public-facing or internal use (non-911 incidents, damage reports, emergency notifications)
Power Apps (Canvas App)	Dispatchers use to dispatch responders, and responders use to modify incident status, location, and field notes
Dataverse	Stores incident information, timestamps, priority codes, GPS coordinates, responder history logs, equipment usage, and inventory status
Power Automate	Directs incidents to the appropriate responder teams, sends out alerts/notifications, and escalates outstanding cases
Power BI	Dashboards that display active incidents, response times, asset allocation, and region-wise risk mapping

Workflow Overview

1. **Intake of Incident**

   - The report is submitted through Power Pages (or the dispatcher logs it in Power Apps). Data includes type, location, urgency, and attachments (e.g., photo of damage).

2. **Auto-Triage and Dispatch**

   - Power Automate routes based on incident type, units' proximity, and asset availability. Disatch orders that are sent to responder mobile apps.

3. **Field Logging of Response**

- Field staff status: "En route," "On Scene," "Resolved." Include photos, GPS check-in, and resources used to log.

4. **Asset Tracking and Reallocation**

- The availability of vehicles and equipment in Dataverse is updated automatically. Shortages trigger restocking alerts.

5. **Reporting and Analytics**

- Power BI displays an ongoing map of incidents, team response time averages, equipment use, and trends of incident category.

Dashboards and Reporting Views

- **Live Incident Tracker**: Map display of open incidents by location and status filters

- **Response Time Dashboard**: Dispatch time, arrival time, and resolution time averages by responder unit

- **Asset Inventory Tracker**: Deployed and available units, equipment, and supply kits

- **Incident Trend Dashboard**: Counts by incident category, time of day, severity, and zone

Results and Measurable Impact

Metric	Before	After
Average dispatch time	7–10 minutes	< 2 minutes
Resource availability tracking	Manual	Real-time updates
Incident report turnaround	2–3 days	Within 30 minutes after the incident
Regional incident visibility	Disconnected	A unified dashboard with GIS overlays

- **Outcome**: Improved dispatch speed, improved field coordination, reduced incident closure time, and improved readiness in city and regional emergency departments

Use Case 2: Disaster Shelter Management and Evacuee Tracking System

Overview and Context

In the event of natural disasters—wildfires, floods, hurricanes, or earthquakes—emergency responders need to establish shelters rapidly, register evacuees, handle capacity, and coordinate supplies. But, the majority of jurisdictions continue to rely on paper forms, spreadsheets, or standalone systems to manage shelter activities.

This contributes to confusion, duplication, over/underuse of shelters, and insufficient visibility into emergency population needs.

This use case involves an application of **Disaster Shelter Management and Evacuee Tracking System** on Microsoft Power Platform to provide automated shelter registration, real-time capacity monitoring, logistics management, and precise reporting to aid in recovery planning.

Who It Helps

Stakeholder	Benefit
Shelter Coordinators	Enroll evacuees, view available beds, monitor medical/support needs, and monitor inventory
Emergency Operations Centers (EOC)	Obtain real-time visibility into shelter status by region and coordinate supply delivery
Volunteers and Field Teams	Use mobile apps to confirm families, assign rooms, and refer medical/social care
Public Health Officers	Monitor at-risk populations (elderly, disabled) and offer timely intervention
FEMA/State Partners	Obtain consistent digital reports for post-disaster funding, audit, and resource allocation

Key Drivers for Modernization

- **Manual Registration**: Evacuee details are recorded on paper forms—susceptible to loss and delays.

- **No Capacity Visibility**: Central coordination doesn't have real-time visibility into bed availability or requirements.

- **Disconnected Case Tracking**: Medical, child care, accessibility, and dietary notes are not associated with individual records.

- **Logistics Inefficiency**: Supplies are allocated on assumption rather than demand at the shelter level.

- **Poor Post-Incident Reporting**: Shelter data is not complete or reliable for reimbursement and planning.

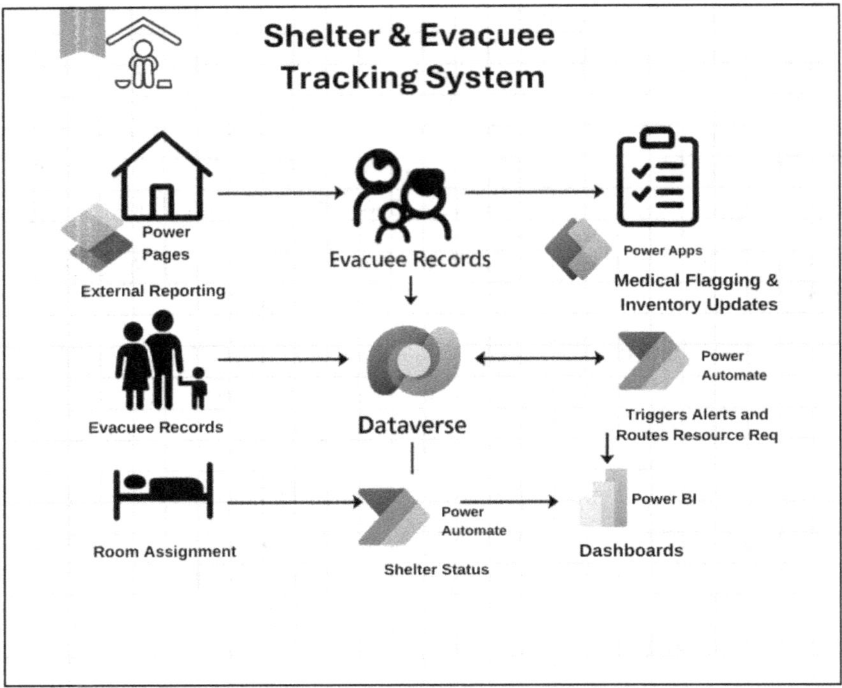

Figure 7-23. *Architecture Diagram—Shelter and Evacuee Tracking System*

Technical Solution Architecture

Component	Role
Power Apps (Canvas App)	The volunteers and the shelter staff use it to check in evacuees, allocate rooms, record medical/access needs, and monitor the usage of resources
Dataverse	Stores records of evacuees, shelter assignments, inventory histories, medical alerts, and status

(continued)

Component	Role
Power Automate	Triggers shelter capacity alerts, increases special needs instances, and handles requests for resources
Power BI	Interactive, real-time occupancy, demographics, resource use, and shelter trend dashboards
Power Pages (Optional)	Used to post shelter availability to regional partners or publish to the general public

Workflow Overview

1. **Evacuee Registration**

   - Staff utilize Power Apps to track simple details, family size, and special needs and allocate rooms or cots.

2. **Tracking Capacity and Needs**

   - Power Automate keeps capacity counters current and notifies regional commands when shelters are almost full or require supplies.

3. **Regular Case Updates**

   - Field workers input updates (medical care given, food served, status changes) directly into the app with timestamped comments.

4. **Resource Management**

   - Stock levels (food, bedding, hygiene packs) are monitored and recorded; low stock alerts are triggered.

5. **Reporting and Analytics**

- Power BI dashboards display the status of shelter, counts of evacuees, trends according to age or medical status, and recovery stage changes.

Dashboards and Reporting Views

- **Shelter Capacity Dashboard:** Available beds, total residents, check-in/check-out history

- **Demographic Breakdown:** By age, disability, pet ownership, language

- **Medical and Special Needs Tracker:** Active number of cases in need of care and response time

- **Resource Utilization Monitor:** Number of meals served on a daily basis, consumed, and available.

Results and Measurable Impact

Metric	Before	After
Average evacuee check-in time	10–15 minutes	< 3 minutes
Real-time shelter visibility	Not available	Fully integrated
Manual supply records	Paper-based	Real-time digital monitoring
Overlooked critical care alerts	Common	Resolved within 1 hour

- **Outcome:** Safer, more effective shelter operations, improved emergency coordination, enhanced public confidence, and recoverability-defensible reporting

Use Case 3: Public Emergency Notification and Alert Management System

Overview and Context

During emergencies—wildfires, chemical spills, storms, active shooter situations, or evacuations—emergency agencies must rapidly inform the public of accurate, location-specific directions. Existing systems consist of radio, reverse 911 calls, or third-party mass notification systems, which are separate from internal incident tracking systems.

This use case presents a **Public Emergency Notification and Alert Management System** developed on the Microsoft Power Platform. It allows local governments to send targeted alerts, control templates, synchronize incident triggers, and monitor public engagement in real time from one integrated system.

Who It Helps

Stakeholder	Benefit
Emergency Operations Centers (EOC)	Generate and deliver alerts quickly to multiple channels (email, SMS, portal, social media)
Public Information Officers (PIOs)	Coordinate message templates, notify citizens, and manage public narratives using real-time dashboards
City/County IT Teams	Track usage of systems, audit effectiveness of alerts, and provide system uptime
Citizens	Receive on-time, actionable information according to their location, subscription choice, and language
First Responders	Gain situational awareness of public counsel that is being offered to the impacted area

Main Drivers for Modernization

- **Manual Alerting devices**: These notify independently of different systems without an audit trail or are built from scratch.

- **One-Size-Fits-All Alerts**: Notifications cannot be sent to individual ZIP codes, school districts, or neighborhoods.

- **Restricted Multilingual Options**: Language constraints thwart the effectiveness of public alerting.

- **Lack of Engagement Analytics**: The agencies are unaware of who opened, responded to, or received notifications.

- **Disconnection from Incident Systems**: Lacking any connection between the actual incidents and the public information that is being sent out.

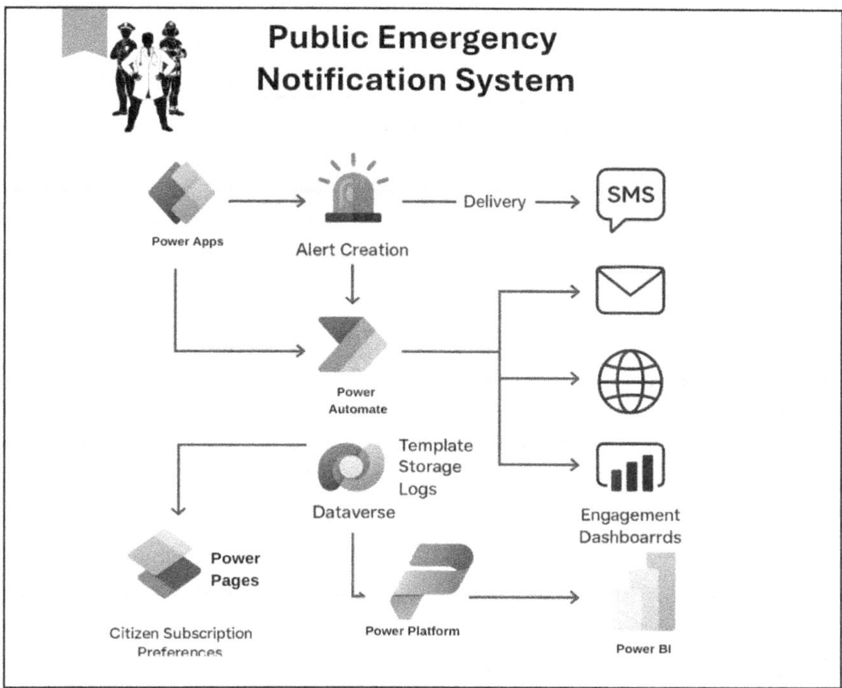

Figure 7-24. *Architecture Diagram—Emergency Alert Management System*

Technical Solution Architecture

Component	Role
Power Apps (Model-Driven App)	Used by EOC staff and PIOs to create alerts using pre-approved templates, customize regions, and deliver notifications
Dataverse	Stores templates, target groups, history of alerts, recipient logs, translations, and opt-in preferences
Power Automate	Sends alerts through SMS, email, and push notifications and connects to Twitter/Facebook or city websites

(continued)

Component	Role
Power BI	Dashboards to monitor alert delivery success, read rates, engagement, and gaps in coverage
Power Pages	Public-facing portal for citizens to sign up for alert receipt, designate language choice, and display last messages

Overview of Workflow

1. **Alert Trigger**

    - Incident data (fire, chemical spill, weather accident) to trigger a new alert using Power Apps.

2. **Composition of Messages**

    - PIO selects a template, fills in location/zone, and modulates by language/audience.

3. **Delivery**

    - Power Automate sends the message through several channels via API connectors (Twilio, Outlook, social edia).

4. **Audience Engagement**

    - Power BI monitors delivery logs, bounce reports, read rates, and click-throughs.

5. **Subscription and Feedback**

    - Subscriptions, favorite topics, or opt-out are managed by citizens through the Power Pages portal.

Dashboards and Reporting Views

- **Alert Coverage Dashboard**: Areas covered vs. gaps (e.g., no subscriptions in high-risk zones)

- **Message Performance Report**: Sent, opened, clicked, unsubscribed

- **Language and Accessibility Metrics**: Messages sent in several languages, percentages opting-in by demographic

- **Alert Type Trends**: Number and timing of alerts by type (weather, active threat, infrastructure failure)

Results and Measurable Impact

Metric	Before	After
Average time to compose and deliver alert	20–30 minutes	< 5 minutes using templates
Geo-targeted delivery	Not available	Enabled with ZIP or GIS filters
Engagement tracking	Manual sampling	Real-time dashboards
Multilingual coverage	Limited	Fully supported with template library and translation workflows

- **Outcome**: Accelerated and more comprehensive emergency messaging, enhanced public safety results, elevated community trust, and audit-ready transparency to crisis response

Use Case 4: Emergency Volunteer Coordination and Credential Management System

Overview and Context

In disaster scenarios—wildfires, floods, or mass shelter operations—government organizations must rapidly mobilize, onboard, and dispatch large numbers of volunteers. Affiliated (e.g., Red Cross, CERT) or spontaneous, these volunteers must be allocated by skills, credentials, place, and availability.

Legacy volunteer management uses paper sign-ins, phone trees, emails, and manual badge printing, which results in slow deployment, credential mismatches, and underutilization of valuable skills.

This solution introduces a **Volunteer Coordination and Credential Management Platform** on the Microsoft Power Platform to automate onboarding, credential verification, auto-assignments, and engagement tracking.

Who It Helps

Stakeholder	Benefit
Volunteer Managers	Review applicants, assign roles, validate certifications, and monitor engagement status
Volunteers	Register online, upload credentials, choose availability, and receive real-time assignments
Emergency Operations Center (EOC)	View volunteer rosters, fill critical positions based on skill gaps, and track field team makeup
Credentialing Authorities	Verify and validate submitted FEMA/NIMS certifications, background checks, and submitted licenses
Public Safety and HR	Provide liability and safety with credential matching, badge creation, and audit logging

Major Drivers for Modernization

- **Manual Sign-Up Processes**: Volunteers sign up in person or via PDF/email forms.

- **Credential Risk**: No live credential verification before assigning critical roles.

- **Uncoordinated Deployment**: Difficult to coordinate volunteers with shelters, supply lines, or medical jobs at scale.

- **No Volunteer Tracking**: Inability to monitor hours, tasks worked, or debrief feedback.

- **Compliance Gaps**: Reduced capability to audit participation for grants, reimbursements, or liability cases.

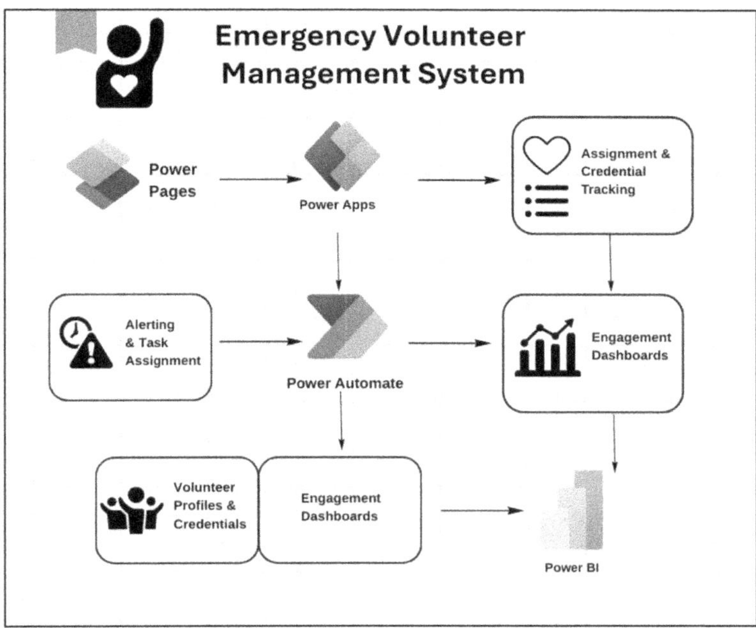

Figure 7-25. *Architecture Diagram—Volunteer and Credentialing Platform*

Technical Solution Architecture

Component	Role
Power Pages	Volunteers sign up, upload certifications, define availability, and see assignments
Power Apps (Model-Driven)	Used by coordinators to see applications, verify credentials, allocate tasks, and record volunteer hours
Dataverse	All volunteer data, credentials, availability, task assignments, participation logs, and compliance flags are stored here
Power Automate	Sends approval reminders, task assignment reminders, credential reminders, and shift notifications
Power BI	Dashboards to track active volunteers, credential deficits, geographic deployment, and after-action feedback

Workflow Overview

1. **Volunteer Signing Up**

   - Volunteers sign up on Power Pages, upload documents (CPR, background check, etc.), and choose their favorite tasks.

2. **Credential Verification**

   - Power Apps workflow allows approved approvers to approve, reject, or request clarification.

3. **Task Assignment and Check-In**

   - Based on skills and availability, Power Automate sends deployment info and assigns volunteers to locations (shelters, supply points, etc.).

4. **Field Operations**

- Check-in/check-out through the mobile app and enter field notes or photographs. Badge IDs are tracked through a QR scan or lookup.

5. **Engagement Analytics**

- Power BI dashboards roll up total hours contributed, assignment rate of completion, and skill gap fill.

Dashboards and Reporting Views

- **Volunteer Availability Map**: Region, skill, shift time, and assignment status

- **Credential Gap Tracker**: Percent of volunteers with needed certifications missing by role type

- **Shift Fulfillment Dashboard**: Work completed vs. available slots by location or incident

- **Volunteer Hours Log**: Total hours contributed, categorized by team, location, or time frame

Results and Measurable Impact

Metric	Before	After
Time to onboard volunteer	1–2 days	< 30 minutes
Unverified assignments	Common	Eliminated through credential gating
Shift fulfillment visibility	Manual	Real-time with automated reporting
Volunteer performance reporting	Ad hoc	Centralized with audit trails

- **Outcome**: Safer deployment of volunteers, accelerated emergency scaling, better grant documentation, and better engagement with the community.

Use Case 5: Damage Assessment and FEMA Reporting Automation System

Overview and Context

Disaster recovery is significantly dependent on proper and timely estimation of damage to determine costs, restore critical areas, and retrieve funds from FEMA or state funding. It typically consists of field workers entering damages, examiners quantifying severity, and administrators writing down reports—increasingly resulting in inconsistencies, delays, and underreporting damages.

This solution proposes the use of a **Damage Assessment and FEMA Reporting Automation System** on Microsoft Power Platform for the automation of field inspections, their validation in an effective way, and the automatic production of funding and policy response reporting packages.

Who It Helps

Stakeholder	Benefit
Field Inspectors and Survey Teams	Utilize mobile apps to log damages, snap photos, and allocate severity tags with GPS locations
Assessment Coordinators	Validate field input, prioritize zones, and build real-time impact dashboards
FEMA and State Partners	Get formal, auditable, geo-tagged reports that facilitate speeded funding decisions
Recovery Planning Teams	Get rolled-up impact data to drive repair schedules and policy reactions
Local Officials	View damage areas, public infrastructure affected, and displacement at population levels on real-time dashboards

Drivers of Modernization

- **Paper-Based Test**: Photographs, comments, and forms are stored separately and compiled manually.

- **Inconsistent Reporting**: Inconsistent formats and blank fields slow approvals and audits.

- **Geographic Confusion**: No real-time map-based visibility into damage clusters or coverage of assessments.

- **Slow FEMA Reporting**: Report turnaround can take weeks, delaying disaster declarations and aid.

- **Absence of Trend Data**: Previous disasters are not comparable between events or analyzed to determine resilience planning.

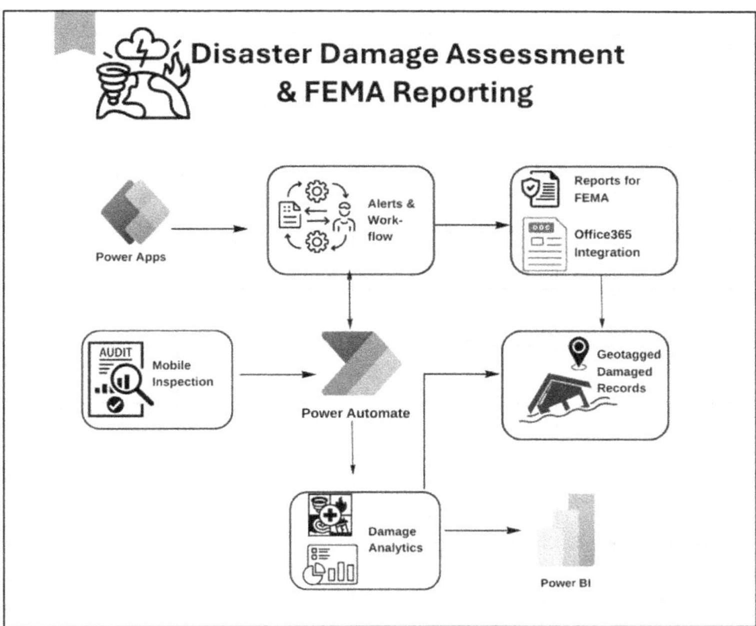

Figure 7-26. *Architecture Diagram—Damage Assessment and FEMA Automation Platform*

Technical Solution Architecture

Component	Role
Power Apps (Canvas App)	Mobile form for inspectors to log structure type, damage level, photos, GPS, and comments
Dataverse	Central repository for damage records, locations, asset types, costs, and affected population metadata
Power Automate	The triggers review process, stamps incomplete submissions, and produces reports to FEMA/state agencies
Power BI	Live damage heatmaps, cost estimates, zone coverage, and unmet needs dashboards
Office 365 Integration	Direct export to Word/Excel from Dataverse ready for FEMA

Workflow Overview

1. **Initiation of Damage Survey**

   - Field teams use Power Apps to report where damage is, enter the extent of damage (e.g., minor, major, destroyed), and attach photos.

2. **Review and Validation**

   - Assessment coordinators utilize Power Apps dashboards to review submissions, pose follow-ups, and complete severity ratings.

3. **Automated Reporting**

   - Daily dollar values of damage and lost coverage areas are captured by Power Automate and auto-fills FEMA report templates with dynamic data.

4. **Analytics and Planning**

- Power BI disseminates damage severity by census tract or zip code, estimated cost zone, infrastructure, and progress by recovery phase.

Dashboards and Reporting Views

- **Damage Intensity Map**: Filterable map with filters by severity, location, or structure type

- **Assessment Progress Tracker**: % covered zones, reinspect flagged, or completed

- **Cost Estimation Summary**: Summarized cost estimates by zone, structure type, or department

- **FEMA Reporting Queue**: List of validated reports ready for export and waiting for validations

Results and Measurable Impact

Metric	Before	After
Average time to assemble FEMA package	10–14 days	< 48 hours
Field entry consistency	Very variable	Standardized, validated in app
Missed areas of coverage	Common	Monitored and marked with GPS
Post-disaster funding slowdowns	Substantial	Cut by >60% via quick reporting

- **Outcome**: Sooner recovery funding, less administrative overload, dependable effects analysis, and greater trust in federal-state cooperation.

7.6 Department of Finance, Treasury, and Accounting

Use Case 1: Expense Reimbursement and Workflow Automation System

Overview and Context

The government employees often incur travel, training, procurement, and emergency operations costs. The process of reimbursing the costs is manual and time-consuming. It also requires paper forms, Excel files, authorization through email, and delayed payment.

This use case brings in a **Power Platform-Driven Expense Reimbursement and Workflow Automation System** to automate the entire process from request submission to approval to payment reconciliation. It ensures policy compliance, quicker reimbursements, and improved visibility into budgets.

Who It Helps

Stakeholder	Benefit
Employees	Submit electronic expense reports along with receipts and automatically calculated amounts
Supervisors/Approvers	Approve or reject claims from mobile or desktop, with audit trail and policy compliance indicators
Accounts Payable Teams	Process claims faster and confirm that the data is verified before it goes into financial systems
Auditors and Compliance Officers	Gain access to electronic logs, policy exceptions, and real-time reports to review
Finance Leadership	Visualize total reimbursed expenses, departmental segregation, and pending claim backlog

208

Key Drivers for Modernization

- **Paper Forms:** Reimbursement claims are primarily submitted in PDFs or printed forms.

- **Approval Delays:** Lack of standardized workflow allows for bottlenecks in threads or lost papers.

- **Policy Violation Non-detection:** Missing documents or policy infractions are not discovered until after payment.

- **No Reporting in Real Time:** The accounting staff has to manually prepare summaries to the department managers or auditors.

- **Repetitive Submissions**: Since there is no central authentication, it allows resubmission of a single receipt.

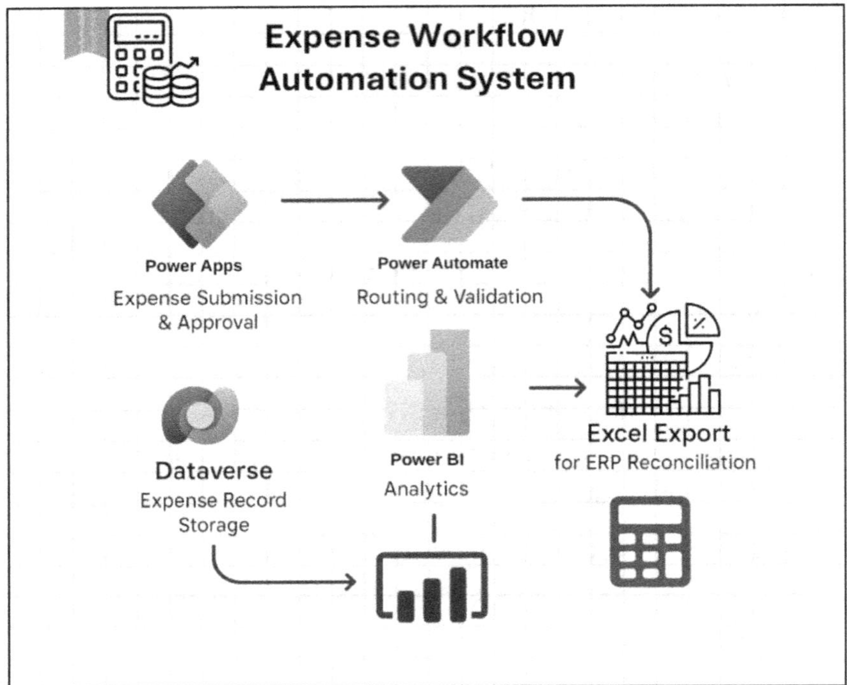

Figure 7-27. *Architecture Diagram—Expense Workflow Automation System*

Technical Solution Architecture

Component	Role
Power Apps (Canvas App)	The staff use it to submit their claims and upload the receipts for the approvers to view and approve or reject the claims
Dataverse	Store transaction information such as a receipt, approval history, expense category codes, employee profiles, and budget tags

(continued)

Component	Role
Power Automate	Forwards to approvers, flags overdue, identifies submissions, policy duplications, or policy violations
Power BI	Finance dashboards vividly show the number of claims, awaiting approvals, out of policy transactions, and departmental trends
Excel/ERP Connector	Facilitates the exchange of finance exports that can be integrated with SAP, Oracle, or Dynamics 365 Finance systems

Workflow Overview

1. **Submission of Expense**

   - Employee logs into Power Apps and submits expenses with receipts and details, chooses categories such as meals or travel, and submits.

2. **Approval Routing**

   - Power Automate validates expense amount and type and then sends to the respective department head or supervisor for approval.

3. **Validation and Compliance**

   - Flows validate missing receipts, duplicate claims, policy limits, and date discrepancy.

4. **Finance Review and Export**

   - In PowerApps, Accounts Payable Team validates approved claims and then exports them to Excel or syncs them with the ERP system.

5. **Dashboards And Audits**

- Power BI will track processing time, total claims, department-wise breached violations, and cycle time taken from submission to payment.

Dashboards and Reporting Views

- **Claims Summary Dashboards**: Total submitted, approved, rejected, and pending.

- **Cycle Time Tracker**: Average time taken from submission to payment.

- **Policy Violation Report:** Claims submitted without receipt, over category limits, or with past submission dates.

- **Department-wise Analysis**: Expenses paid by department, user, and quarter.

Results and Measurable Impact

Metric	Before	After
Repayment time	15–20 working days	5 days
Policy violation anomalies detected	Ad hoc	Automated during submission
Duplicate expense submission	Typical	Blocked and flagged
Quarterly reporting time	1–2 weeks	Immediate with dashboards

- **Outcome:** Faster reimbursement with lower errors and noncompliance risk with improved visibility of economic flow across departments

Use Case 2: Budget Request and Allocation Approval Workflow

Overview and Context

Budget planning and appropriation systems within the government agencies traditionally involve numerous cycles of review, justification reports, multilevel approvers, and strict compliance to fiscal calendars. Many agencies still handle this process today via spreadsheets, email communication, and siloed databases. This results in delays, low openness, and poor audibility.

This use case presents the **Budget Request and Allocation Approval Workflow** built on Microsoft Power Platforms to digitize budget proposals, automate routing according to a fiscal policy, and enable real-time visibility to approvals, rejections, and financial commitments.

Who It Helps

Stakeholder	Benefit
Department Heads	Just submit budget requests digitally with justifications and supporting papers
Budget Officers	Review requests, monitor allocations, compare with available funds, and route to senior authority
Finance Executives	Make choices with backed data and have concentrated visibility into every pending and authorized budget request
Auditors	With time stamps, auditors can view the entire history of submissions, approvals, comments, and papers
Grant and Capital Program Teams	Grant and capital program teams track phased releases, conditional budgets, and matching fund requirements

Modernization Key Drivers

- **Disjointed Submissions**: Requests submitted via paper forms or email increase processing time and data loss risk.

- **No Standard Workflow**: Approval paths vary across departments and are usually not documented.

- **Lack of Real-Time Visibility**: Finance lacks aggregate pending budget visibility or committed versus accessible fund ratios.

- **Missed Approvals:** Missing reminders and escalations lead to bottlenecks and missed approvals—events occurring on a regular basis.

- **Poor Audit Trails:** Approval notes, versions, and justifications are difficult to rebuild during an audit or assessment.

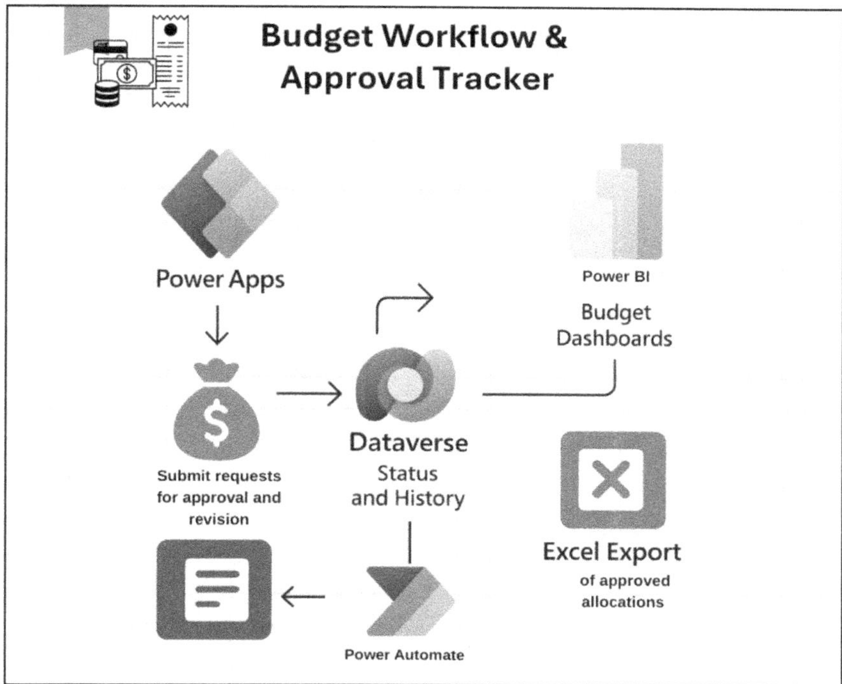

Figure 7-28. *Architecture Diagram for Budget Workflow and Approval Tracker*

Technical Solution Architecture

Component	Role
Power Apps (Model-Driven App)	Departments use it to submit requests and finance to review, comment, approve, or request changes
Dataverse	Centralized database for request forms, justifications, allocation history, status logs, and approver comments in Dataverse

(continued)

Component	Role
Power Automate	Send requests to approvers based on thresholds and policy, reminder notifications for deadlines, and sends overdue actions for escalation
Power BI	Power BI dashboards present submitted versus approved budgets pending by department, allocation by fund category, and bottleneck
Excel Integration	Approved allocations can be exported into standardized budget templates or financial systems thanks to Excel Integration

Workflow Summary

1. **Submission**

   - The department head selects the funding category and fiscal year and uploads justifications in Power Apps.

   - **Routing**

   - Power Automate routes based on the amount requested, type of fund, and organization either financial analysts or executives.

2. **Review and Comments**

   - Approvers review requests, comment or add conditions, approve, reject, or return for revision.

3. **Final Allocation**

   - Approved allocation data can be exported to ERP systems, displayed in budget dashboards, or saved in Dataverse.

4. **Oversight and Analytics**

- The Power BI dashboards display unallocated fund balances, category totals, time to approval, and allocation performance.

Views for Reporting and Dashboard

- **Budget Request Tracker**: Total submitted, pending, approved, rejected by department or quarter

- **Overview of Fund Allocation**: Visual of committed vs. accessible budgets

- **Approval SLA Dashboard:** Max and avg approval times by reviewer or team

- **Top Budget Categories**: Roll-up of purpose-driven requests (e.g., IT, infrastructure, training, hiring)

Outcomes and Measurable Effects

Metric	Before	After
Average approval cycle	2–3 weeks	4 business days
Request visibility	Siloed by department	Centralized and searchable
Missed funding deadlines	Common	Rare (automated reminders/ escalations)
Availability of audit trail	Manual logs	Completely electronic, time-stamped, searchable

- **Outcome**: Live insights will speed up budget approvals, improve planning, boost fiscal policy compliance, and enable strategic decision-making.

Use Case 3: Invoice Processing and Vendor Payment Automation

Overview and Context

A very crucial financial role that is done often is vendor invoice handling. In a month, government departments may receive numerous invoices from suppliers, service providers, and contractors. The typical process consists in invoice manual data input, approval pathway via emails, and timely payments paper or PDF invoices. This creates backlogs, late charges, audit risks, and strangled vendor relationships.

This use case offers a **Power Platform-Based Invoice Processing and Payment Automation System** to digitize invoice intake, route approvals, auto-validate against purchase orders, and integrate with ERP/payment systems for quicker, error-free payments.

Who It Helps

Stakeholder	Benefit
Accounts Payable (AP) Staff	Invoice auto-ingestion, elimination of manual data entry, and the ability to focus on exceptions are up sides for accounts payable (AP) staff
Departmental Approvers	Reminder emails for policy verifications and invoices to be approved are sent to approving departments
Vendors/Suppliers	Track bills and payments live as you get the real-time status update of your invoices submitted and payments from vendors/suppliers
Finance Directors	Track accounts payable performance, identify issues, and keep tabs on payment cycles and fines
Auditors	Auditors benefit from real-time access to searchable invoice records, approval history, and supporting documents

Significant Modernization Motivation Factors

- **Manual Invoice Entry**: Financial systems manually input PDF invoices via manual invoice entry. This increases error rates and cycle times.

- **Slow Approvals**: Without automatic reminders or routing, late and missed due dates result.

- **Policy Violations**: No automated checks for duplicate invoices, tax errors, orbudget overages.

- **Suppliers Have No Visibility**: Vendors need to call or email AP for status updates.

- **Audit Challenges**: For audit purposes, tracking approvals, exceptions, or non-PO invoices either raises challenging or error-prone questions.

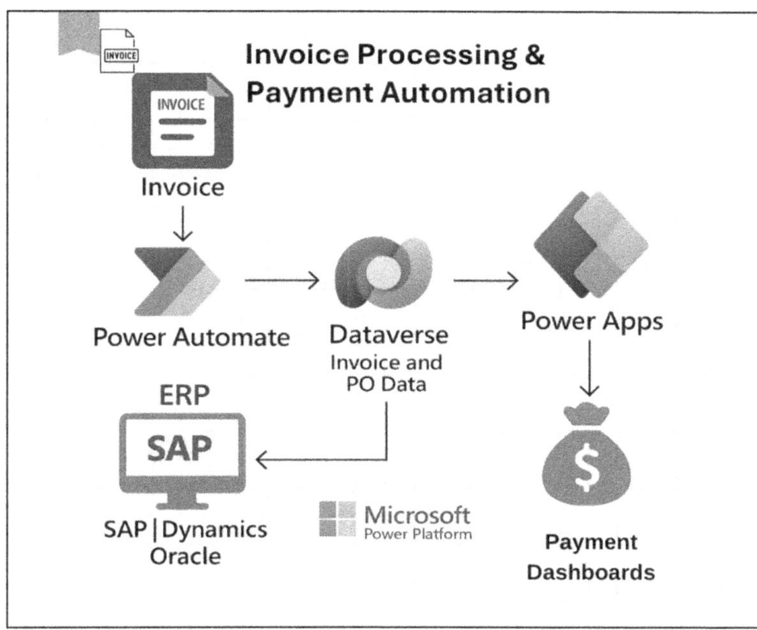

Figure 7-29. *Architectural Diagram—Invoice Processing and Payment Automation*

Architectural Technical Solution

Component	Role
Power Automate	Reads incoming invoices from email or API, uses AI Builder to extract essential data, and forwards for approval Power Automate
Dataverse	Dataverse stores attachments, invoice records, PO references, vendor profiles, GL codes, and payment status
Power Apps	Finance and department managers access Power Apps to view, approve, deny, or comment on invoices
ERP Connector	Approved invoices are synchronized by ERP Connector to the payment run system such as Dynamics 365, SAP, or Oracle
Power BI	Dashboards in Power BI for top vendors, duplicate detection, open invoice status, and payment turnaround time

Workflow Overview

1. **Invoice Submission**

   - Invoices are received via email or uploaded to a portal; data is then extracted by Power Automate with AI Builder and verified for the format of the invoice.

2. **PO Routing and Matching**

   - The system matches invoice data if a PO exists. Based on department/fund code, the invoice is sent to the proper approver.

3. **Approval and Evaluation**

   - Approvers sign in Power Apps to approve/reject with comments. Power Automate tracks actions and timestamps.

4. **Payment Handling**

   - Approved invoices are either processed in a payment batch run or sent to the ERP system.

5. **Compliance and Reporting**

   - Power BI displays exceptions, invoice quantity, vendor-specific data, and delays.

Reporting Views and Dashboards

- **Invoice Aging Report**: Average approval time, days outstanding, overdue counts

- **Top Vendor Summary**: By vendor, invoiced, handled, and delayed amounts

- **Duplicate and Error Flag Dashboard**: AI-detected problems, flagged duplicates, mismatches

- **Cash Flow Forecasting**: Based on due dates and approved/pending invoices

Results and Measurable Impact

Metric	Before	After
Average invoice processing time	15–20 days	5 days
Late payment fines	Frequent	Cut by more than 90%
Manual data entry	High	Eliminated via AI Builder
Time of audit resolution	Weeks	Real-time searchable logs

- **Outcome**: Reduced errors, quicker vendor payments, streamlined AP processes, and total compliance visibility across divisions.

Use Case 4: Tracking Financial Grant Management and Its Disbursement

General View and Context

Government agencies run state and federal grant programs that help with education, infrastructure, health, economic development, and emergency response. These initiatives demand close accountability of results reporting, budgetary appropriations, grant submissions, and payments. Usually, this is done using paper forms, emails, and spreadsheets. This complicates control of compliance, tracking of disbursement phases, and measure impact.

This application scenario aims to simplify the complete life cycle from grant intake to award, fund release, progress reporting, and compliance audit preparation by using a **Power Platform-Based Grant Management and Disbursement Tracking System**.

Who It Helps

Stakeholder	Benefit
Grant Program Officers	Single dashboard lets program managers handle grant applications, reviews, approvals, and fund disbursement phases
Applicants (e.g., Nonprofits, Agencies, Schools)	Applicants track their status in real-time, submit applications online, upload papers.
Finance Teams	Track fund use, release timetables, and match criteria connected to budgets or federal finance rules will help finance teams
Auditors and Compliance Teams	For audit readiness, auditors and compliance teams access all digital logs, submission timestamps, reviewer comments, attached financials
Policy and Oversight Boards	Make funding choices by visualizing grant effects across programs, jurisdictions, and agencies

Key Drivers for Modernization

- **Manual Submission Method**: Paper or email forms result in delays and missing papers.

- **Disbursement Delays**: Missed deadlines and unspent money result from lack of automated workflow.

- **Compliance Risks**: Disparate records can lead to failed audits or rejected or disqualified matching funds.

- **No Central Oversight**: Grant performance, fund status, and effect are unseen until manual compilation.

- **Inadequate Transparency**: Applicants lack adequate transparency and no timely updates on the status of their applications or funds.

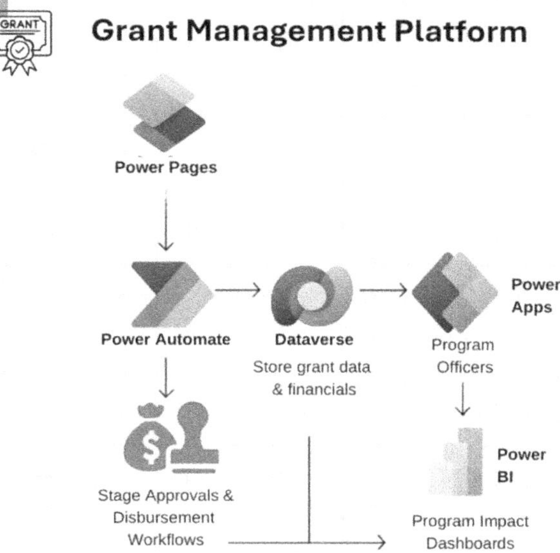

Figure 7-30. *Architecture Diagram—Grant Life Cycle and Disbursement Management*

Technical Solution Architecture

Component	Role
Power Pages	Public or internal portal for candidates to submit grant forms, upload supporting materials, and check status
Power Apps (Model-Driven App)	Grant officers that review applications, record comments, assign scores, and monitor stages utilize Power Apps
Power Automate	Power Automate handles application routing, sends deadline alerts, manages disbursement triggers, and escalates overdue reports
Dataverse	Stores all grant data—applications, scoring history, award amounts, disbursement dates, usage reports, audit logs—Dataverse
Power BI	Dashboards in Power BI display region, fund usage trends, pending awards, and impact reports

Workflow Overview

1. **Application Intake**

   - Applicants submit program applications with supporting documents and financials using Power Pages.

2. **Evaluation and Scoring**

   - Grant officers consult Power Apps to review submissions, assign scores, and route approval depending on funding limits.

3. **Approval and Disbursement**

- Dataverse keeps track of approved grants; Power Automate plans payments in stages (e.g., 50% up front, 50% after milestone).

4. **Reporting of Progress**

- Grantees provide follow-up reports; Power Automate checks for absences reports and sends reminders.

5. **Analytics and Oversight**

- Power BI offers program impact, grantee performance, deadline tracking, and fund distribution dashboards.

Dashboards and Reporting Views

- **Grant Award Tracker**: Real-time filtering of Grant Award Tracker shows application results—approved, pending, rejected.

- **Disbursement Schedule Dashboard**: Fund release by project and stage (committed vs. disbursed) is shown on the disbursement schedule dashboard.

- **Compliance Status**: Missed reports, overdue milestones, fund usage versus plan define compliance status.

- **Impact Metrics Viewer**: Program outcomes (e.g., students served, housing built, jobs created).

Outcomes and Measurable Effects

Metric	Before	After
Average time for grant application processing	4–6 weeks	< 10 business days
Disbursement delays	Frequent	Reduced with automated triggers
Application status visibility	Low	Real-time portal access
Audit readiness	Manual files	Instant, exportable audit packages

- **Outcome**: Improved program outcomes across funding agencies, efficient and auditable grant management, quicker fund use, and improved reporting

Use Case 5: Revenue Collection and Payment Reconciliation System

Overview and Background

State and local governments may generate money in several ways: permit fees, taxes, licensing, utilities, citations, service charges, and grants. Different systems, divisions, or suppliers could handle each of these sets, hence contributing to a disparate and mistake-prone reconciliation process. Manual payment matching against invoices or ledger accounts results in delayed financial reporting, errors are emphasized, and compliance with auditing is compromised.

This application is a Revenue Collection and Payment Reconciliation System on Power Platform that aims to automate reconciliation of bank/payment processor accounts, automate collection tracking, and generate accurate forecasting and reporting.

Who It Helps

Stakeholder	Benefit
Revenue Officers	Revenue officers will monitor every payment received through multiple channels and connect it to services, bills, or accounts
Finance Analysts	Automated internal systems reconciliation with bank/payment feeds assists finance analysts
Treasury Managers	Monitor cash flow, identify real-time mismatches, and manage treasury distributions are Treasury Managers
Auditors	Have access to validated, timestamped transaction records with cleansing history
Departmental finance teams	Detect revenue shortfalls, trends, and differences between expected and collected amounts

Key Drivers for Modernization

- **Numerous Collection Systems:** No single perspective throughout courts, tax portals, utilities, and licensing systems.

- **Manual Reconciliation:** Payments processors, banks, and financial systems require manual reconciliation—frequently in spreadsheets.

- **Delayed Closeouts:** Unreconciled entries and suspect data sources lead to delayed month-end or quarterly closeouts.

- **Risk of Error or Fraud:** Manual processes heighten the risk of incorrect distribution, double entry, or forgotten payments.

- **Inability to Report in Real Time:** Revenue figures may be days or weeks behind actual receipts.

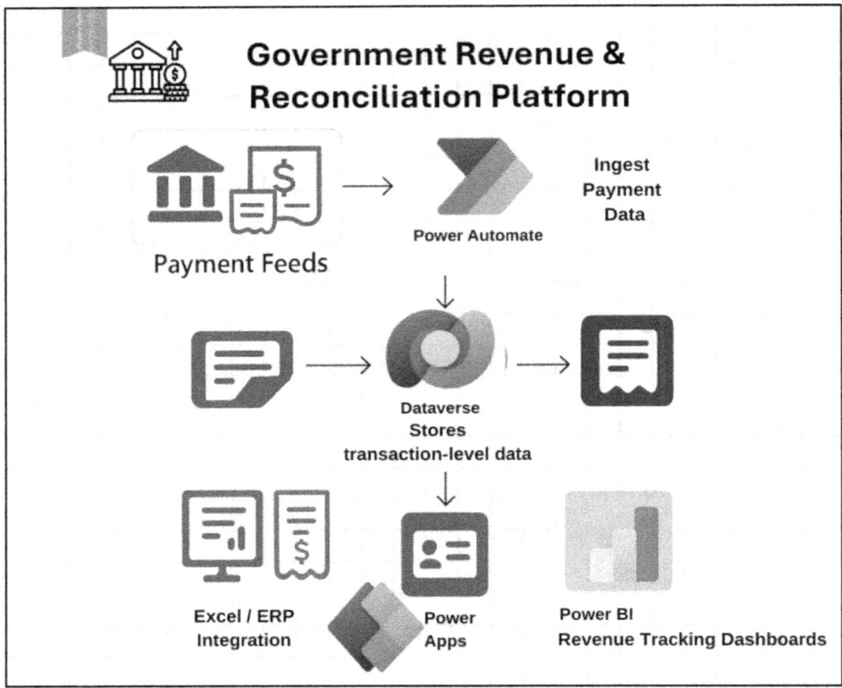

Figure 7-31. *Revenue and Reconciliation Platform Architectural Diagram*

Architectural Design of Technical Solutions

Component	Role
Power Automate	Power Automate connects with merchant APIs, banks, and payment portals to consume payment information
Dataverse	Dataverse stores transaction-level data on payer information, service codes, amount, channel, and matching status
Power Apps	Finance teams use Power Apps to check unpaid invoices, flag red flags, and approve ledger reconciliations
Power BI	Power BI offers dashboards for real-time revenue tracking, matched/unmatched reports, fund balances, and monthly trends
Excel/ERP Integration	Enabling financial system exports or bulk imports for cross-system matching, Excel/ERP

Workflow Overview

1. **Payment Ingestion**

   - Power Automate stores transactions from payment banks, APIs, or uploaded CSVs in Dataverse.

2. **Auto-Matching Logic**

   - Using rules (e.g., invoice number, payer ID, date/ amount tolerance), automatically match payments to services or invoices.

3. **Review and Change**

   - Power Apps flags manual review of exceptions such as partial payments or mismatched services.

4. **Ledger Synchronization and Approval**

   - Locked, approved matched entries will go to ERP or treasury systems.

5. **Reporting and Projections**

   - Power BI dashboards display matched/unmatched rates, channel collections, revenue projections, and compliance gaps.

Dashboard and Report Perspectives

- **Real-Time Revenue Dashboard**: Channel, date, source, and department gathered revenue

- **Reconciliation Summary**: Total matched, unmatched, exceptions needing review.

- **Cash Flow Forecasting Tool**: Based on seasonal collections and revenue trends

- **Exception Tracker**: Tagged transactions by category—duplicates, incorrect codes, failed matches, etc.

Outcomes and Quantifiable Effect

Metric	Before	After
Monthly reconciliation completed time	7–10 days	Less than 48 hours
Automated matching payment match rates	65–75%	Exceeding 95%
Unmatched transaction backlog	High	Reduced by >80%
Manual spreadsheet use	Standard	Eliminated with Dataverse automation

- **Results**: Real-time cash visibility, faster period closeouts, enhanced data accuracy, and total auditability of government revenue streams.

7.7 Department of Labor and Employment

Use Case 1: Unemployment Claim and Eligibility Verification Process

Summary and Context

During job loss, economic downturns, and events like the COVID-19 epidemic, unemployment insurance programs are a lifeline. Still, many state systems managing claims intake, eligibility verification, and disbursement depend on obsolete legacy technology. This leads to overloaded systems, false claims, lengthy wait periods, and public discontent.

This use case illustrates a **Power Platform-Powered Unemployment Claims Intake and Eligibility Workflow**. It enables digital processing of claims, automates verification, and keeps people updated on the status of applications and claims. This can even reduce fraud and administrative delays.

Who Benefits From This?

Stakeholder	Benefit
Job Seekers	Submit claims online, upload documents, and track claim status in real time
Claims Officers	Review submitted claims, check eligibility criteria, and mark fraud signals
Labor Department Analysts	See claim duration statistics, denial reason analysis, and volume trends
Finance/Disbursement Teams	Finance/Disbursement Teams handle payments linked to validated claims with transparent audit trails
State Leadership	Real-time tracking of claims backlog, benefit distribution, and economic impact will help state leadership

Modernization Key Drivers

- **Overwhelmed Legacy Systems**: Claims spikes (e.g., during COVID) crash old and outdated portals.

- **Manual Verification**: Human checks of identity, job history, and eligibility cause delays in manual verification.

- **Fraud Risk**: No automated duplicate detection or anomaly scoring results in incorrect payouts.

- **Lack of Status Transparency**: Applicants lack knowledge of the status of their claim—pending, denied, or approved.

- **Bad Analytics:** Leaders lack real-time dashboards to grasp program impact or obstacles.

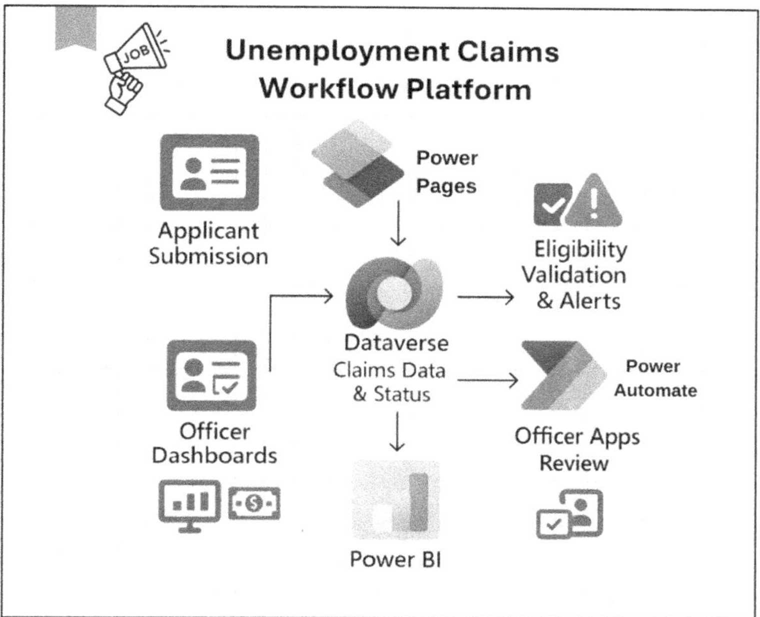

Figure 7-32. *Architectural Diagram—Unemployment Claims Workflow Platform*

Technical Architecture for Solutions

Component	Role
Power Pages	Public portal for applicants to submit claims, check eligibility, upload ID/work documents, and track status
Power Automate	Performs background checks (SSN, work history), duplicates claim screening, and refers to officers for examination
Dataverse	Dataverse securely stores history logs, verification results, payment status, appeal details, and application records
Power Apps	Claims processors use Power Apps to review applications, check documents, make decisions, and trigger questions
Power BI	Dashboards in Power BI show fake alerts, claim volume, approval rates, average benefit cycle, and funding use

Workflow Overview

1. **Claim Submission**

   - Applicant completed guided form Power Pages, uploads identification and proof of prior employment.

2. **Eligibility Check**

   - Power Automate checks ID, compares it to currently available claim records, and searches for missing data.

3. **Claims Officer Review**

   - Claims Officer Review Status (e.g., Auto-Cleared, Needs Review, Flagged) claims show up in Power Apps queue. Officer checks and approves or rejects.

4. **Payment Trigger**

   - Approved claims are tagged for disbursement via linked finance system; appeals go into secondary review queue.

5. **Monitoring and Supervision**

   - Power BI dashboards display overall trends in the economy, claims inflow/outflow, payment delay, and high-risk profiles.

Reporting Views and Dashboard

- **Claims Volume Dashboard:** Trend lines of claim type and geography by day, week, and month on the Claims Dashboard

- **Processing Time Tracker:** Average time to decision; outstanding claims over SLA

- **Dashboard for Fraud Monitoring:** Suspicious IP activity, anomaly detection, duplicate SSNs

- **Economic Impact Summary**: Total paid; average benefit length; field of prior work

Outcomes and Measurable Effect

Metric	Before	After
Average time to process a claim	10–15 days	< 3 days
Fraud detection	Limited	AI-supported anomaly checks at submission
Claim status visibility	Not available	Real-time portal view
Benefit distribution accuracy	85–90%	> 98% confirmed approvals

- **Outcome**: Simplified backend processes, more public trust in the unemployment benefits system, faster relief to unemployed people, and less fraud

Use Case 2: Workforce Program Enrollment and Case Management System

Overview and Context

The government operates multiple workforce development initiatives. This includes training programs alongside reskilling opportunities and apprenticeship pairings with assistance for veterans and disability support. The enrollment and case tracking procedures for these programs exist either as paper-based systems or separate disconnected systems. This makes it hard to follow participant progress, measuring outcomes, and maintaining coordinated servicing.

This use case introduces a **Power Platform-Based Workforce Program Enrollment and Case Management System** to centralize participant data, streamline program intake, automate follow-ups, and track milestones in a secure, digital environment.

Who It Helps

Stakeholder	Benefit
Job Seekers and Participants	Job seekers can enroll in programs through online platforms which will notify them about their progress and connect them with program advisors
Case Managers	Staff members handle multiple cases by monitoring client progress and writing appointment records as well as assigning service programs
Program Administrators	Program administrators need to track how enrollment changes over time together with participant drop-off rates and program completion rates
Partner Organizations	The organization provides service coordination by delivering training and counseling and education along with reporting participation statistics
State/Federal Auditors	The system enables users with secure access to review program compliance and funding utilization and measure program impact

Key Drivers for Modernization

- **Siloed Intake Processes**: Each program operates with its own separate system. This results in fragmented data across different programs.

236

- **No Cross-Agency Visibility**: Participants being enrolled across multiple programs but lacking a unified record system.

- **Manual Milestone Tracking**: Case managers currently track milestones through handwritten records and Excel spreadsheet systems.

- **Delayed Reporting**: Program outcome reporting exists as a manual process that deal reporting.

- **Limited Participant Engagement**: Job seekers have no access to see their program progress or steps.

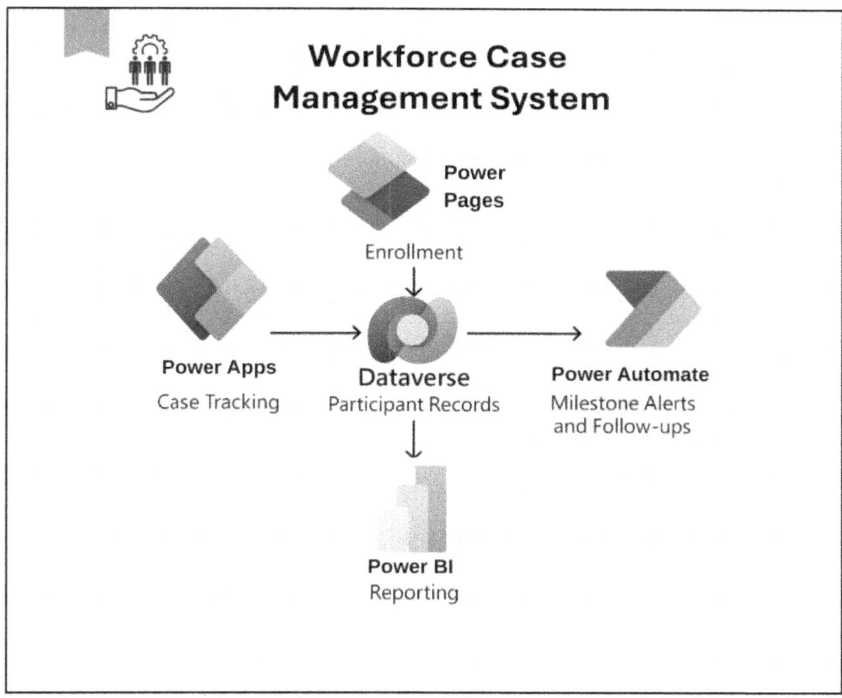

Figure 7-33. Architecture Diagram—Workforce Case Management System

Technical Solution Architecture

Component	Role
Power Pages	The system features a web-based interface that allows residents to join programs and upload requirements while checking their application progress
Power Apps (Model-Driven App)	The case management hub serves as an advisor tracking system for appointments, service assignments, outcome tracking and case note management
Dataverse	The Dataverse database securely maintains records of participants together with program enrollment data, service logs, and contact history and program milestones
Power Automate	The system automatically provides session alerts, deadline warnings, document expiration notices, and non-participation escalation alerts
Power BI	The system includes Power BI dashboards that show program enrollment patterns alongside participant advancement, completion statistics, and population-based data

Workflow Overview

1. **Participant Enrollment**

   - The enrollment process through Power Pages enables applicants to submit their documents and choose their programs of interest.

2. **Case Assignment**

   - The Power Automate system distributes participants to case managers according to their selected programs and regional locations.

3. **Goal and Milestone Tracking**

   - The case manager builds goal plans through Power Apps. This can track each individual step such as resume workshops and job interviews and training modules.

4. **Appointment and Engagement Logs**

   - Every contact between the case manager and participant (meeting, call, workshop) gets recorded in Dataverse with attendance records and feedback details.

5. **Progress Reporting**

   - Using Power BI software displays program metrics. It measures cohort completion statistics along with employment duration and benefit maintenance results.

Dashboards and Reporting Views

- **Enrollment Trends Dashboard:** By age, region, program type, and employment sector.

- **Case Progress Tracker**: The tracker displays participant status on track, behind schedule, and completion.

- **Workforce Impact Summary**: It describes the employment transition rate, placement duration data, and post-placement retention statistics.

- **Program Equity Scorecard**: The Scorecard provides information about access rates along with outcome results based on racial, gender, disability, and veteran demographics.

Results and Measurable Impact

Metric	Before	After
The case notes entry method	manual	Digital and searchable with standardized formats
Enrollment visibility for all program participants	Disconnected	The system now presents unified enrollment in one system
The program completion rate	Variable	Improved with milestone monitoring and reminder systems
Quarterly reporting effort	Manual aggregation	Manual aggregation

- **Outcome**: The outcome produces better participant success while enhancing grant guidelines adherence, rising workforce involvement and better training program coordination.

Use Case 3: Employer Portal and Job Posting Validation Workflow

Overview and Context

State labor departments maintain public job boards and conduct employer engagement activities. This helps residents discover local employment opportunities. The job posting process requires employer submissions that undergo manual review at present while wage fairness checks, discrimination screening, and labor law compliance verification are absent from the current system.

This use case demonstrates how Microsoft Power Platform enables an **Employer Portal and Job Posting Validation Workflow**. Through its self-service portal, employers can submit job postings. These are then automatically routed for approval, while regulatory compliance checks are conducted and the postings become accessible on public job seeker portals.

Who It Helps

Stakeholder	Benefit
Employers	Online job posting allows employers to track progress and obtain guidance on compliance requirements and tax benefit opportunities
Job Seeker Program Teams	Ensure all postings must be relevant and fair-wage and nondiscriminatory and delivered on a timely basis
Job Boards and Workforce Agencies	The system automatically publishes approved postings on public sites and training programs
Legal/Compliance Officers	The team responsible for reviewing flagged postings must verify their compliance with state and federal labor laws
Analysts and Workforce Planners	Access dashboards that present data about job demand, employer engagement levels, and industry trends

Key Drivers for Modernization

- **Email-Based Submission**: Employer-submitted job postings as attachments lead to prolonged processing time.

- **No Validation Logic**: The job descriptions have components that violate wage laws and labor standards and accessibility requirements.

- **Manual Approval Chains**: There is no standard workflow system to ensure both consistency and timeliness throughout the process.

- **Poor Tracking of Outcomes**: Agencies lack the ability to track which employers use their referrals or determine the duration of posted listings.

- **Lack of Integration**: Postings are not synced with training programs or regional initiatives.

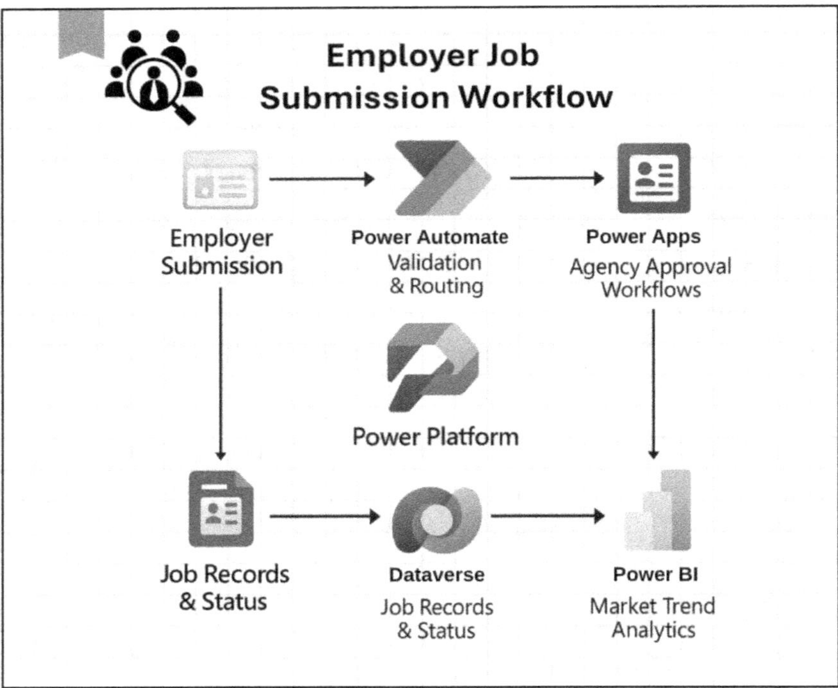

Figure 7-34. Architecture Diagram—Employer Job Submission Workflow

Technical Solution Architecture

Component	Role
Power Pages	Through the employer-facing portal, users can post jobs and check guidelines and see their submission records
Power Automate	Validates required fields (e.g., wage, EEO compliance), routes to reviewers, flags risky terms or expired listings
Power Apps	Staff use this tool to conduct reviews, approvals, rejections with additional commenting features, and link postings to program and job boards
Dataverse	The system keeps all the employer records along with job postings, review history, posting tenure, and placement information
Power BI	The team of workforce planning gets dashboards that show regional job vacancies in addition to approval times and top hiring industries

Workflow Overview

1. **Job Posting Submission**

   - Employers through Power Pages utilize a step-by-step form to input job information such as pay, benefits, and job location information.

2. **Policy Validation**

   - Power Automate examines for missing information, discriminatory language, incorrect wage ranges, and flags accordingly.

3. **Review and Approval**

- Power Apps are utilized by workforce agency staff to review highlighted postings and comment or give instant approval.

4. **Publication and Promotion**

- Approved job postings will be automatically uploaded to state job boards, training providers and partner agencies.

5. **Employer Engagement Analytics**

- The Power BI system tracks employer engagement, monitoring position filling, approval time, and job market performance.

Dashboards and Reporting Views

- **Active Job Postings Tracker**: The tracker gives job postings details based on the type of employer and status in the sector. It also reveals approval status.

- **Approval Time Dashboard**: Average review times along with flagged apps and returned submissions are tracked by the system.

- **Hiring Outcomes Dashboard**: The dashboard displays information regarding the fill rate for positions along with employer feedback as well as average hiring times.

- **Market Demand Report**: The system can show job openings by location, wage band, and role type.

Results and Measurable Impact

Metric	Before	After
Average time to approve job postings	3–5 days	Less than 24 hours
Invalid/incomplete submissions	Frequent	Reduced with validation flows
Manual tracking spreadsheets	Used heavily	Replaced with centralized Dataverse
Employer satisfaction	Moderate	Increased with self-service portal and status transparency

Outcome: A faster and more transparent engagement system for employers, high-quality job listings, compliance to employment laws, and workforce data improvement

Use Case 4: Labor Market Intelligence and Skills Gap Analytics Dashboard

Overview and Context

The responsibility of labor departments includes monitoring employment trends and finding workforce gaps while matching training programs to current market requirements. However, labor market intelligence exists in fragmented form. The system relies on outdated reports and static surveys along with isolated job board data. This prevents organizations from making decisions based on data.

This use case presents a **Labor Market Intelligence and Skills Gap Analytics Dashboard** built on the Power Platform framework. The system combines job data employment positions with unemployment claims statistics, training performance metrics and economic measurement results to generate useful workforce development planning.

Who It Helps

Stakeholder	Benefit
Policy Makers and Labor Commissioners	Commissioners determine top in-demand jobs, local skill gaps, and employment patterns to develop policy design
Training Providers and Schools	Curriculum should align with real-world job requirements as well as industry trends
Workforce Boards and Economic Developers	Organizations can utilize the ethical application of trends to entice employers and focus workforce investment and improve placement outcomes
Employers	Employers obtain local hiring information in order to develop talent pipelines or employee relocation plans
Citizens	View career pathways combined with job growth data to make better training decisions

Key Drivers for Modernization

- **Lagging Indicators**: The majority of reports present historical information which does not link to current job vacancies or claims data.

- **Disconnected Data Sources**: Job board data, training completions, and unemployment trends are in separate silos.

- **Limited Regional Insights**: Statewide statistics do not show local skill deficits or employment expansion areas.

- **No Predictive Trends**: Agencies lack the ability to predict future workforce requirements through economic changes or industry growth patterns.

- **Poor Program Alignment**: Training programs fail to adapt to labor market needs because they lack intelligence.

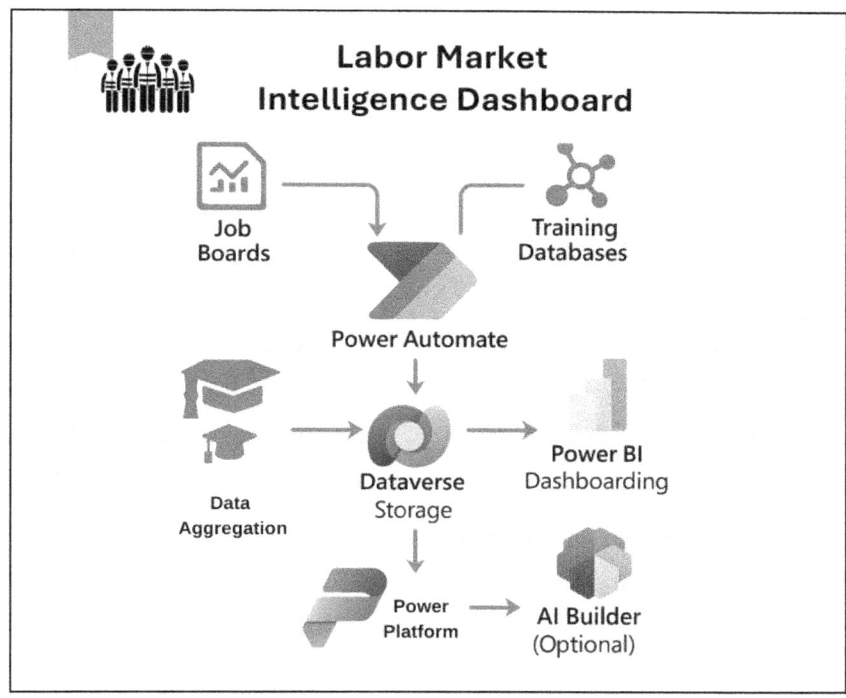

Figure 7-35. *Architecture Diagram—Labor Market Intelligence Dashboard*

Technical Solution Architecture

Component	Role
Power Automate	The system collects job board postings, training completions, and unemployment claim data by multiple sources including CSV, APIs, and Excel
Dataverse	The system stores workforce data in a single model that combines job demand, required skills, sector trends, and education program results
AI Builder (Optional)	It uses time-series forecasting and seasonal patterns to make workforce predictions for the future
Power BI	The system provides real-time labor market dashboards alongside maps for demand-supply analysis and actionable data insights

Workflow Overview

1. **Data Aggregation**

   - Power Automate operates on a schedule to retrieve real-time job postings, training data and unemployment records which are stored in Dataverse.

2. **Data Enrichment and Normalization**

   - The job database connects jobs to skill codes (such as O*NET) which further allows users to access occupational information and nearby training programs.

3. **Trend Forecasting**

- AI Builder applies time-series analysis to establish future demand projections for core industries and job markets.

4. **Dashboarding and Decision Support**

- Power BI employs visuals to display job market information such as available jobs, training capacity, claims activity, and anticipated workforce shortages.

Dashboards and Reporting Views

- **In-Demand Occupations Dashboard**: Real-time job postings by region, role, and salary range.

- **Skills Gap Report**: The assessment evaluates necessary skill sets against training program end results.

- **Unemployment Trend Analytics**: By county, industry, and claimant demographics.

- **Workforce Forecasting Dashboard**: 6–12 month projections by sector and geography.

Results and Measurable Impact

Metric	Before	After
Skills gap identification	Annual or static	Real time and dynamic
The process of data consolidation time	Manual, days	Automated scheduled flows decreased these times
Training alignment with job requirements	Low	Streamlined with dashboards
Workforce investment ROI measurement	Weak	Transparent, KPI-based insights

Outcome: Evidence-based workforce strategy, diminished skill mismatches, more intelligent training investments, and measurable impact across labor and economic development programs.

Use Case 5: Benefits Eligibility Screener and Case Routing Automation

Overview and Context

The government offers different benefits in its labor departments. These benefits include unemployment insurance, job training subsidies, disability benefits, and child care benefits. But the residents are still uninformed regarding their benefit eligibility and application process. On the other hand, the caseworkers are plagued with the problem of a fragmented intake process, duplication of data entry, and delay in routing.

This use case offers a **Benefits Eligibility Screener and Case Routing Automation System** created using Microsoft Power Platform technologies. It leads residents through an interactive eligibility screening, identifies real-time qualification status, and directs suitable cases to processing teams.

Who It Helps

Stakeholder	Benefit
Residents	Residents can complete a guided multilingual screener to identify eligible benefits while using a single portal to submit documents
Case Managers	The system delivers pre-screened applications that are categorized to help case managers process applications faster and avoid duplication of work

(continued)

Stakeholder	Benefit
Call Centers	The online platform provides self-service screening combined with clear next step instructions. This reduces the number of support calls entering the system
Program Admins	Track demand, caseload distribution, and eligibility patterns by program and demographic
Compliance Officers	The system ensures eligibility is consistent with policy guidelines and has a full audit trail for every case

Key Drivers for Modernization

- **Complicated Program Navigation:** Applicants must navigate several websites and forms to determine their program eligibility.

- **Manual Case Assignment**: The use of email and shared spreadsheets for referral transmission results in lost applications.

- **Redundant Data Entry**: Users need to provide identical information multiple times across different service platforms.

- **Delayed Processing**: The combination of assignment bottlenecks and absent documents causes delays in the approval process.

- **No Central Oversight**: Leadership has no clear view of overall demand levels and regions.

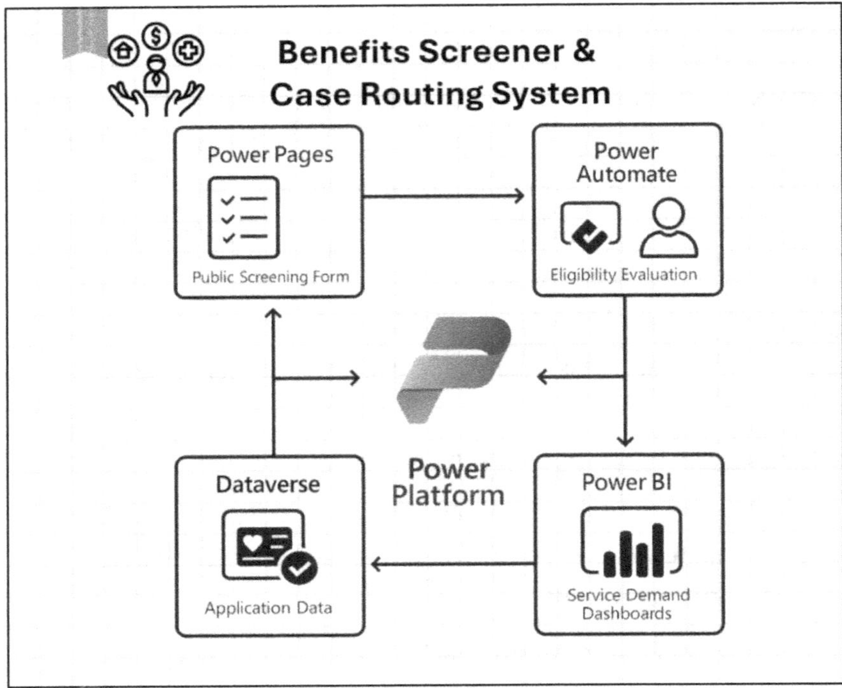

Figure 7-36. *Architecture Diagram—Benefits Screener and Case Routing System*

Technical Solution Architecture

Component	Role
Power Pages	The system features an interactive portal that enables residents to handle dynamic questions and submit necessary documents
Power Automate	The system applies eligibility criteria through age, income, employment, and residency standards to direct qualified applications to appropriate departments

(continued)

Component	Role
Dataverse	Centralized storage for application data, program eligibility outcomes, routing status, and case history
Power Apps (Model-Driven App)	Used by staff to check their assigned cases while verifying documents and updating statuses and completing benefit onboarding procedures
Power BI	Dashboards to view total screeners completed, eligibility distribution, routing SLA performance, and regional benefit demand

Workflow Overview

1. **Screener Completion**

   - The residents use Power Pages to complete a questionnaire about income, employment, dependents, and housing while adding their verification documentation.

2. **Eligibility Assessment**

   - Power Automate utilizes logic trees to establish preliminary program eligibility for UI, child care, TANF and training benefits.

3. **Case Routing**

   - The case system routes every assignment to its respective team and shows it in Power Apps with all pertinent information already populated.

4. **Verification and Communication**

- Caseworkers sift through papers while calling applicants when needed to verify service eligibility for approval or rejection.

5. **Performance Analytics**

- The Power BI tool shows three performance analysis components such as the funnel conversion (screened ➤ routed ➤ approved) and average routing time and most-requested programs by area.

Dashboards and Reporting Views

- **Eligibility Funnel Dashboard**: The system tracks the numbers of total screeners and eligible residents and routed cases and approved applications.

- **Top Requested Programs**: Users can filter data through ZIP code selections together with demographic categories and specific time intervals.

- **Case Routing SLA Tracker**: The system routes few percentages of applications within one day while maintaining workload distribution across teams.

- **Underserved Region Map**: Locations with high ineligibility rates or access gaps.

Results and Measurable Impact

Metric	Before	After
The average time needed for eligibility	5–10 days	Instant at pre-screening
Case routing errors	Frequent	Nearly removed case routing errors eliminated via automation
Program overlap and missed benefits	High	Reduced through single-entry workflow
Staff workload imbalance	Untracked	Balanced using dashboards and SLA routing logic

- **Outcome**: Better access to benefits with faster processing and greater openness to applicants, thus allowing for better resource utilization across the labor and social services departments.

7.8 Department of Technology Services/IT Shared Services

Use Case 1: IT Service Request Intake and Ticket Management System

Overview and Context

Internal IT departments of government agencies help them handle digital services, system failures, user access, software, and hardware. Most IT service desks, however, operate with antiquated email-based request systems or out-of-date ticketing software that is not integrated, automated, or even self-service enabled.

This use case brings in an **IT Service Request and Ticketing Management System on the Power Platform.** It assists in automating the request intake, triage, SLA tracking, and service performance insight visibility for both the end users and the IT staff.

Who It Helps

Stakeholder	Benefit
End Users (Employees)	End users can submit IT requests via a basic self-service portal and track real-time status
IT Help Desk Teams	Receive well-classified tickets, prevent duplicates, and give priority depending on urgency or impact
IT Managers	Real-time dashboards help monitor team performance, SLA compliance, and resource load by IT managers
Security and Access Teams	Handle system onboarding, device provisioning, and user access requests using audit-ready workflows
Agency Leadership	Understand IT trends, service usage, and support demand across departments

Key Drivers for Modernization

- **Unorganized Intake**: Requests mainly come via emails or phone calls. This results in unclear or lost tickets.

- **No Triage Workflow**: IT personnel manually read and route each ticket, therefore delaying the response.

- **No Status Transparency**: End users have no idea of request progress or what projected resolution time is.

- **Manual SLA Tracking**: No automated compliance checking or escalation in manual SLA Tracking.

- **Restricted Analytics**: Manual reporting may or may not be related to performance metrics or ticket volume.

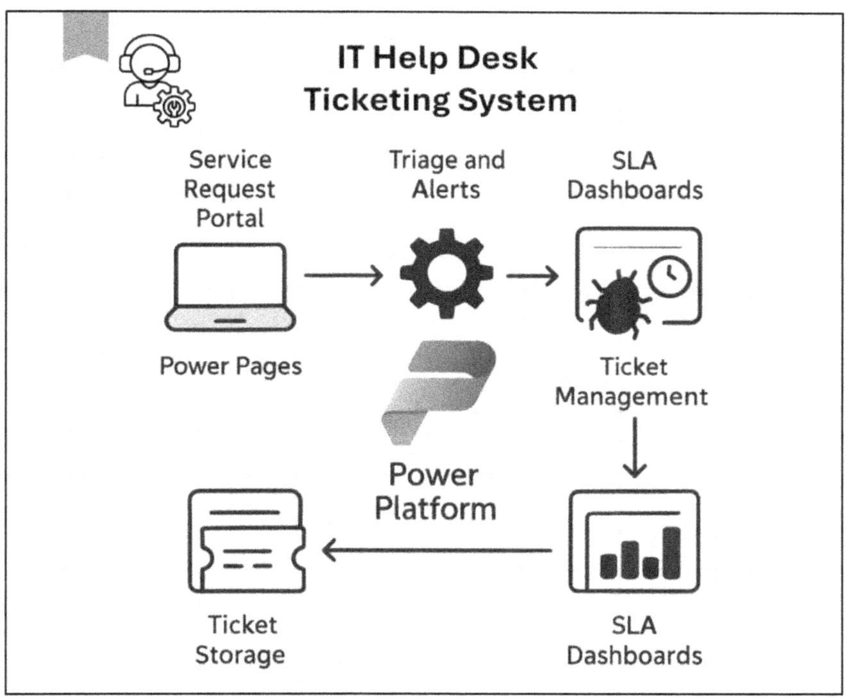

Figure 7-37. *Architecture Diagram—IT Help Desk Ticketing System*

Technical Solution Architecture

Component	Role
Power Pages	Self-service IT portal for submitting requests like device troubleshooting, password resets, software installation
Power Automate	Triage based on keywords, categories, and urgency; routes ticket and sends SLA alerts in Power Automate
Dataverse	Stores timestamps, resolution notes, response logs, attachments, user contacts, and ticket metadata in Dataverse
Power Apps (Model-Driven App)	Utilized by IT personnel to handle tickets, queue management, reassign tasks, and case closing
Power BI	Power BI gives an overview of the open tickets according to categories, performance of the teams, resolution time, and SLA compliance

Workflow Overview

1. **Ticket Submission**

   - Power Pages allows the user to submit requests, including software, hardware, and access, from a dropdown.

2. **Automated Categorization**

   - Power Automate reads the description to route tickets to a suitable IT queue based on triage logic.

3. **Service Team Response**

   - Power Apps enables IT personnel to see assigned tickets, update them, log internal notes, and close or resolve tickets.

4. **User Notifications**

- Notifications through email or SMS sent by Power Automate inform users of any status update to the ticket or when it gets resolved.

5. **SLA Management and Reporting**

- On Power BI dashboards, frequent request types, backlog, overdue tickets, resolution time of tickets, and volumes are displayed.

Reporting View and Dashboards

- **Dashboard for Ticket Volume:** Categories, departments, day/time requests

- **SLA Compliance Report**: Average resolution time, overdue tickets, escalations

- **Dashboard of Technician Performance:** Average handle time, tickets closed per Agent

- **Trends in Service Demand:** Software and hardware requests, repeating top issues

Results and Measurable Impact

Metric	Before	After
Average ticket resolution time	4–7 days	< 2 days
Duplicate/uncategorized tickets	Common	Auto-tagged and sorted
User happiness with IT	Low	Portal and openness will help to raise it
SLA breach rate	>30%	<5% with real-time escalation

- **Outcome:** This will lead to faster IT resolution, improved user experience, centralized ticketing visibility, and measurable IT support effectiveness.

Use Case 2: IT Asset Inventory and Life Cycle Management System

Overview and Context

Government IT departments are responsible for managing thousands of assets—from laptops and mobiles to network setups and software licenses. These assets must track from acquisition through assignment, maintenance, and eventual retirement. Without a centralized system, departments rely on spreadsheets or disconnected tools. This results in losses, underutilization, and compliance risks.

This use case introduces a **Power Platform-Based IT Asset Inventory and Life Cycle Management System** to enable an end-to-end tracking, assignment, audit readiness, and life cycle automation for all IT assets.

Who It Helps

Stakeholder	Benefit
IT Asset Managers	Keep a single source of truth regarding asset locality, assignment, warranty, and life cycle status
Procurement Teams	Predict replacement needs upcoming to avoid over/under-purchasing
End Users	End users know assigned devices and request upgrades or repairs via portal
Security and Compliance Teams	Ensure all devices are accounted for and meet policy standards
Auditors	Auditors Access historical records of asset ownership, location, and service logs

Key Drivers for Modernization

- **Spread Asset Registry**: Spreadsheets in teams or un-updated regularly.

- **No Assignment Tracking**: Giving out devices—no formal logging or digital acknowledgment.

- **Late Life Cycle Management**: Warranty expiration unnoticed; old devices remain in circulation.

- **Security Holes**: Compliance and cybersecurity risks created from having equipment that is just inactive or ill-managed.

- **Manual Audits**: Auditing of assets from different departments now takes much ground work and time.

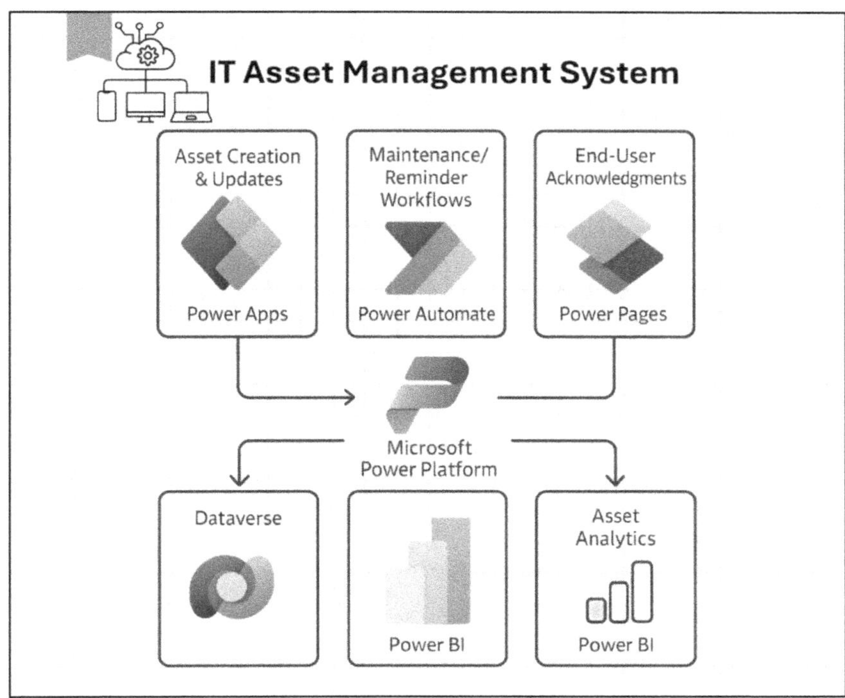

Figure 7-38. *Architecture Diagram—IT Asset Management System*

Architecture of Technical Solutions

Component	Role
Power Apps (Model-Driven App)	Used by the IT staff to register new assets, assign them to users, log service events, and decommission items
Dataverse	Stores the entire asset metadata, that is, type, serial number, date of purchase, user assigned, service history, warranty status
Power Automate	Sends reminders for maintenance, warranty expiring, and asset audits and triggers workflows for automatic reassignments
Power Pages	Allows users to acknowledge their assigned devices, ask for replacements, or view asset history
Power BI	Dashboards for total assets, aging devices, upcoming refreshes, audit status, and policy compliance

Workflow Overview

1. **Asset Onboarding**

   - Once the new asset is procured, the IT team logs into Power Apps the details of the new asset (vendor, warranty, category, cost).

2. **Assignment and Acknowledgment**

   - The assigned worker receives an email through Power Automate with a link to Power Pages to acknowledge the assignment.

3. **Maintenance and Life Cycle Updates**

   • Prespecified triggered workflows for maintenance, renewal of warranty, or retirement based on age/condition.

4. **Asset Transfer or Decommission**

   • Power apps records when assets are transferred, returned, or scrapped with a full audit log and condition pictures.

5. **Reporting and Compliance**

   • These Power BI dashboards show total inventories by department and warranty risk, along with assignment status and assets up for replacement.

Dashboards and Reporting Views

• **Asset Inventory Summary**: Total asset per category (laptops, routers, licenses)

• **Life Cycle Stage Overview**: Assets in use, maintenance, refresh, or retired

• **Assignment Tracker:** Against available devices, acknowledgment status by user

• **Audit Readiness Report:** Complete vs. missing records of assets, compliance violations

Results and Measurable Impact

Metric	Before	After
Missing assets	Common	Almost eliminated with assignment audit trail
Warranty/maintenance alerts	Manual	Automated via Power Automate
User acknowledgment rate	<50%	>90% by email prompt and portal
Inventory reconciliation time	Weeks	<48 hours with live dashboards

- **Outcome:** Visibility of assets in an effective manner, life cycle management automated, and security posture improved to faster audit cycles.

Use Case 3: Access Request, Provisioning, and Deprovisioning Automation

Overview and Context

Providing user access to applications, systems, and secured data is a fundamental IT function. For multiple government agencies, such requests are made manually mostly through emails, spreadsheets, as well as general ticketing systems, often with hardly any tracking, inconsistent approval chains, and no automated offboarding whenever the employees leave or change jobs.

This use case brings a **Power Platform-Based Access Request and Provisioning Automation System**. This simplifies access management, policy-based routing, and timely offboarding to mitigate risk and maintain compliance.

Who It Helps

Stakeholder	Benefit
Employees and Contractors	Use a standardized guided form, including status tracking, to submit access requests
IT and Security Teams	View the entire audit log along with the convenience of automated approval routing
Managers	Have access with clear visibility over the requested resources and assigned roles
Compliance Officers	Ensure system access is restricted to only the users who are authorized, with timely revocation and log updates
HR/Onboarding Teams	Association to recruitment and separation processes for initiating access provisioning/ deprovisioning automatically

Key Drivers for Modernization

- **Email-Based Access Requests**: Lack of standard format, mandatory information, and routing logic.

- **Delayed Provisioning:** New hires end up waiting for days to be granted system access.

- **No Role-Based Visibility**: Managers approving access might have no idea what permissions are involved.

- **Manual Deprovisioning**: Staff do not cut off access to data when leaving the organization.

- **Audit Gaps:** Cannot track the authorization from original source, when access was granted and currently being used.

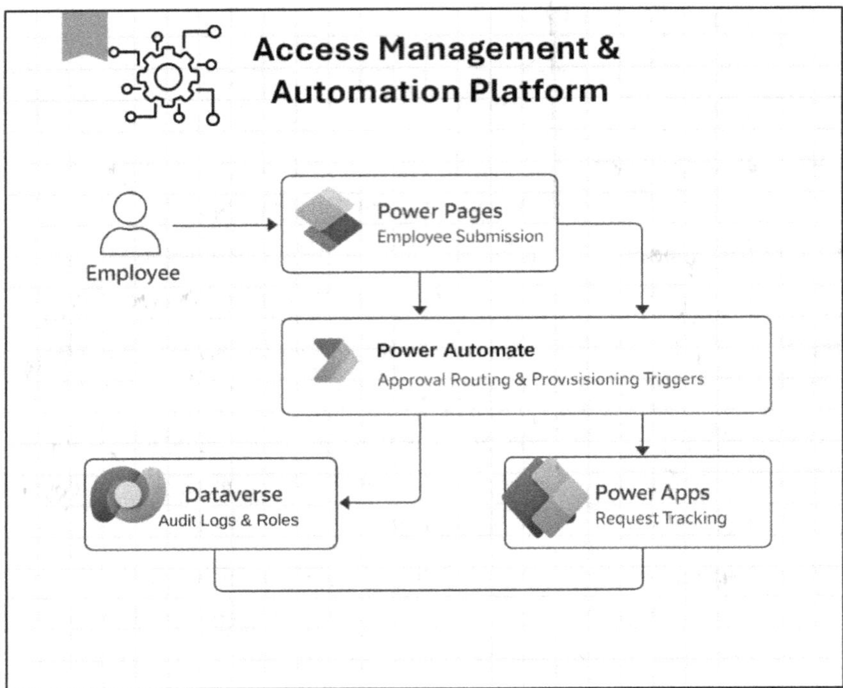

Figure 7-39. *Architecture Diagram—Access Management and Automation Platform*

Technical Solution Architecture

Component Role	Role
Power Pages	Self-service portal where employees request access to systems, data folders, or tools with justification and role selection
Power Automate	It applies rule of routing based on request and role, sends to managers or teams security, triggers provisioning by APIs or scripts glued outside

(continued)

Component Role	Role
Dataverse	Maintains request history, chain of approvals, assigned access roles, expiration date, and user metadata
Power Apps (Model-Driven App)	Used by IT and security personnel to view and manage incoming/approved requests, change ownership, and register accessibility changes
Power BI	Dashboards of provisioning timings, time for pending requests, risk on unauthorized access, and compliance toward de-provisioning

Workflow Overview

1. **Access Request Submission**

   - The user chooses a resource, such as SharePoint, VPN, Dynamics, or Power BI, and provides justification through Power Pages.

2. **Approval Workflow**

   - Power Automate routes the request to the appropriate approver(s) based on the department, sensitivity, and role type, along with notifications and deadlines.

3. **Access Granting**

   - Following approval, the connector or script provides access automatically or notifies IT for manual follow-up. Dataverse records all such events.

4. **Scheduled Deprovisioning**

   - Automatically, an access will be marked for removal on the contract end date, employee separation, or project completion.

5. **Review and Audit Reporting**

- Power BI presents outstanding requests, role access by user, elevated risky privilege escalations, and expired access that still needs removal.

Dashboards and Reporting Views

- **Access Request Tracker**: Pending, approved, rejected, overdue

- **Provisioning SLA Dashboard**: Avg. time to grant access per system and per role

- **Deprovisioning Risk Report**: Users with expired role or with no end date

- **Role Access Overview**: Users with administrative or sensitive access by department

Results and Measurable Impact

Metric	Before	After
Approvals for access	3–7 days	< 1 day
Missed deprovisioning events	Frequent	95% reduction via automation
Audit trail completeness	Low	100% with centralized tracking
Role visibility	Limited	Complete role-user mapping by Power BI

- **Outcome**: Streamlined onboarding/offboarding, improved security posture, faster IT response, and full audit-ready access governance.

Use Case 4: Citizen-Facing Digital Service Catalog and Request Fulfillment System

Overview and Context

When state and local government agencies are digitizing public service, the citizens expect centralized and friendly portals where they can make requests, get information, and track requests for such things as a business license, inspection, utility connection, or record. However, most agencies are operating individually in a silo, with respective websites, forms, and workflows.

This use case introduces a **Citizen-Facing Digital Service Catalog and Request Fulfillment System** built using Microsoft Power Platform. It helps to provide a one-stop portal for government services where residents can track request statuses and enjoy automated fulfillment across departments.

Who It Helps

Stakeholder	Benefit
Citizens and Businesses	Gain access to all services from a unified portal, submit requests, upload supporting documents, and enjoy real-time tracking
Agency Service Teams	Receive and carry out requests using standardized forms. This reduces manual effort in processing requests
IT and Integration Teams	Bring together several departmental workflows into one platform for coordination and visibility
Leadership	Real-time dashboard to monitor service delivery metrics, residents' satisfaction, and bottlenecks
Call Centers and Public Desks	Offer transparent self-service digital options to reduce inquiry calls and foot traffic

Key Drivers for Modernization

- **Siloed Service Portals**: Every department is using its own forms and submission methods. This results in confusion among citizens.

- **No Transparency in Status**: The applicants are in the dark regarding the fulfillment of their requests.

- **Manual Workflows**: Service teams use email or paper forms for request management, which is prone to delays and errors.

- **Inconsistent Service Levels**: Certain requests flow through with a minimal or no delay, but other requests are delayed without tracking.

- **No Data for Optimization**: The agencies cannot analyze request patterns and gauge the effectiveness of SLAs in terms of service delivery.

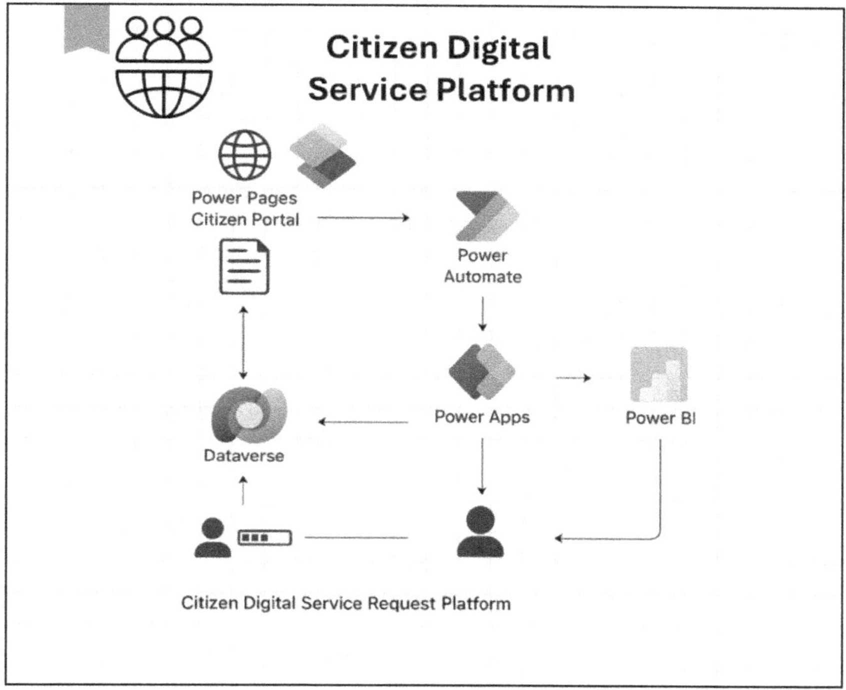

Figure 7-40. *Architecture Diagram for Citizen Digital Service Platform*

Architecture of Technical Solutions

Component	Function
Power Pages	A portal for citizens supported with a categorized service catalog (e.g., permits, licenses, records, inspections) and submission of requests through forms
Power Automate	Automates routing by request type, location, and department, sends confirmation and SLA countdowns
Dataverse	Service requests, supporting documents, user data, time stamps, and fulfillment histories are stored in Dataverse

(continued)

Component	Function
Power Apps	Used by staff members to view and fulfill requests, provide updates, add comments, or redirect
Power BI	Dashboards provide fulfillment time, pending requests, citizen satisfaction surveys, and service volume management

Workflow Overview

1. **Service Request Initiation**

   - Citizens select a service from the Power Pages catalog, fill in a dynamic form, upload documents, and obtain a request ID.

2. **Automated Routing and Acknowledgment**

   - Power Automate manages routing of request to the benefiting department/staff and confirms to the user with expected resolution time.

3. **Reprocessing of Requests**

   - IT personnel use PowerApps to examine the application, reach out to the candidate as needed, and fulfill the service fulfillment.

4. **Alerts and Escalation**

   - Every step brings an update to the citizen; overdue requests are reassigned and raised.

5. **Dashboards and Service Supervision**

   - Power BI offers live metrics with SLA compliance, request volume by category, and satisfaction rating analytics.

Dashboards and Reporting Views

- **Service Request Dashboard:** Total submitted, in progress, completed, overdue with regard to category.

- **Request Map by Geography**: Density of Requests by ZIP code or service area.

- **SLA Performance Dashboard**: Fulfillment rate and average handling times by service teams.

- **Resident Satisfaction Scorecard**: Based on the voluntary feedback survey and service timeline.

Results and Measurable Impact

Metric	Before	After
Time to route citizen requests	2–5 days	<1 hour
Request status visibility for citizens	None	Real time through the portal
Missed SLA thresholds	High	Tracked and diminished by more than 70%
Citizen satisfaction with services	Low	Increased through updates, access to the portal, and speed

Outcome: A citizen experience, increased transparency for the service, reduced overhead for the agency, and measurable improvement in the responsiveness of government services

Use Case 5: IT Governance and Project Portfolio Management Dashboard

Overview and Context

Government IT organizations tend to operate dozens of concurrent technology projects, from simple system upgrades and migration to cloud environments, cybersecurity programs, and application development. Without centralized portfolio approach, it is a challenge for leadership to track projects, resource allocation, budgets, and business impacts.

This use case introduces the **Power Platform-Based IT Governance and Project Portfolio Management (PPM) Dashboard**. It allows PMOs and IT leadership to track all their projects, risks, timeframes, and KPIs all in one place, thus supporting strategic alignment, transparency, and decision-making.

Who It Helps

Stakeholder	Benefit
IT Project Managers	IT project managers can do the above, using a centralized tool to track timelines, tasks, deliverables, budgets, and risks
CIOs/IT Leadership	Have visibility on all projects, real-time utilization of resources, and performance in delivery
Finance Officers	Track Spending vs. Budget: can trace the funds availability and manage capital expenditure
Governance Boards	Create comparative appraisals of alignment with strategy, portfolio health, and risk exposure for prioritization decisions
Auditors and Reviewers	Auditors and reviewers can access historical project data, logs, approvals, and status changes with full traceability

Modernization Key Drivers

- **Siloed Project Tracking Tools**: Each team has different formats such as Excel, SharePoint, or old systems.

- **Unreliable Reporting**: PMs send slides or status reports by email, but without a standard and precise template.

- **No Real-Time Dashboard**: Leadership does not have portfolio-wide visibility of project progress, issues, or risks.

- **No Resource Utilization View**: Difficult to identify teams either working beyond capacity or not using some of the staff completely.

- **Poor Strategic Visibility**: Projects could not match agency objectives or even quantifiable business value, hence undermining strategic visibility.

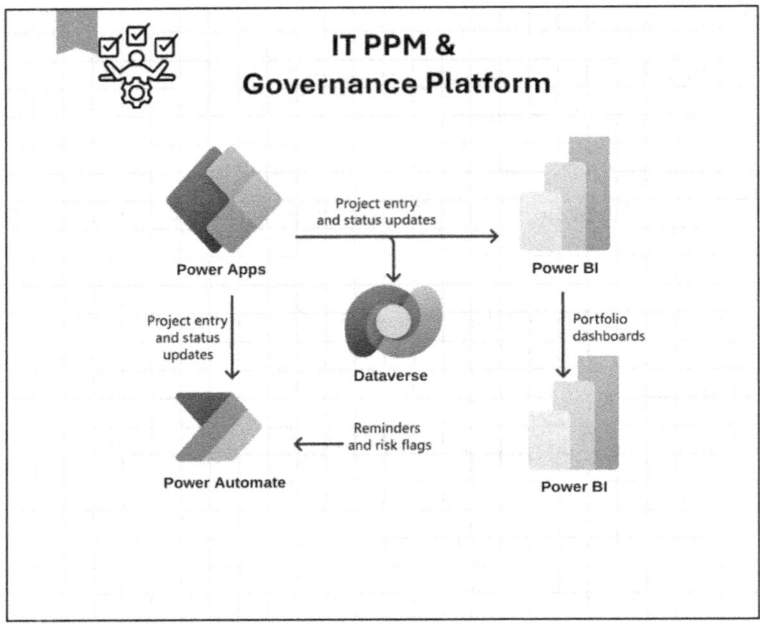

Figure 7-41. *Architecture Diagram—IT PPM and Governance Platform*

Technical Solution Architecture

Component	Role
Power Apps	Project managers utilize Power Apps to input project charters, timelines, budget data, milestones, risks, and weekly updates
Dataverse	Dataverse is the place for governance notes, status reports, resource assignments, budget changes, and standardized project metadata
Power Automate	Power Automate notifies governance reviewers and sends reminders for updates, overdue milestones, or risks
Power BI	Visualizes the entire project portfolio with respect to health status, timeline, risk level, and alignment to strategic goals

Workflow Overview

1. **Planning and Project Implementation**

   - PM Power Apps have project data entry capability. It covers scope, goals, timetable, stakeholders, and budget.

2. **Weekly or Monthly Status Report**

   - An automatic guided form with PM updating milestones, RAG rating, risks, and resource usage. Power Automate imposes update deadlines.

3. **Portfolio Management**

   - Power BI rolls all the individual project data up into dashboards on the overall progress, risk zones, underperforming projects, and available capacity.

4. **Governance Analysis**

   - Governance team leverage the dashboard to determine performance, make go/no-go checks, or re-allocate resources.

5. **Strategic Reporting and Auditing**

   - For long-term performance measurement and audit protection, Dataverse keeps the entire update history along with comments and approvals.

Reporting View and Dashboard

- **Portfolio Health Dashboard**: % of on-track delayed and at-risk projects

- **Project Timeline View**: Gantt-style display with filter options by departmental, sponsor, or financing source.

- **Actual Spend vs. Forecast**: Project-based actual spending compared to projected allocations

- **Risk and Issues Register**: All projects with open hazards, escalations, and mitigations entries in the register

Outcomes and Measured Impact

Measurement	Before	After
Time to compile status reports	Days/weeks	Updates in real time on dashboard
Visibility into portfolio risks	Manual	Automated alerts and flags
Executive decision-making	Based on slide decks	Based on live data and KPIs
Audit trail completeness	Fragmented	100% centralized and timestamped

Outcome: Centralized oversight of all IT projects, strategic alignment of resources, enhanced on-time/on-budget delivery, and audit-ready governance throughout the agency are outcomes.

7.9 Department of Justice And Corrections

Use Case 1: Electronic Inmate Intake, Classification, and Facility Assignment System

Overview and Context

The intake of inmates is one of the most vital processes in the corrections system. Establishing the legal documentation, medical and psychological screening processes, and suitable facility assignments are all involved in this process. Largely, these have been managed by paper-based processes and limited data sharing across departments. In such instances, these cause delays, misclassification, and security risks.

In this use case, we would like to introduce a **Power Platform-Based Digital Inmate Intake and Facility Assignment System** to standardize admissions, automate classifications, and facilitate placements in facilities. This ensures better safety, compliance, and data integration.

Who Benefits This

Stakeholder	Benefits
Intake Officers	Digitally process new inmates with real-time data validation and facility recommendations
Classification Teams	View complete profiles of inmates (criminal history, medical, psychological, risk assessments) are used to decide placements
Wardens/Facility Managers	Placement requests are accurate and capacity optimal, with full background
Incorporation into the Justice System	Align with courts, public defenders, parole officers, and health systems
State Supervision/Auditors	Central access to the record for audit, compliance, and demographic analysis

Major Drivers of Modernization

- **Paper-Based Intake**: Delays resulting from processing of handwritten forms, lack of signatures, and transporting physical files on and off.

- **Facility Mismatches**: There isn't any intelligent logic involved in matching risk level with facility security.

- **Stand-Alone Records**: Judicial systems, medical providers, and correctional facilities each have separate data stores.

- **No Digital Audit Trail**: Most intake approvals and risk assessments and classification notes appear lost or are difficult to search.

- **Limited Data for Planning**: Difficulties include forecasting population flow or tracking recidivism by intake patterns.

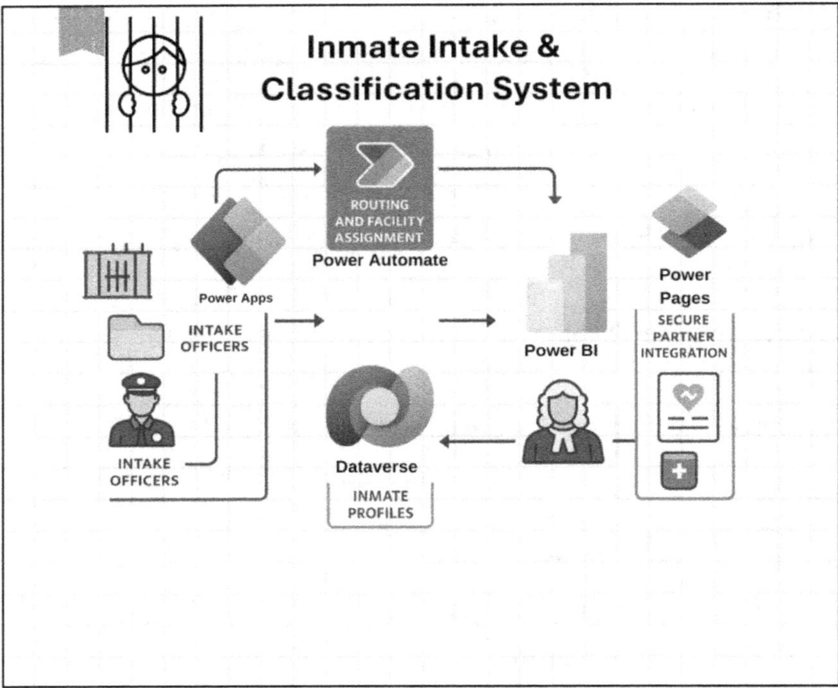

Figure 7-42. Architecture Diagram—Inmate Intake And Classification System

Technical Solution Architecture

Component	Role
Power Apps	This app will be used to capture the intake details, risk score, and court documentation and to recommend preliminary placement
Dataverse	A central data model for all records of inmates, screening scores, facilities status, medical flags, and movement history
Power Automate	Applies classification logic, routes to review board, and sends placement notice to receiving facility
Power BI	Real-time dashboards for said facility population, inmate flow by crime type, classification errors, and audit readiness
Power Pages	A secure portal for court liaisons, public defenders, and pretrial partners to upload documents and review intake status

Overview of Workflow

1. **Intake Interview**

   - In the interview, the officer enters the new inmate info into Power Apps (court case ID, medical summary and behavioral screening results, with prior history).

2. **Automated Classification**

   - Power Automate applies configurable rules to assign initial security level, flag health issues, and recommend facility based on location and capacity.

3. **Assignment to Review Board Classification**

   - The facilities team makes the classification decisions in Power Apps; they are logged for confirmation in Dataverse.

4. **Facility Notification**

   - If there is an incoming inmate, they would notify the facility along with the digital intake packet, where also scheduled arrival and risk indicators would lie.

5. **Auditing and Oversight**

   - Power BI breaks down populations according to duration of intake, health risks, and predictions about capacity.

Dashboards and Reporting Views

- **Facility Assignment Dashboard**: New intakes categorization based on crime type, risk level, and facility capacity

- **Population Forecast Dashboard**: Projections for 30/60/90-day periods classified by intake volume and discharge schedules

- **Medical Risk Flags**: Intake trends for inmates suffering from chronic illness/disability or mental illness

- **Audit Trail and Timeliness Report**: Period from intake to classification and documentation completion rates

Results and Measurable Impact

Metric	Before	After
Average time to assign facility	3–5 days	<24 hr
Mismatches in classification	Frequent	80% reduction by automated logic
Intake files lost/incomplete	Common	Digitally complete with an audit log
Interagency cooperation	Low	Enabled with secure Power Pages integration

- **Outcome**: Quicker, safer, and more accurate intake process, optimized usage of facilities, better cooperation among agencies, better adherence to justice and civil rights policies

Use Case 2: Court Case Routing, Judge Assignment, and Hearing Scheduling Automation

Overview and Context

With all the cases building up in the courts, there is much work to be done and many overheads to be managed. This includes a lot of manual work in case-routing, judge-assigning, and scheduling of hearings—typically with the use of spreadsheets, email chains, or legacy docketing systems. And all of it can lead to some deadlines being missed, trials being delayed, and inconsistent case assignment.

This use case proposes a Court Case Routing and Hearing Scheduling System based on the Power Platform. It automates the court workflows and ensures balance of workload across judges and operates transparency to all legal stakeholders.

Who Benefits For it

Stakeholder	Benefit
Clerks of Court	Automation of case routing and calendar scheduling across divisions and courtrooms
Judges	Receiving a balanced case assignment and operating their dockets more efficiently
Attorneys/Public Defenders	Access to hearing schedules with automated reminders and digitized requests for continuances
Court Administrators	Track caseload distribution, judge utilization, and percentages of on-time hearings
Auditors/Justice Oversight Bodies	Access to routing logs for the case, history of judge assignment, and delays in schedule

Main Drivers for Modernization

- **Scheduling Is Manual**: Clerks will spend time going through their calendars and making conflicting schedules and over-assigning judges.

- **No Uniformity in Case Route**: Judges may be assigned according to their availability instead of jurisdiction or specialty.

- **No Alert System**: Attorneys and court staff frequently miss notifications or rely on phone calls.

- **No Visibility**: They do not have any dashboards to tell court management about backlog, delay, or court performance.

- **Paper-Based Logs**: Audits trails in approvals, reschedules, and continuances are nonexistence.

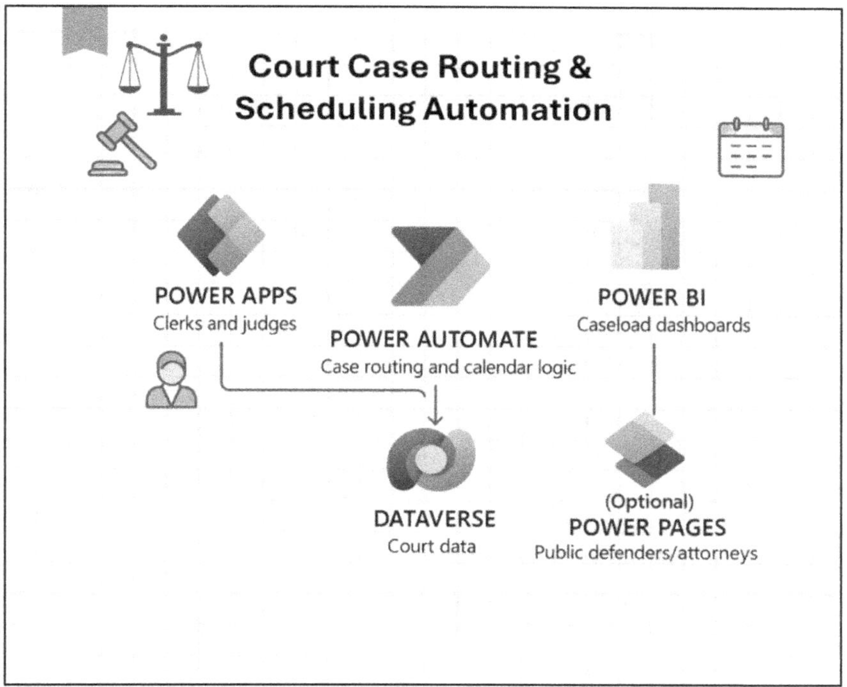

***Figure 7-43.** Architecture Diagram—Court Case Routing and Scheduling Automation*

Technical Solution Architecture

Component	Role
Power Apps	This app is used by the clerks to enter new cases, assign judges, and schedule courtrooms based on availability and jurisdiction
Power Automate	Automatically routes cases to the judge assigned, creates events for hearing, and sends reminders to all the parties
Dataverse	Store case metadata, assignments, schedules, requests for continuance, and routing logic with full logs

(continued)

Component	Role
Power Pages	(Optional) Portal for attorneys to request dates, upload documents, or track upcoming court appearances
Power BI	Online dashboards for volume of open cases, time to hearing, judge workload, and trends in trial backlogs

Workflow Overview

1. **New Case Entry**

   - Clerk enters a case into the Power Apps with the details like jurisdiction, severity, and parties involved.

2. **Judge Assignment Power**

   - Power Automate shall implement rules like rotation, division of court, specialty to assign judges to respective courtroom slots.

3. **Hearing Scheduling**

   - Court calendar auto-update, Power Automate to send notification to all parties and add events to judge's and staff's calendar.

4. **Requests and Reschedules**

   - Through Power Pages, attorneys can request continuances or file motions. Workflows would route these requests to clerks or judges for their approval.

5. **Caseload Analytics**

   - Power BI provides transparency into scheduling delays, the time that it takes to hear a case by division, and the weight of judges' dockets.

Dashboards and Reporting Views

- **Courtroom Utilization Dashboard**: Percentage of filled slots, rates of rescheduling, and average wait times by courtroom

- **Judge Assignment Metrics**: Total Active Cases Assigned for Each Judge, Workload Equity Indicators

- **Case Life Cycle Tracker**: Average time from filing to hearing, disposition rate, and frequency of requests for continuances

- **Scheduling Conflict Heatmap**: Dates/times showing overload risk, visualized across divisions

Results and Measurable Impact

Metric	Before	After
Time to assign judge and courtroom	1–3 days	< 1 hour (automated)
Missed or overlapping hearing times	Frequent	Rare with centralized calendar logic
Visibility into court workloads	Manual	Real-time dashboards by judge or division
Continuance processing time	Manual, multi-day	Streamlined with portal and routing workflows

- **Outcome**: Efficient, fair, and auditable court scheduling, better access to justice, reduced clerical burden, and more transparency in case management

Use Case 3: Analysis of Recidivism and Tracking of Offender Rehabilitation Programs

Overview and Context

Vocational training, substance abuse treatment, education, and mental health services are examples of effective rehabilitation programs. These are quite helpful to lower recidivism. Many correctional systems, however, lack universal instruments to enroll inmates, monitor program progress, and assess post-release results. Without definite statistics, it is impossible to evaluate which programs really helped to lower re-offense rates.

This use case shows a **Power Platform-Enabled Rehabilitation Program Management and Reoffence Analytics System** designed to monitor offender participation and evaluate long-term results through integrated dashboards and performance metrics.

Who It Helps

Stakeholder	Benefit
Rehabilitation Program Coordinators	Enroll inmates, assign courses, and monitor session attendance and results
Correctional Officers	Officers can view inmate progress, flags problems, and record behavior milestones
Probation and Reentry Officers	Post-release support services are coordinated by probation and reentry officers depending on pre-release program involvement
Policy Makers and Justice Leadership	Justice Leadership and Policy Makers Apply data analysis to determine which programs most successfully cut recidivism
Auditors and Grant Funders	Grant funders and auditors access organized program data to help with reporting and compliance needs

Incentive Forces for Modernization

- **Manual Enrollment Logs**: Program participation is recorded either on paper or spreadsheets. This results in inconsistent data and loss.

- **Program Standardization's Lack**: No coordinated record of program options, curriculum, or progress milestones.

- **Restricted Outcome Measurement**: Post-release monitoring is not connected to in-facility events.

- **Misses Intervention Opportunities**: Staff may not notice dropouts or noncompliance until it is too late or unless they are notified.

- **Absence of ROI Metrics**: Justifying program costs is hindered by the inability to relate program cost to real recidivism reduction achieved.

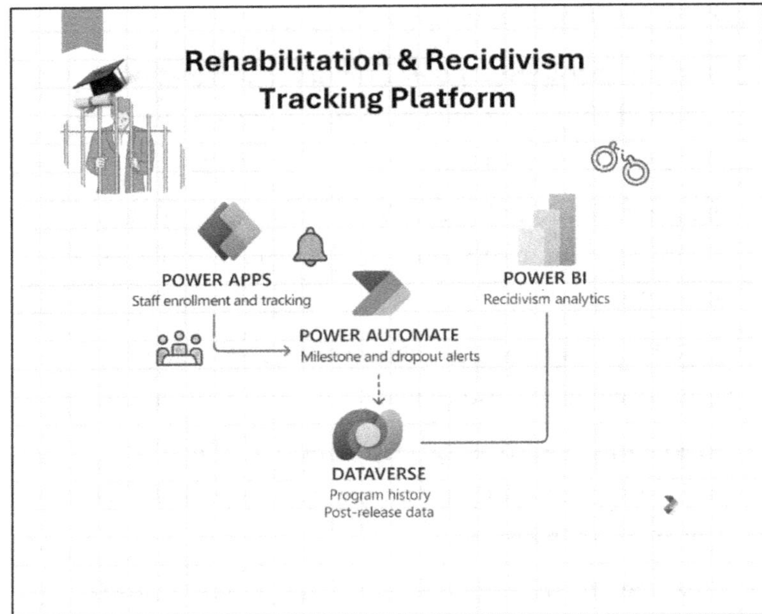

Figure 7-44. Architectural Diagram—Platform for Tracking Rehabilitation and Recidivism

Technical Solution Architecture

Component	Role
Power Apps	Coordinators use Power Apps for inmate enrollment, attendance monitoring, progress documentation, and certification or accomplishment logging
Dataverse	Dataverse keeps track of post-release tracking metrics, store logs from sessions, program history for offenders, and reentry support
Power Automate	Send alerts for missed sessions, high-risk participants marked, and post-release follow-ups using Power Automate
Power BI	Dashboard suite monitors program enrollment patterns, success, and long-term recidivism statistics

Overview of Workflows

1. **Program Participation**

   - An inmate enrolls in the rehabilitation program through Power Apps; information of interest includes session schedule, assigned instructor, and program goals.

2. **Milestone Tracking and Attendance**

   - Power Automate alerts missed sessions or dropout risks by monitoring session attendance, behavioral changes, and credentials earned.

3. **Pre-Release Preparation**

   - Summaries of program completion will be prepared by coordinators for community partners or probation officers.

4. **Post-Release Monitoring**

   - Linked records in Dataverse help reentry teams monitor employment, housing, or re-offense incidents.

5. **Reporting and Analysis**

   - Dashboards in Power BI. Program performance by category, site, demographic group, and recidivism outcome is presented here.

Dashboards and Reporting View

- **Program Participation Endowment Dashboard**: Offender profile, program type, and facility-based enrollments

- **Program Completion and Progress Tracker**: % of participants who finished every program

- **Recidivism Effect Dashboard**: Program completion versus dropouts' re-offense rates comparison

- **ROI and Funding Justification**: Program cost relative to savings from marginally decreased incarceration will help define ROI and funding.

Outcomes and Measurable Effects

Metric	Before	After
Records of inmate program attendance	Disconnected or paper-based	Centralized and easily accessible in real time
Session attendance management	Manual	Automated with alerts
Siloed support coordination post-release	Siloed	Connects via justice and community advocates
Recidivism insights by program	Not measurable	Completely seen in Power BI with filters

- **Outcome**: Improve rehabilitation tracking, target reentry planning, make data-driven policy decisions, and create firmer evidence of program impact on reducing reoffending behavior.

Use Case 4: Probation Case Management and Compliance Monitoring System

Overview and Context

Supervised departments are in charge of pupils who are freed from incarceration and have yet to prove their ability to live without going back to prison. A lot of the paperwork for managing caseloads and documenting check-ins or violations is done manually—filed, phone logs, unstructured notes, etc. There ends up being a whole lot of inefficiencies, gaps in compliance, and lots of missed chances to intervene.

This case is about a **Power Platform-Based Probation Case Management and Compliance Monitoring System**. This will assist probation officers to digitize supervision workflow and track compliance across community-based justice programs.

Who Is It Helping?

Stakeholder	Benefit
Probation Officers	Efficient management of caseloads through real-time dashboards, automated follow-ups, and case history logs
Court and Judges	Get compliance summary, violation report, and court-order fulfillment status
Probationers	Check in digitally, upload documents, receive reminders for appointments and conditions
Supervisors	Monitor caseload balance, high-risk offenders, and intervention effectiveness
Auditors and Oversight Bodies	Assess full audit trails of their programs in relation to effectiveness and risk

Key Drivers for Modernization

- **Manual Case Notes:** Heavy dependence on handwritten or poorly designed informal digital notes increases fragility in reporting.

- **None Automated Alerts:** Missed appointments, failed drug tests, and violations of curfews are without alerts.

- **Less Data in Risk Management:** Agencies are unable to flag chronic offenders quickly or prioritize high-risk individuals.

- **Too Many Cases:** Supervisors remain ignorant of their staff's workloads and trends in regional supervision.

- **Divergent Systems:** Different tools for check-ins, test results, and court reporting definitely increase inefficiencies.

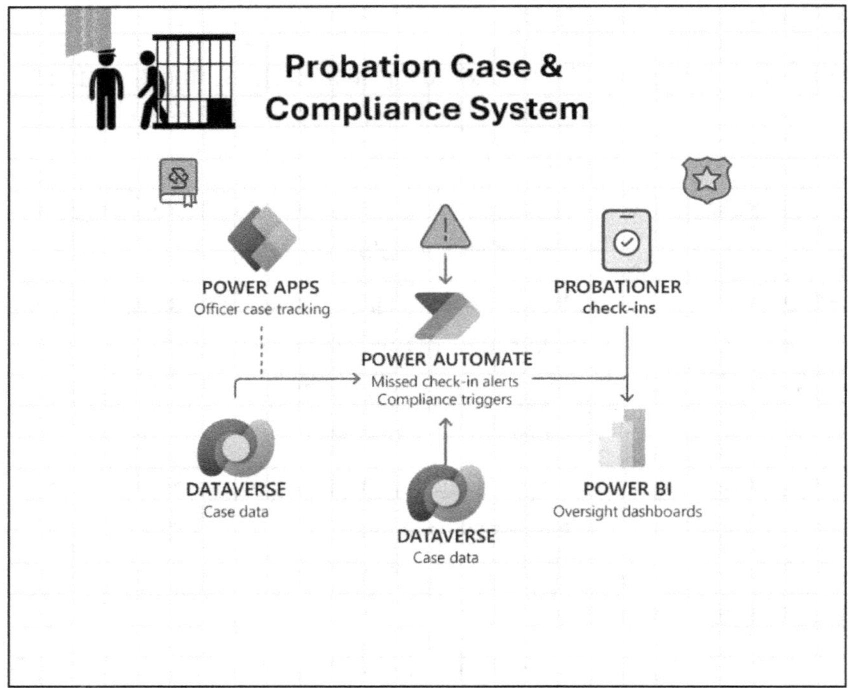

Figure 7-45. *Architecture Diagram—Probation Case and Compliance System*

Technical Solution Architecture

Component	Role
Power Apps	The apps are used by probation officers to manage their caseloads, record notes, appointments, and supervision progress
Power Pages	A secure portal for probationers to check in online, submit proof of employment or participation in a program, and view next steps
Dataverse	Storage for supervision histories, the client's conditions of release, and breaches of each client with officer assignments and automated alerts
Power Automate	Monitors missed check-ins or incomplete milestones or violations flagged to trigger alerts and workflows
Power BI	Dashboards viewing live supervision cases, regional compliance rates, high-risk flags, and officer workload analytics

Workflow Overview

1. **Case Assignment**

   - New probationers are assigned in Power Apps with initial conditions, risk rating, and meeting specifics.

2. **Check-In and Monitoring**

   - Probationers check in via Power Pages portal or mobile device, logging employment, housing, or program status.

3. **Violation Tracking**

   - Power Automate flags any missed check-ins or failed drug tests and escalates them either to the officer or to the court as needed.

4. **Progressing Updates and Reviews**

   - Officers enter their session notes, updates on court matters, along with their completed milestones (for instance, community service hours) into Power Apps.

5. **Reporting and Oversight**

   - Power BI shows regional case load figures, trends in noncompliance, and metrics on officer performance.

Dashboards and Reporting Views

- **Active Case Tracker**: Status by officer, by compliance level, and by type of supervision

- **Violation Dashboard**: Missed appointments, positive test results, curfew violations

- **Completion Metrics**: % of probationers completing the court-required milestones

- **Caseload Management by Officer**: Assignments based on geography, risk level, and case type

Results and Measurable Impact

Metric	Before	After
Missed check-in identification	Held up or not tracked	Real time via Power Automate
Case documentation consistency	Low	Structured, timestamped in Dataverse
Transparency of officers' workloads	Minimal	Real-time dashboards with risk filtering
Violation escalation response time	2–3 days	<1 day (automatically flagged)

- **Outcome:** Enhanced effectiveness of supervision in the community, with early interventions on violations, balanced caseloads per officer, and total visibility to court and oversight teams

Use Case 5: Victim Notification, Rights Management, and Case Communication Portal

Overview and Context

Crime victims are entitled to be notified of the status of their case, custody changes, and release of the offender. The majority of corrections and the justice system, however, use antiquated victim communication techniques, such as sending letters by mail or making phone calls. Such outdated means create chances for notifications to be missed, which in turn can infringe on victims' rights laws.

This use case presents the description of a **Power Platform-Based Portal for Victim Notification and Case Communication** that seeks to automate the proper notification to victims, facilitate secure self-service access, and ensure the compliance of all victim rights statutes.

Who It Helps

Stakeholders	Benefit
Crime Victims and Survivors	Get secure real-time notifications about custody status changes, court dates, and release information
Victim Services Coordinators	Victims' enrollment, consent forms, and communication preferences can be managed from a single interface
Corrections and Parole Officers	Automatic alerts are triggered where offender status changes (e.g. parole granted, escape, transfer)
Legal and Compliance Teams	Legal teams willing to notify victims and keep auditable records in accordance with legal requirements
Advocacy Organizations	Advocacy groups help victims by up-to-date alerts and real-time case timeline access

Modernization Key Drivers

- **Manual Notification Approaches**: Call and letter messages are prone to delays and inconsistencies.

- **Compliance Risk**: Missed alerts could violate victims' rights legislation, therefore exposing the agency to liability.

- **Lack of Victim Control**: Victims cannot control how or when they are updated.

- **Fragmented Systems**: Information from victims, perpetrators, and their corresponding courts is kept in separate systems.

- **No Central Access**: The victims lack a reliable way to check case status or establish contact preferences.

Figure 7-46. *Architectural Diagram—Victim Notification And Rights Management Platform*

Technical Solution Architecture

Component	Role
Power Pages	Portal for the victim to register, choose notification preference (SMS, email), and monitor case milestones
Power Apps	The app is used by victim coordinators in managing communication, validation of consent, and updates to case linkages
Power Automate	To issue automated alerts for major events—updates about parole board, transfers, escapes, release/approval, and court hearings
Dataverse	Stores case details, victim preferences, notification logs, consent forms, and current status of custody of offenders
Power BI	Dashboards give advance notification timeframes, success of delivery, and outreach by region or case type

Workflow Overview

1. **Enrollment of Victims**

   - Victims are enrolling through Power Pages using validated case information and consent to communications and notification preferences.

2. **Event Monitoring and Alerts**

   - Power Automate is listening for triggers (status changes, hearings, transfers) from connected systems and notifying victims.

3. **Coordinator Oversight**

- Victim service staff use Power Apps to help high-risk cases; questions are answered and then put into the system for another layer of support.

4. **Actual Access in Real Time**

- Victims can safely log in to verify notification history, check upcoming court dates, or get safety planning guidance.

5. **Reporting and Compliance**

- Power BI tracks victim service enrollment, missed alerts, and notification historical performance.

Reporting Reviews and Dashboard Views

- **Notification Compliance Dashboard**: Timely vs. late or failed alerts

- **Overview of Outreach and Enrollment**: By offense type and region, victims registered

- **Notification Type Report**: Victim profile breakdown of SMS, email, and portal usage

- **High-Risk Monitoring Panel**: Cases marked for priority attention or recurring system contact

Outcomes and Measurable Effects

Metric	Before	After
Missed notifications for victims	Common	Automated reduced by over 95%
Manual notification tracking	Spreadsheet-based	Automated and logged in Dataverse
Access by victims to case info	None	Real-time portal access to full history
Timeliness in compliance with statutory deadlines	Inconsistent	Near-total adherence checking with alerts and tracking

- **Outcome**: Legally compliant, victim-centered messages, quicker alerts, better safety planning, and openness by means of real-time tracking and audit trails.

7.10 Department of Human Services

Use Case 1: Advantages of Integrated Family Support System and Case Intake

General Introduction and Context

Essential safety-net programs offered by the Human Services departments include SNAP, TANF, Medicaid, child care subsidies, housing assistance, and family crisis services. Applicants typically have to submit paperwork to various offices, which complicates their ability to comprehend the services they are eligible for.

This use case introduces a **Benefits Intake And Integrated Family Support System** based on Power Platform, allowing for centralized case intake and a consolidated view of the household across all benefit programs.

Who It Helps

Stakeholder	Benefit
Low-Income Families and Individuals	Submit one application for multiple benefits, guided eligibility checks with real-time status' updates
Caseworkers	Advanced access to all household information, management of multiple services from a single screen, and the possibility of auto-triggering referrals
Supervisors and Program Managers	Conduct monitoring of caseloads, trends on incoming applications, and track on effective service bundling
Policy Analysts and Funders	View unified reports on family types receiving benefits by region and outcome metrics
Call Centers and Community Navigators	Decrease client wait times and provide guidance through data-driven assistance

Key Factors for Modernization

- **Broken-Down Program Applications**: Clients must go from one office to another for each benefit and input the same information repeatedly.

- **Erratic Intake Processes**: Paper and manual interviews differ from program and location.

- **No Family View**: Siloed systems produce no way to understand household needs and support in the overlapping areas.

- **Insufficient Data for Coordination**: Departments struggle to track families receiving some assistance at risk of slipping through the cracks.

- **Delay in Case Opening**: Long wait, delay in assistance, and increase in abandonment rates are because of the manual process.

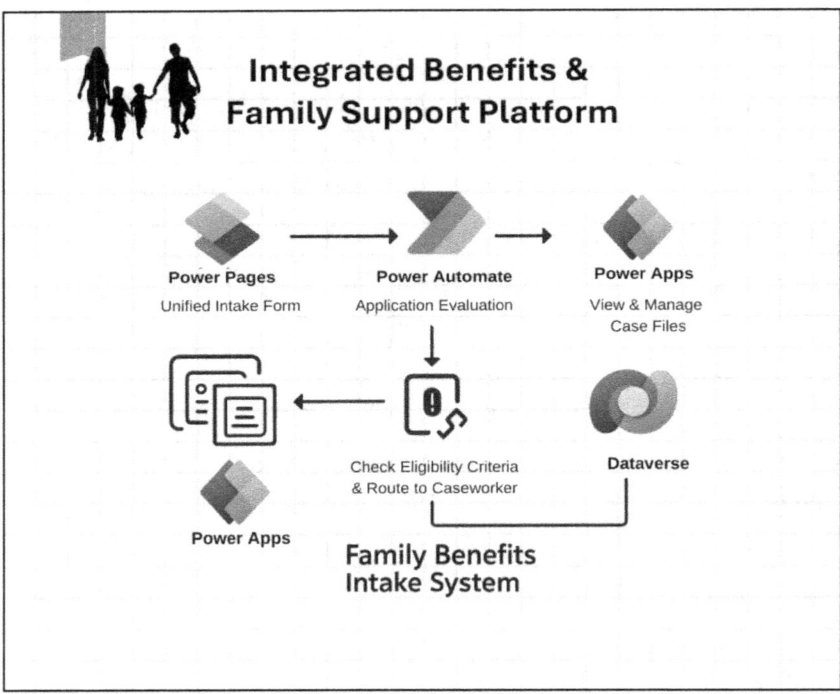

Figure 7-47. Architecture Diagram—Integrated Benefits and Family Support Platform

Technical Solution Architecture

Component	Role
Power Pages	Multilingual portal through which the applicant completes a single intake questionnaire for multiple forms of benefits with document upload
Power Automate	Evaluates responses against eligibility criteria and attaches cases to the relevant program or caseworker team
Dataverse	All comprehensive household profiles containing benefits history, documentation, referral status, and engagement logs
Power Apps	The app is used by staff to view and manage integrated case files, assign programs, and collaborate with other teams
Power BI	Dashboards monitoring service bundling, application turnaround time, household need clusters, and case abandonment

Workflows Summarized

1. **Unified Intake Submission**

   - The client submits a dynamic application through Power Pages with conditional questions and auto-saved progress.

2. **Eligibility Evaluation and Routing**

   - Power Automate matches responses to eligibility matrices in areas like SNAP, TANF, housing, child care, and routes staff accordingly.

3. **The Caseworker Dashboard**

   - Power Apps are utilized by caseworkers to access all data for the household, add notes, flag verified documents, and refer to other agencies when necessary.

4. **Multi-Program Assignment**

   - The client is enrolled in eligible benefits for program follow-up actions that Dataverse is tracking.

5. **Monitoring and Reporting**

   - Power BI presents performance results by household type, demographic, location, and actual effectiveness of the benefits bundles.

Dashboards and Reporting View

- **Benefits Bundled Dashboard**: Clients receiving 1, 2, or 3+ services together

- **Application Turnaround Time**: Average time and days since application submission to approval with respect to the benefit type

- **Abandonment and Reentry Metrics**: Percent of incomplete/paused applications with successful follow-ups

- **Household Needs Cluster Map**: Service Request Mapping by neighborhood or demographic

Results and Measurable Impact

Metric	Before	After
Average application time per benefit	60–90 minutes	<25 minutes with unified application
Visibility to enroll concurrently in different programs	None	Full cross-benefit tracking
Abandonment rate	High	Reduced by 60% with guided application form and save/resume
Caseworker assignment time	2–5 days	Same day via Power Automation Routing

- **Outcome**: Greater equity in service delivery across supports, rapid access to multiple supports for clients, enhanced cooperation among caseworkers, and better data for policy and investment decisions.

Use Case 2: Foster Care Case Management and Provider Collaboration Hub

Overview and Context

Foster care agencies exist to protect vulnerable children, work with the foster families and the legal entity, and provide continuous support for the children and caregivers. Usually, case tracking is quite fragmented—spreadsheets, binders, and case notes. Unfortunately, it's responsible for gaps in care, miscommunication, and delayed interventions.

This use case brings a **Power Platform-Based Foster Care Case Management and Provider Collaboration Hub** that provides an integrated environment for tracking child cases, managing placements, coordinating with external providers, and ensuring the delivery of services across the foster care life cycle.

Who It Helps

Stakeholder	Benefit
Caseworkers	Manage child cases, update assessment data, track placements, and coordinate with foster providers in one highly secure system
Foster Families and Providers	Submit reports, request services, and track milestones of children through a very secure portal
Supervisors	To monitor caseload distribution, placement stability, and critical incident reports
Legal and Compliance Teams	To review all audit-ready records, timelines for court, and visitation documentation
Health and Education Coordinators	To make sure that the therapies, tutors, and healthcare are provided timely and in continuity

Drivers Toward Modernization

- **Severely Disjointed Case Files:** Notes, placements, and referrals are in completely distant systems or physical files.

- **Limited Coordination of Roster Provider:** There are no available means for foster parents and outside providers to communicate together.

- **No Real-Time Supervision**: Supervisors are not
  able to get instant information on high-risk or high-
  turnover cases.

- **Instability of Placement**: Alerts and history analytical
  recordings fail to avert a breakdown or an unnecessary
  transfer.

- **Problems with Compliance**: Incomplete files have
  resulted in a delay in court proceedings and regulatory
  reviews.

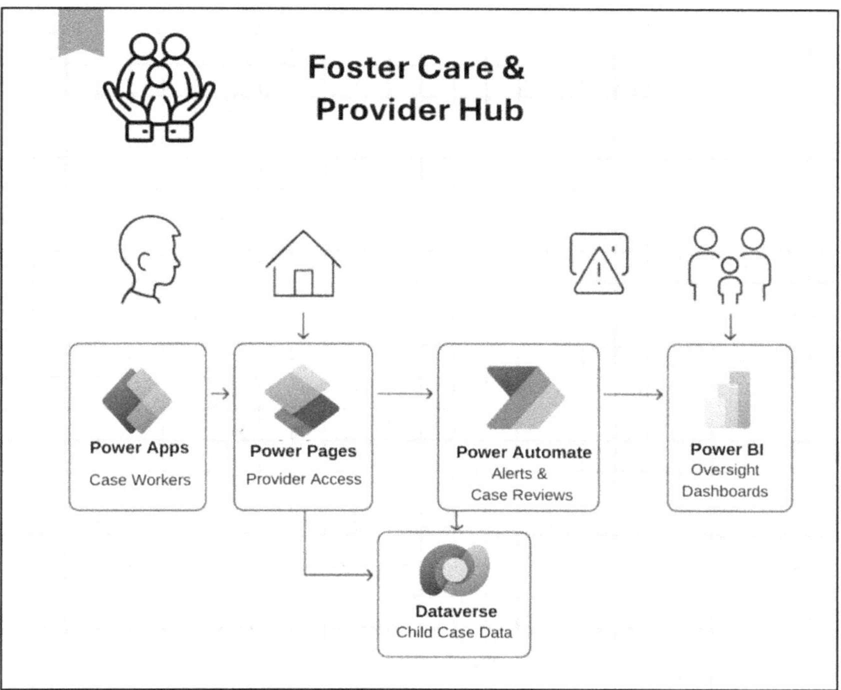

Figure 7-48. *Architecture Diagram—Foster Care and Provider Hub*

Technical Solution Architecture

Component	Role
Power Apps	The application is used by caseworkers to manage child profiles, track placements, log notes, schedule reviews, and submit assessments
Power Pages	Secure portal for foster families and providers to report issues, update status, and view placement data
Power Automate	Alerts overdue visits, missing documentation, service gaps, and placement disruption risks
Dataverse	Stores child history, placement logs, incident reports, service referrals, education/health plans, and court dates
Power BI	Dashboards for placement stability, service compliance, caseload trends, and critical incident analytics

Workflow Overview

1. **Case Initiation**

   - Caseworker opens a new case in Power Apps, enters intake info, assign the initial placement, and log initial safety plan.

2. **Provider Collaboration**

   - Foster families access Power Pages to upload progress notes, to flag incidents, and to submit requests for appointments.

3. **Milestone and Incident Tracking**

- Power Automate generates alerts to staff when check-ins are overdue, there are safety risks, or placement transfers. All actions logged into Dataverse.

4. **Court and Compliance Preparation**

- All the documents clearly related to legal matters like hearing schedules, provider certifications are tracked and exported as necessary.

5. **Monitoring and Analytics**

- Display child-level and program-level metrics on Power BI to spot problems soon to improve caregiver outcomes.

Dashboards and Reporting Views

- **Placement Stability Dashboard**: The number of placements per child, duration of care, reunification goals

- **Incident Report Summary**: Events logged, time taken for resolution, and escalation flags

- **Service Coordination Tracker**: Therapy appointments tracked by child and provider; medical, educational appointments

- **Caseload and Review Metrics**: Total cases per worker and reviews due ahead and compliance overdue tasks.

Results and Measurable Impact

Metric	Before	After
Placement tracking method	Manual logs or spreadsheets	Fully digitized and centralized
Provider communication method	Phone/email only	Real-time portal and alerts
Missed documentation for court	Often	<5% with automatic reminders
Placement disruptions	Unmonitored	Visualized and decreased using trend analytics

- **Outcome**: Safer and stable placements, stronger family-provider coordination caseworker reality, improved compliance, and improved outcomes for children in the care

Use Case 3: SNAP/TANF Redetermination and Benefit Recertification Automation

Overview and Context

Eligibility for critical benefits such as SNAP (food assistance) and TANF (temporary assistance for needy families) should be certified periodically. Clients do not meet deadlines, and agencies did not do well in managing recertification waves due to paper notices, manual interviews, and poor tracking, resulting in benefit interruptions, increased appeals, and administrative strain.

This use case presents **Power Platform-Based Redetermination and Recertification Automation System** to effectively reckon benefit renewal processes so that they are compliant and enhance client communications.

Who It Helps

Stakeholder	Benefit
Beneficiaries (Clients)	Have automatic reminders for renewals, completed recertification online, and tracking of status
Eligibility Workers	Review cases with pre-filled type forms, verify all documents accessed in one interface, and assure reduced errors
Supervisors	Manage volumes of recertification, overdue cases, and staff workload on real-time dashboards
Call Center Staff	Quickly answer client status questions using centralized case data
Program Administrators	Track compliance with federal reporting rules and renewal cycle KPIs

Key Drivers for Modernization

- **Missed Deadlines**: Paper notices are now missed, causing benefits cutoffs or reinstatement backlogged.

- **High Appeal Volume:** Poor communication and delayed renewal lead to contested case closures.

- **Repeat Data Entry**: Clients keep submitting the same data again and again.

- **Workload Peaks**: No agency can assess and see upcoming renewals volumes.

- **Manual Reporting**: All of the recertification compliance reports which are quarterly or annual are compiled manually.

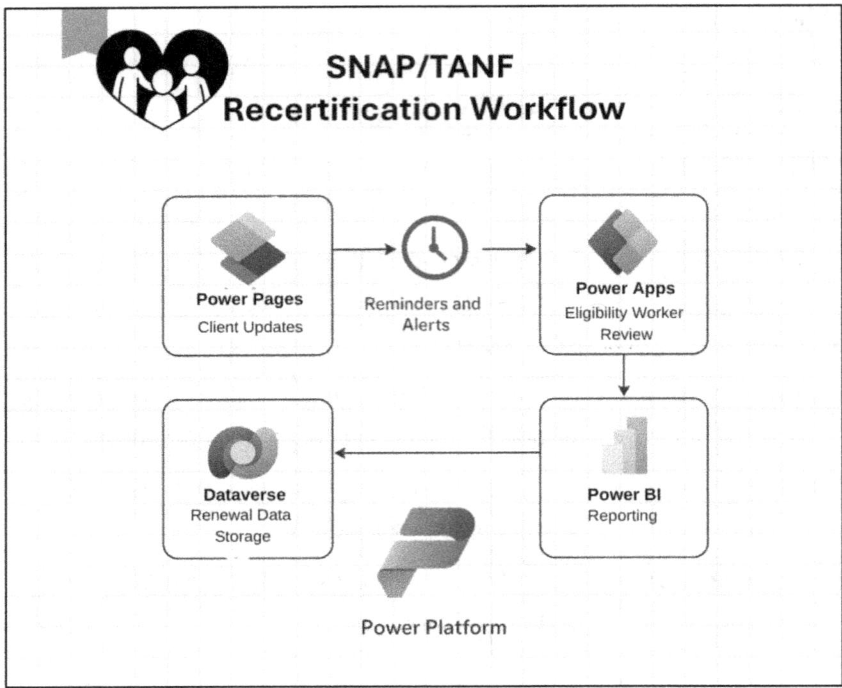

Figure 7-49. *Architecture Diagram—SNAP/TANF Recertification Workflow*

Technical Solution Architecture

Component	Role
Power Pages	Client portal for recertification submission, document upload, and appointment scheduling
Power Automate	Early bird reminders, notices regarding deadline due dates, escalated missed deadlines, and interview schedules

(continued)

Component	Role
Power Apps	Case workers review the forms submitted, validate the documents, and finally take eligibility decisions
Dataverse	Redetermining history, document logs, case status, sent notifications, and appeal outcomes are stored
Power BI	Dashboards for recertification rates, case backlog, SLA performance, and outreach effectiveness

Workflow Overview

1. **Renewal Notification**

   - Notices before redetermination deadline will be sent through SMS/email using Power Automate on 45, 30, and 15 days before the deadline.

2. **Submission by Client**

   - The clients fill out the recertification form through Power Pages upload income or residency documents and request time for interviews.

3. **Eligibility Assessment**

   - Power Apps used to access forms, missing data automatically flagged, and approvals or denials source is logged for tracking purposes.

4. **Update on the Case Plus Case Integration**

   - Dataverse updates case records and syncs with external benefits systems (e.g., eligibility engine payment processor).

5. **Analytics and Compliance**

- Power BI shows the renewal success rate as well as denial trends and timeliness benchmarking.

Dashboards and Reporting Views

- **Upcoming Renewals Calendar**: Households due in the next 30/60/90 days

- **Recertification Completion Rate**: % submitted on time, late, or missed

- **Denial, Appeal Trends**: Top reasons for denial and reentry outcomes

- **Worker Assessment Performance**: SLA metrics and case volume distribution

Results and Measured Impact

Metric	Before	After
On-time renewal submission	60–70%	% > 90% with reminders and digital portal
Average processing time	15–20 days	< 7 days
Client complaints and appeals for missed renewals	High	Reduced by >75%
Tracking of recertification	Manual logs	Fully automated and visible in real time

- **Outcome**: Renewals benefit faster, fairer, fewest terminations, best compliance, best client satisfaction, and the least employee burden through redetermination cycles

Use Case 4: Homeless Services Coordination and Housing Placement System

Overview and Context

Human service departments are mainly coordinators for the support system available for people and families without homes, getting them into shelters, transitional housing, healthcare, food programs, and permanent supportive housing. The problems, however, arise for clients, with many intake procedures being shared among providers with tracking of bed availability done manually and clients being asked to retell their stories at every contact.

The use case introduces the **Homeless Services and Housing Coordination System** based on the Power Platform. It aims to provide real-time shelter bed tracking, an automated referral mechanism across a community-wide service network, and setting data-driven placement decisions.

Who It Helps

Stakeholder	Benefit
Case Managers and Outreach Workers	Single dashboard to intake clients, assess risk, refer to services, and track placement into housing
Shelter and Housing Providers	Update units in real time and get referrals with full context of client
Clients	Avoid repeating their story; faster referral to available housing or emergency support
Program Coordinators	Monitor shelter capacity, referral success, service gaps, and time-to-housing metrics
Public Health and Mental Health Teams	Coordinate with housing staff to support complex or high-needs clients

Key Drivers for Modernization

- **Repeated Intake**: Clients are screened multiple times by different providers.

- **Paper-Based Bed Tracking System**: Updates on shelter capacities happen with telephone calls or emails, which sometimes are hours away from the real-time data.

- **No Referral Logic Acceptable:** Case assignment is accomplished through manual intervention without any audit trail or prioritization logic.

- **Some Follow-Ups Are Missed:** Clients fall through the cracks as cases are handed over from one program or provider to another.

- **No Analytics Pertaining to Housing Outcomes**: Management has no visibility into successful uses and stays in homelessness.

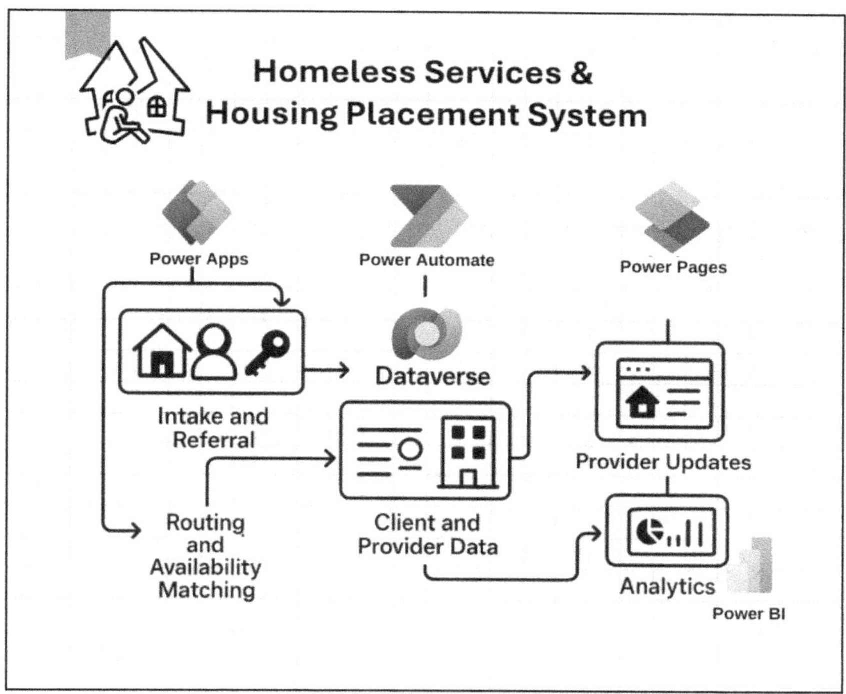

Figure 7-50. *Architecture Diagram of the Homeless Services and Housing Placement System*

Technical Solution Architecture

Component	Role
Power Apps (Canvas App)	The app is used by outreach teams and caseworkers to intake clients, log services needed, and initiate referrals
Power Pages	Provider portal for shelters and housing organizations to update availability and manage referrals
Power Automate	Matches clients to the appropriate shelter or housing resource based upon needs, location, and priority

(continued)

Component	Role
Dataverse	Stores client data (with confidentiality controls), provider records, availability logs, and placement history
Power BI	Dashboards to track service demand, time to placement, bed utilization, and outcomes at the program level

Overview of the Workflow

1. **Client Intake**

   - Outreach worker fills in the intake Power Apps for client demographics, risk factors, needs, and last known housing.

2. **Matching and Referral**

   - Power Automate checks for real-time availability in the Dataverse, applies prioritization rules, and refers to the shelter or housing provider.

3. **Provider Response**

   - Providers access the referral through Power Pages and accept/decline it, while also updating the bed status and check-in information.

4. **Service Coordination**

   - The caseworker tracks the progress of the service, logs support services, and also coordinates with the healthcare, addiction, or employment teams.

5. **Performance Reporting**

   - All the metrics from intake to housing are shown in Power BI dashboards showcasing frequent users of the shelter service, turnover ratio for the shelter, and outcome indicators after exit.

Dashboards and Reports Views

- **Live Bed Availability Map**: Availability of shelters and units across the city/region

- **Referral Outcome Dashboard**: % of referrals placed, declined, or expired

- **Housing Stability Scorecard**: % of clients retained in housing 30/60/90 days after placement

- **Frequent Service Users Tracker**: Identifying high-need clients who enter and exit shelters or emergency services frequently

Results and Measurable Impact

Metric	Before	After
Time from intake to referral	1–3 days	<1 hour
Accuracy of shelter capacity	Manual adjustments	Real time with Power Pages
Data re-collection	Redundant	Eliminated with one case profile being shared
Tracking of placements	Informal logs	Digitally tracked with audit trail

- **Outcome:** Achieving swifter, more equitable housing placements, improved inter-agency coordination, lessening of administrative work, and strengthened outcome reporting for funding and strategy alignment

Use Case 5: Automation of Payment Workflow and Child Support Case Management

Overview and Background

Managing child support responsibilities involves coordinating court orders, non-custodial parent payments, enforcement activities, and interstate concerns. Still many agencies use legacy systems, manual case tracking, and paper payment processes. As a consequence, payments are delayed, creating compliance gaps and administrative inefficiencies.

Thus, this use case is a **Power Platform-Based Child Support Case Management and Payment Workflow Automation System** to track obligations systematically, enabling quick payment processing. This enhances transparency for all parties involved.

Affected Parties

Stakeholders	Benefit
Custodial Parents	Receive child support payments on time and view case/payment history online
Non-custodial Parents	Follow up responsibilities, get reminders, and see payment history clearly and simply
Case Workers	Streamline court orders, payment schedules, enforcement measures, and communications from a centralized dashboard
Finance and Treasury Teams	Automate payment routing and disbursement to qualified custodial recipients
Judicial and Compliance Bodies	Ability to interrogate court order records, delinquency rates, and enforcement actions with a full audit trail

Key Drivers of Modernization

- **Old Payment Tracking**: Old systems or paper files hold up reconciliation and reporting.

- **Manual Entering of Court Orders**: These court-ordered modifications are manually entered in an inconsistent way into different systems.

- **Disbursement Delays**: Execution of payment can be potentially thwarted by document gap(s) or processing failures.

- **Restricted Parent Access**: Custodial/non-custodial parties are still required to call to inquire about case status or come into the office.

- **Enforcement Complexity**: Missing payments are difficult to detect and bring to attention in real time.

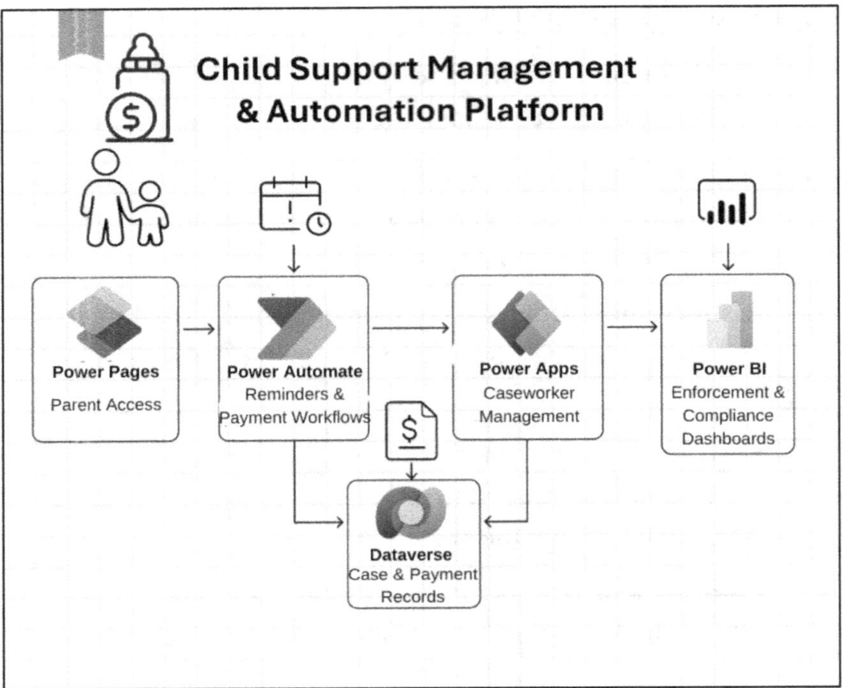

Figure 7-51. *Architecture Diagram—Child Support Management and Automation Platform*

Technical Architecture Solution

Component	Role
Power Apps	The app is used for the case workers to manage court orders, track payment activities, initiate actions undertaken for enforcement, and communicate with the involved parties
Power Pages	Portal securely lets parents see case status, submit updates, and check payment history

(continued)

Component	Role
Power Automate	Alerts when payment is due, court hearing reminders, and starts compliance workflows
Dataverse	Stores audit log, financial history, parents' information, court documentation, and case records in Dataverse
Power BI	Dashboards in Power BI help to monitor payment rates, compliance problems, enforcement reactions, and collections in certain areas

Workflow Overview

1. **Case Creation**

   - The case worker enters court order specifics, the obligation amount, payment frequency, and people engaged in the case into Power Apps.

2. **Tracking of Payments**

   - Verification of the scheduled payment dates, matching of amounts received, and marking of underpayment or nonpayment are the responsibility of Power Automate.

3. **Parental Access and Engagement**

   - Custodial and non-custodial parents log in via Power Pages to view payment status, court dates, and communicate with caseworkers.

4. **Enforcement Mechanisms**

   - Dataverse will keep all records, and the missed payment will activate enforcement action (wage garnishment, license hold, court review).

5. **Monitoring Compliance**

- Power BI monitors overall levels of compliance for payment, delinquency trends, and total funds collected/disbursed by the program.

Reporting and Dashboard

- **Payment Compliance Dashboard**: % late payments, average delay, total arrears

- **Delinquency and Enforcement Tracker**: Active enforcement, payment recovery success

- **Parent Activity Summary**: Portal login, message traces, document submissions

- **Regional Program Performance**: Payment volume and disbursement for a county or district

Results and Measurable Impacts

Metric	Before	After
Average payment posting time	2–4 days	Less than 1 day with Automated Tracking
Identification of missed payments	Delay or Miss	Live alerts driven by Power Automate
Parent view of case status	Minimal	Self-service access powered by Power Pages
Collection-to-pay-out rate	Inconsistency	Manual workflows and performance tracking

- **Outcome**: Families and supervising agencies get more openness, improved accountability, more child support order compliance, and faster funds distribution.

CHAPTER 8

Best Practices and Frameworks

8.1 Low-Code Design Thinking

Design thinking is a human-centered approach that enables government agencies to create solutions that fully address user requirements. It minimizes rework and enables innovation even in disciplined public sector settings.

Design Thinking Steps in Government Projects

1. **Empathize**

   - Interview frontline workers and citizens.

   - Observe processes (e.g., intake stations, inspectors, reviewers).

2. **Define**

   - Find root causes (e.g., "Applications are delayed due to manual document routing.")

3. **Ideate**

   - Brainstorm solutions with Power Platform.

   - Collaborate with citizen developer feedback.

© Sarat Piridi 2025

S. Piridi, *GovOps with Microsoft Power Platform and Copilot*, Inside Copilot, https://doi.org/10.1007/979-8-8688-1796-0_8

4. **Prototype**

   - Quickly develop a proof-of-concept in Canvas or Model-Driven Apps.

   - Prototype with internal stakeholders.

5. **Test**

   - Gather feedback.

   - Iterate based on real-time data and user feedback of experience.

Tip   Obtain whiteboarding tools such as Miro or Microsoft Whiteboard to diagram flows prior to building.

8.2 Agile Methodologies

Agile methodologies work naturally well with low-code platforms due to quick prototyping and quick iteration cycles.

Most Significant Agile Practices

- **Two-Week Sprints:** Deliver shippable components frequently.

- **Daily Stand-Ups:** Clear blockers ahead of time.

- **Backlog Grooming:** Prioritized list of app features and bugs.

- **Sprint Demos:** Show progress to business owners and stakeholders.

Note   Use Planner or Azure DevOps to plan and track the backlog for the sprint.

8.3 Templates and Reusability

Reusability and standardization of components speed up development and impose consistency across departments.

Best Practices

- **Power Apps component libraries** for headers, footers, notifications, and default layouts

- **Pre-built flows** for approvals, document uploads, and notification flows

- **JSON templates** for deploying Power Automate and Power Pages

- **Dataverse schema packages** for common tables (e.g., Applicant, Permit, Case)

8.4 Change Management

Low-code transformation is a success when people—not tech—are well managed.

Government Change Management Steps

1. **Establish stakeholders** first (IT, Business, Legal, Security).

2. **Develop a communications plan** (emails, internal portals, FAQs).

3. **Establish a feedback loop** (post-implementation interviews, surveys).

4. **Deliver training workshops** or micro-learning modules.

Tool Tip   Leverage Microsoft Viva Learning and Teams channels to execute awareness campaigns.

8.5 Citizen Developer Governance

Allowing non-technical employees to develop applications has to be done with guardrails.

Governance Framework Includes

- **Learning Paths:** Beginner to advanced learning paths

- **CoE Support:** Help desk or coaching pods to assist citizen developers

- **Policy Enforcement:** DLP, naming conventions, and solution templates enforced

- **Review Boards:** Routine audits or application registration prior to use in production

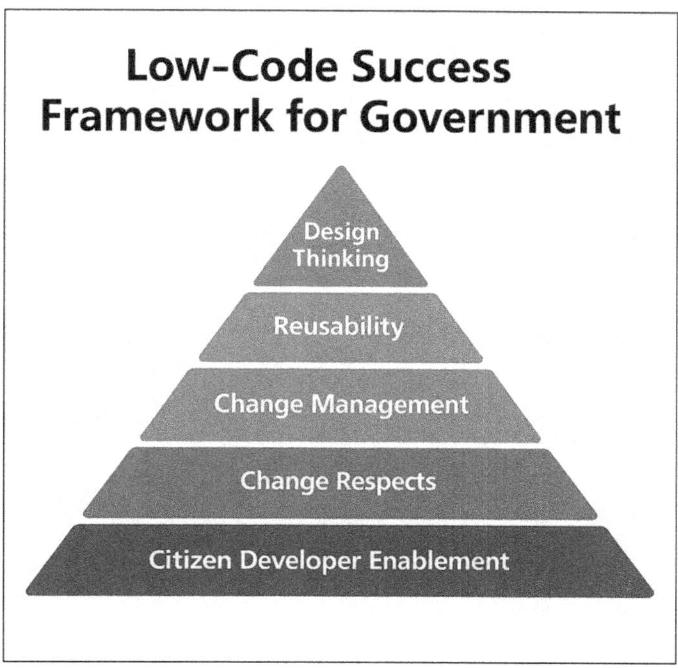

Figure 8-1. *Low-Code Success Framework for Government*

CHAPTER 9

The Road Ahead

9.1 Next-Gen Copilot

Copilot roles will increasingly move from **assistive AI** to **autonomous AI**, transforming how government workers construct solutions and analyze data.

Most Important Breakthroughs on the Horizon

- **Scenario-Based Learning:** Copilot learns context from current data and systems to provide end-to-end workflows (e.g., "You just created an inspection app—do you want to automate scheduling too?").

- **AI-Generated Environments:** Provision Dev, QA, and Prod environments automatically from agency templates.

- **Proactive AI Assistants:** Copilot provides advance feedback of user requests, e.g., "Higher-than-average permit rejection rates for this week in District 3."

Future Focus: Embedding GPT-type models into government-domain policies and data will enable domain-sensitive copilots.

© Sarat Piridi 2025
S. Piridi, *GovOps with Microsoft Power Platform and Copilot,* Inside Copilot,
https://doi.org/10.1007/979-8-8688-1796-0_9

9.2 Future of AI in Government

Trends to Watch

- **Natural Language Processing for Legal Analysis:** AI makes possible the interpretation, summarizing, and comparing legal provisions within policy drafts or contracts.

- **Real-Time Translation:** Multilingual AI-based services by Azure enhance accessibility and equity in service delivery.

- **Predictive Analytics for Policy Decisions:** Budget deficit, spike in service requests, or compliance breach is predicted by models.

Use Case: AI translates public comments, budget trends, and categories of complaints and suggests topics for inclusion in future council meetings.

9.3 Digital Centers of Excellence (CoE)

Digital CoEs will transform from tooling and governance into **hubs of innovation.**

Next-Gen CoE Architecture

- **Solution Architects:** Develop reusable templates and standards.

- **Citizen Developer Coaches:** Mentor business teams with low code.

- **Data Scientists:** Enhance Copilot and AI Builder capabilities.

- **Compliance Leads:** Make all automations regulation-compliant.

Impact: CoEs will determine agencies' digital maturity and drive time to value between departments.

9.4 Leading the Way

Governments need to develop a mindset of **continuous learning and community engagement** to stay agile in a rapidly changing tech environment.

Recommendations

- Join groups such as the Microsoft Power Platform Community.

- Encourage employees to get certified (e.g., PL-900, PL-100, PL-200).

- Conduct low-code "hackathons" or solution demonstrations internally.

- Keep up with Microsoft roadmap releases and participate in public previews.

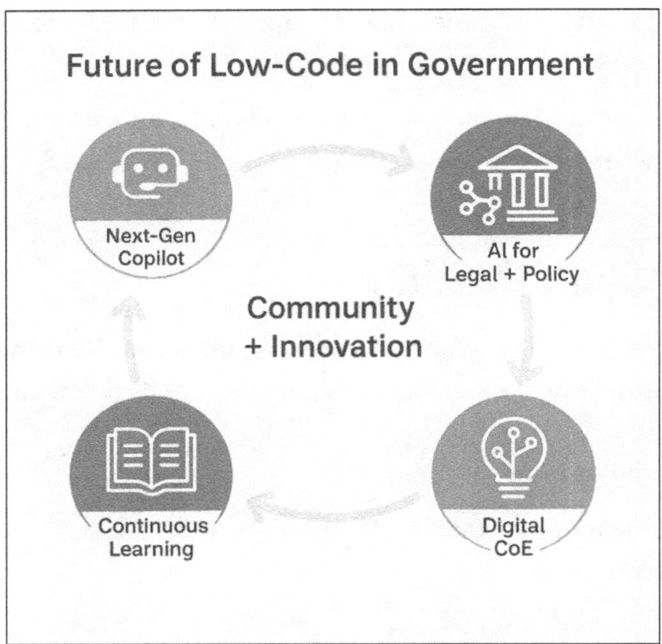

Figure 9-1. *How Low Code in Government Will Evolve in the Future*

CHAPTER 10

Resources and Templates

This chapter offers reference materials, pre-configured assets, and vetted tools to assist government teams in getting started or expanding their low-code automation program on the Power Platform.

10.1 Solution Architecture Diagrams

Reusable stencils and diagrams for typical solution types:

- Permit Processing App Architecture

- Citizen Complaint Portal Flow

- Public Safety Inspection Dashboard

- AI-Powered Help Desk Bot

- Multi-Environment Dev ➤ UAT ➤ Prod Deployment Models

Tool　Utilize Visio or Draw.io templates to enhance the visual aspect of these diagrams.

© Sarat Piridi 2025
S. Piridi, *GovOps with Microsoft Power Platform and Copilot*, Inside Copilot,
https://doi.org/10.1007/979-8-8688-1796-0_10

10.2 ALM Scripts and Tools

Critical automation and life cycle management assets:

- Power Platform Pipelines YAML configuration templates

- PowerShell scripts for exporting/importing solutions

- GitHub workflows for automated deployment

- Environment variable templates

- DevOps task sequence checklist

10.3 Sample User Stories and Use Case Library

Pre-authored user story library for quick backlog creation:

- "As a permit clerk, I want to be able to track submitted applications…"

- "As a constituent, I want to be notified when my request is approved…"

- "As a compliance officer, I want to be able to escalate overdue investigations…"

Bonus: Add prioritization labels (e.g., High Impact/Low Effort).

10.4 App Development Workbook

A printable or digital workbook to walk teams through the development cycle:

- Use case canvas

- Stakeholder matrix

- Environment planning sheet

- Compliance checklist

- Post-launch support tracker

10.5 Whitepapers and Reference Guides

Reading and learning materials required:

- Microsoft Power Platform Adoption Framework

- AI Builder best practices

- Power Apps accessibility guide

- Data governance in the public sector whitepapers

- Government CoE starter kit documentation

10.6 Learning and Community Resources

Stay up to date and active:

- Microsoft Learn for Power Platform courses

- Power Platform Blog

- Government-focused LinkedIn groups and Reddit channels

- Official Power Platform Community Forums

- Microsoft's Public Sector Digital Transformation website

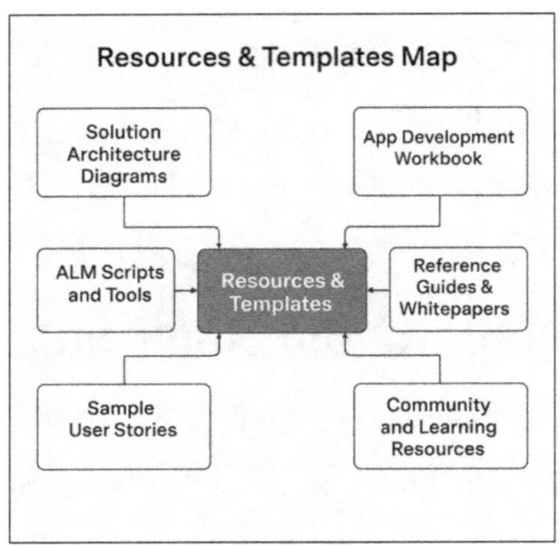

Figure 10-1. *Resources and Templates Map*

CHAPTER 11

Azure AI + AI Builder High-Level AI Model Development

11.1 Introduction

AI is no longer the dream of one "someday," artificial intelligence is today a key capability that underpins government mission operations. To prevent fraud, be in a position to read documents better, and more measure citizen feelings and sentiment, outcomes can speed up while becoming quality-improving and progressively cost-saving.

With **AI Builder** and **Azure AI Services**, government teams can integrate low-code and pro-code AI models into Power Platform solutions without having data science-skilled teams.

S. Piridi, *GovOps with Microsoft Power Platform and Copilot*, Inside Copilot,
https://doi.org/10.1007/979-8-8688-1796-0_11

11.2 AI Use Cases for Government

Use Case	Description
Document Intelligence	Extract and classify data from contracts, forms, and legal documents with Form Recognizer
Case Routing with Prediction	Forecast urgency based on history, route cases automatically
License Plate Recognition	Utilize Azure Computer Vision to examine images for traffic enforcement
Sentiment Analysis	Classify public comment or citizen feedback by text analytics
Anomaly Detection	Detect anomalies in health data, spending, or applications by Azure AI models

11.3 Overview: AI Builder vs. Azure AI

Feature	AI Builder	Azure AI
Ease of Use	No-code user interface in Power Apps/Automate	Pro-code APIs, SDKs, Azure Portal
Use Cases	Forms, classification, sentiment, object detection	Custom NLP, vision, audio, translation
Integration	Native to Power Platform	Requiring connectors or custom integration
Licensing	Based on credits	Based on usage (Cognitive Services billing) for Azure

11.4 Example AI Builder Features

- **Form Processing:** Train a model to pull fields out of scanned PDFs.

- **Prediction:** Predict renewal risk, citizen churn, or eligibility.

- **Object Detection:** Detect objects in inspection photos (e.g., safety equipment).

- **Text Classification:** Classify incoming emails or public comments.

- **Business Card Reader:** Automate contact management in field outreach.

11.5 Advanced Use: Azure AI + Power Platform

Integrations Include

- **Azure Form Recognizer** with Power Automate for high-volume docs

- **Azure OpenAI** to auto-summarize or provide decision support insights

- **Azure Translator** for multilingual citizen services

- **Azure Cognitive Search** integrated into Power Pages

- **Azure Custom Vision** to use in inspections or surveillance

Use custom connectors or Azure Functions to bridge pro-code models into low-code flows or apps.

11.6 Responsible AI for Public Sector

- **Bias and Fairness Audits** for trained models

- **Explainable AI** tools to enable transparency in public decisions

- **Human-in-the-Loop Workflows** for override and escalation

- **Compliance Logging** with Dataverse + Power Platform Admin Tools

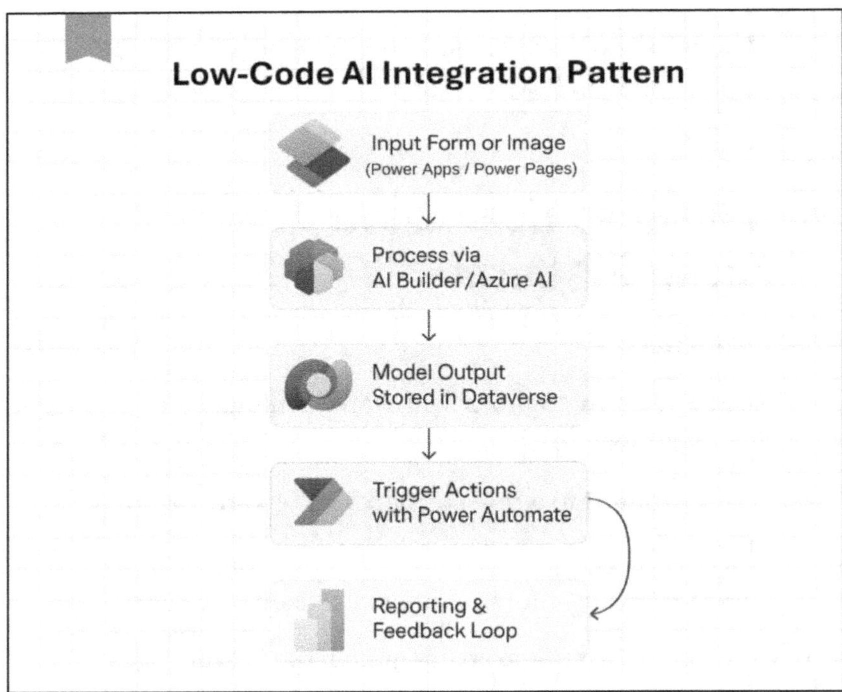

Figure 11-1. *Low-Code AI Integration Pattern*

CHAPTER 12

Copilot Studio In-Depth Tutorial: Bots, Prompts, and Custom Skills

12.1 Introduction

Government agencies can create **AI bots** and **natural language copilots** with ease, utilizing Microsoft's **Copilot Studio** (previously called Power Virtual Agents) that direct citizens and employees to obtain information, fill out forms, and access systems—all without coding.

Combined with Power Automate, Dataverse, and Azure OpenAI, however, such copilots can transform from simple chatbots into strong digital assistants who are capable of deciding, summarizing, or starting workflows.

S. Piridi, *GovOps with Microsoft Power Platform and Copilot*, Inside Copilot,
https://doi.org/10.1007/979-8-8688-1796-0_12

12.2 Core Concepts in Copilot Studio

Feature	Description
Topics	Pre-determined or AI-created conversation flow from question and intent
Triggers	Keywords or questions serving as a cue for a topic
Entities	Structured data types pulled from user input (date, zip code)
Variables	Save answers for the conversation context
Power Automate Integration	Trigger flows to retrieve information, update systems, or alert through notifications
Hand-Off to Human	Pass to Teams or a live agent through escalation triggers

12.3 Government Use Cases for Copilot Studio

Use Case	Description
Permit Status Inquiries	Assist citizens with check of application status or required documents
FAQ Bots	Deal with frequent questions such as hours, rules, or requirements
Employee HR Assistants	Allow employees to inquire about leave, payroll, or policy
Crisis Response Bots	Direct users to safety information, shelters, or emergency forms
Public Health Screeners	Triage symptoms or provide health resources in outbreaks

12.4 Building Bots with Copilot Studio

1. **Create Topics** with AI or preexisting templates.

2. **Insert Questions and Messages** with visual authoring.

3. **Utilize Conditions** for branching (e.g., "Do you need to upload a file?").

4. **Trigger Flows** to push questions (e.g., ID-based case lookup).

5. **Test with Copilot Emulator** and deploy to channels (Power Pages, Teams, web).

12.5 Enhancing Copilot with Custom Skills

- Summarizing citizen petitions through integration with **Azure OpenAI**

- Including **semantic search** by means of Azure Cognitive Search

- Calling **custom APIs** for external data lookup or input validation

- Implementing **custom connectors** for calling internal legacy systems

- Translation of dialogues through **Azure Translator API**

12.6 Tips for Prompt Engineering

- Keep the questions concise and to-the-point ones (e.g., "Summarize the following...").

- Make use of **role-specific prompts** for compliance or legal use cases.

- Test **edge cases and multi-language inputs**.

- Instructions + examples for best AI performance.

- Save reusable question history in Dataverse.

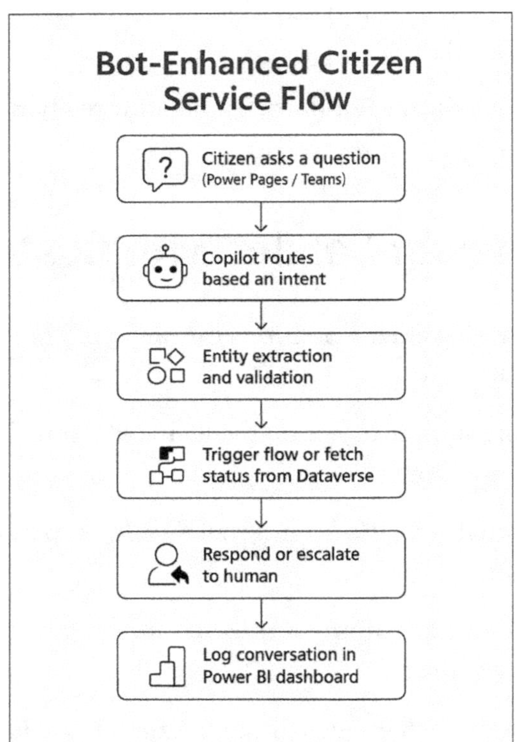

Figure 12-1. Bot-Enhanced Citizen Service Flow

CHAPTER 13

Low-Code + Pro-Code Fusion: When to Extend with Azure Functions

13.1 Introduction

Low-code solutions have huge potential right out of the box. But government applications tend to integrate with legacy applications, complex data processing, or custom business rules that are not available through connectors and flows.

That's when **pro-code extensibility** to the rescue. With the Power Platform and **Azure Functions, APIs**, or custom connectors, organizations get the benefit of both: power and speed.

S. Piridi, *GovOps with Microsoft Power Platform and Copilot*, Inside Copilot, https://doi.org/10.1007/979-8-8688-1796-0_13

13.2 When Low-Code Isn't Enough

- Sophisticated data transformations that are outside the capability of Power Fx

- API calls that demand advanced headers, tokens, or chained logic

- Processing secure or sensitive data using custom encryption

- Integration with on-prem or third-party systems not exposed via standard connectors

- Constructing reproducible microservices or integrations at scale

13.3 Common Scenarios for Fusion Development

Scenario	Low-Code Component	Pro-Code Extension
Address Standardization	Canvas App input	Azure Function with USPS API
Custom Scoring	Model-Driven App	Azure Function with ML Model
Legacy Mainframe Integration	Power Automate Desktop	Custom connector to REST gateway
Advanced Document Parsing	AI Builder Form Processor	Azure Document Intelligence or Azure Content Understanding
Conditional PDF Generation	Power Automate Flow	Azure Function to merge templates

13.4 What Are Azure Functions?

Azure Functions are **serverless computing services** that execute small chunks of code (functions) upon events such as an HTTP request, queue messages, or a timer.

Key Benefits

- No servers to manage

- Automatically scaling

- Pay-you-use costs

- Support for C#, JavaScript, Python, and PowerShell

13.5 Connecting Azure Functions and Power Platform

1. **Expose your function** as an HTTP endpoint, secured properly.

2. **Wrap it in a Custom Connector** with Power Platform Connector Builder.

3. **Call from Power Automate** or **Power Apps** using the connector.

4. **Log inputs/outputs** in Dataverse for traceability.

Tip   Use Azure API Management to manage, monitor, and secure your APIs and Functions at scale.

13.6 Developer + Citizen Developer Collaboration

- Citizen devs create front-ends and workflows.

- Pro devs add back-end logic, custom connectors, and secure APIs.

- Teams work together using **DevOps pipelines, shared repositories,** and **ALM best practices**.

CoE (Center of Excellence) teams enact governance and extension models.

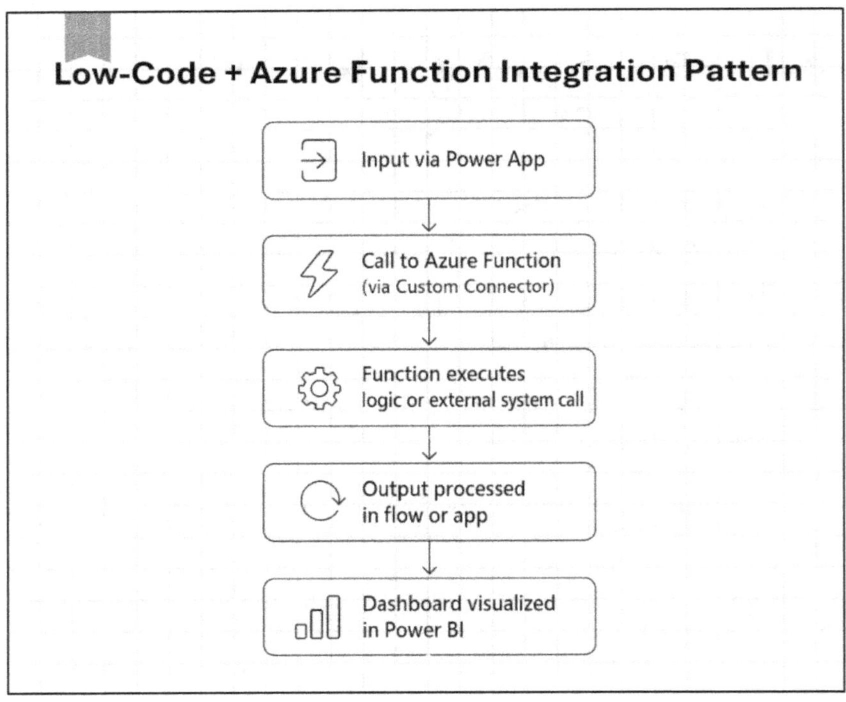

Figure 13-1. *Low-Code + Azure Function Integration Pattern*

CHAPTER 14

Secure External API Integrations in Government Applications

14.1 Introduction

Today's modern government services are required to integrate with many third-party systems—license boards tax authorities and weather APIs. These integrations need to be secure, compliant, and low maintenance in order to protect sensitive data and public trust.

Power Platform allows robust external integrations using custom connectors, Azure API Management, and Power Automate.

© Sarat Piridi 2025

S. Piridi, *GovOps with Microsoft Power Platform and Copilot,* Inside Copilot, https://doi.org/10.1007/979-8-8688-1796-0_14

14.2 Government Integration Challenges

- External systems may not handle existing protocols or standards.

- Authentication and authorization requirements (OAuth2, API Keys, etc.).

- Compliance and data residency (FedRAMP, CJIS, GDPR).

- Handling rate limits, failures, and data discrepancy.

- Traceability and log audit necessity.

14.3 Typical Integration Scenarios

System	Use Case
State Licensing Board	Verify applicant status when processing business license applications
Weather or Traffic API	Emergency alert routing power dynamic
Law Enforcement	Verify IDs or status for background checks
Payment Gateway	Process application fees or fines
GIS Systems	Append location data to permits or inspections

14.4 Power Platform Integration Tools

- **Standard Connectors:** Use when available (e.g., Outlook, SharePoint, SAP).

- **Custom Connectors:** Set up endpoints, auth, headers, request/response structure.

- **Azure API Management (APIM):** Main gateway to enforce policies, log activities, and control traffic.

- **Power Automate:** Act as the workflow engine to link API calls together.

- **Dataverse Virtual Tables:** Access and modify data straight from external systems without replication.

CHAPTER 15

Data Governance and Sovereignty with Dataverse and Azure

15.1 Introduction

Government organizations need to adhere to stringent data governance requirements due to regulations such as CJIS, HIPAA, FedRAMP, GDPR, and state-level legislation. These rules cover how organizations collect, store, share, keep, and audit data.

Microsoft Dataverse and Azure services enable Power Platform solutions to meet compliance requirements, manage access, and exercise data sovereignty—keeping data within particular jurisdictions.

15.2 Key Governance Challenges

- Third-party systems store data beyond state/country borders.

- No one can view who accessed what and when.

© Sarat Piridi 2025
S. Piridi, *GovOps with Microsoft Power Platform and Copilot*, Inside Copilot,
https://doi.org/10.1007/979-8-8688-1796-0_15

- No central mechanism to enforce policies across apps.

- Difficulty fulfilling audit and retention needs.

- Overuse of personal environments or shadow IT.

15.3 How Dataverse Facilitates Data Governance

Feature	Governance Benefit
Role-Based Security (RBAC)	Controls access on a field, record, or table level
Auditing and Logging	Records create, update, delete, and access events
Field-Level Security	Protects sensitive data (e.g., SSNs, PII)
Environment Segregation	Dev/Test/Prod for life cycle and controls
DLP Policies	Prevents connectors that move data outside trusted services

15.4 Azure Services for Sovereignty and Compliance

- **Azure Compliance Portal:** Shows data center compliance by region

- **Azure Key Vault:** Secures credentials, secrets, and keys

- **Azure Purview:** Catalogs, groups, and reports on data governance

- **Azure Information Protection (AIP):** Marks and restricts access to sorted data

- **Azure Policy:** Ensures resources conform to tags, location rules, and policies

15.5 Center of Excellence (CoE) for Governance

- Develop a governance plan that includes

- Naming conventions, solutions, and connectors

- Certification and publishing workflows of apps

- Monitoring unused apps or flows

- Training and onboarding of citizen developers

- Frequently audits of environments and access

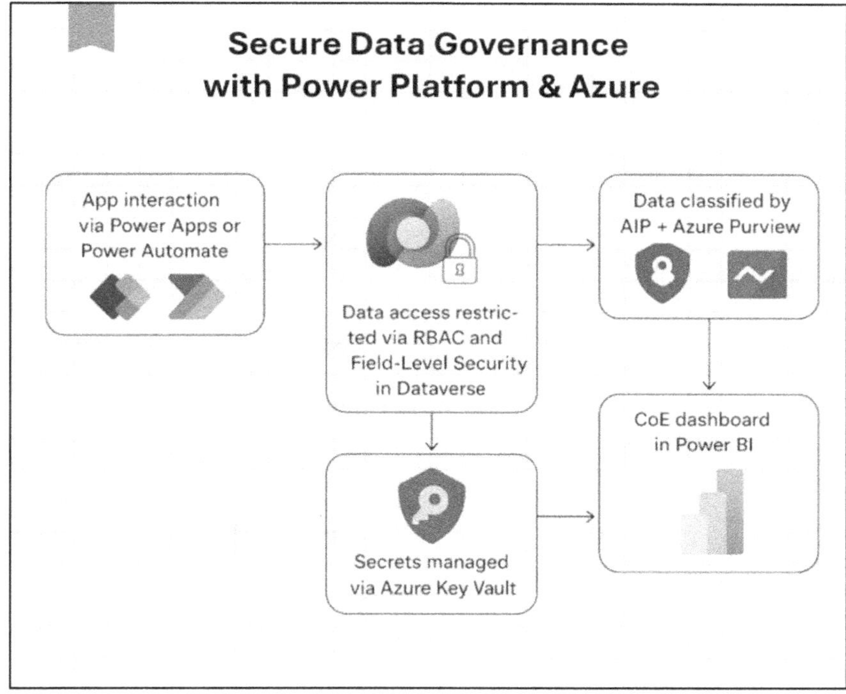

Figure 15-1. *Secure Data Governance with Power Platform and Azure*

CHAPTER 16

Making Power Platform Solutions Run Better

16.1 Introduction

As Power Platform apps scale across departments and handle more users, data, and automation, making them run faster becomes key. An app that loads, a flow that takes too long, or a dashboard that's bloated can frustrate users and undermine adoption in high-volume government operations.

This chapter looks at ways to build Power Apps, Flows, and Dashboards that respond, scale, and work well.

16.2 Common Performance Pain Points

- Canvas Apps that take too long to load because of too many controls or data requests

- Power Automate runs that take a long time or stop working

© Sarat Piridi 2025
S. Piridi, *GovOps with Microsoft Power Platform and Copilot*, Inside Copilot,
https://doi.org/10.1007/979-8-8688-1796-0_16

- Dataverse queries and lookups that don't work well

- Dashboards that slow down because they have too many visuals or filters

- Flows failing because of throttling, retries, or API limits

16.3 Tips to Optimize Canvas Apps

Area	Suggestion
Controls	Reduce visible controls on each screen; use components
Data Calls	Use Concurrent () for parallel calls; don't use Clear Collect () when the app starts
Delegation	Use queries that can be delegated with filters/sorts for large datasets
Pictures	Compress and store if used often
Variables	Use Set () to avoid unnecessary calculations

16.4 Boosting Dataverse Speed and Performance

- Put indexed columns to work for filters and lookups.

- Avoid retrieving unnecessary columns or records.

- Set up business rules instead of complex client-side logic.

- Leverage change tracking to cut down on polling.

- Move old data to separate tables or environments.

16.5 Making Power BI Dashboards Faster

- Trim down the number of visuals on a single report.

- Harness aggregated tables or measures you've calculated beforehand.

- Make smart use of filters and slicers.

- Turn to DirectQuery when necessary, or go for hybrid models.

- Watch your progress with Performance Analyzer in Power BI Desktop.

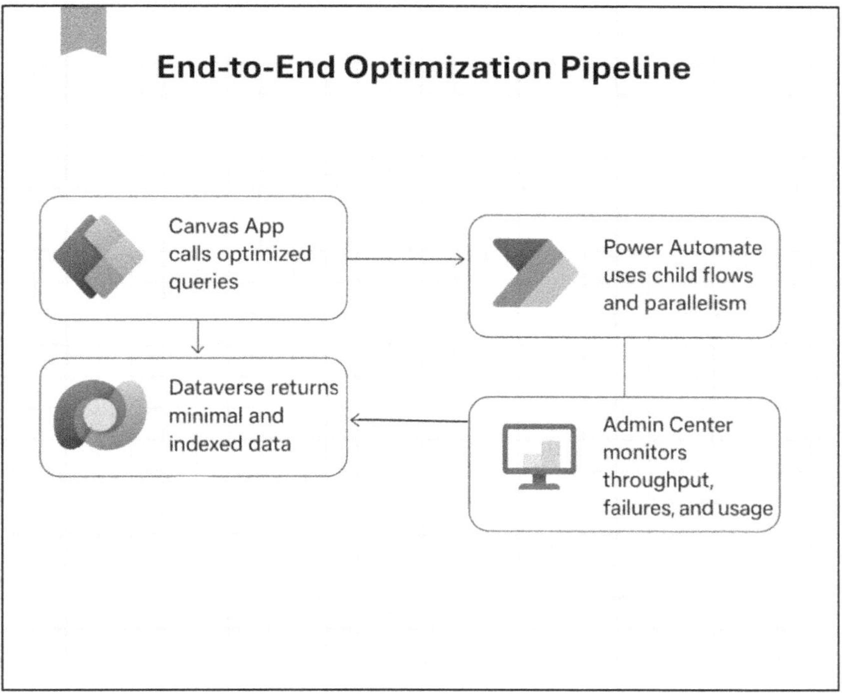

Figure 16-1. *End-to-End Optimization Pipeline*

Monitoring and Logging with Azure Monitor and Power Platform Admin Center

17.1 Introduction

In high-scale government implementations, system behavior visibility is crucial. From flowing failures, application usage, login attempts, or data changes, teams with real-time monitoring and logging are able to monitor uptime, anomalies, and audit needs.

This chapter demonstrates how to construct a solid system to view all of it. You will learn to utilize tools such as the Power Platform Admin Center, Azure Monitor, Dataverse auditing, and Power BI.

© Sarat Piridi 2025

S. Piridi, *GovOps with Microsoft Power Platform and Copilot*, Inside Copilot,
https://doi.org/10.1007/979-8-8688-1796-0_17

17.2 Why Monitoring Matters in Government

- **Proactive Incident Detection:** Find problems before they get worse.

- **User Adoption Metrics:** See how people use apps and why they stop using it.

- **Audit Trail Requirements:** Keep records of access and changes.

- **Performance Troubleshooting:** Find bottlenecks or failures.

- **Security and Compliance:** Watch for unusual behaviors or policy violations.

17.3 Key Monitoring Tools

Tool	Purpose
Power Platform Admin Center	See environment health, capacity, DLP enforcement, and usage stats
Dataverse Auditing	Record and track field-level changes, who/when/what actions people performed
Azure Monitor + Application Insights	Take in logs from flows, apps, and connectors to analyze deeply
Power Automate Analytics	Show run history, errors, and success rates
Power BI Reports	Combine and display trends for leadership

17.4 What to Monitor

- Flow failures, retries, and timeouts

- App launch times, screen loads, and session length

- Unauthorized connector uses or DLP breaches

- Storage and API call use by environment

- User roles, login trends, and access shifts

- Key business records or fields

17.5 Integration with Azure Monitor

1. Turn on telemetry in flows or custom connectors.

2. Send data to Azure Log Analytics.

3. Use Kusto Query Language (KQL) to build dashboards.

4. Create alerts or detect anomalies in patterns (e.g., spikes, failures).

5. Send insights to Power BI or alert via Teams.

17.6 Automation and Alerts

- Create flow-based alerts for failures thresholds.

- Send Teams messages when incidents occur or SLAs are not met.

- Set up automatic processes to clean up users or
  reassign licenses.

- Put together daily reports on system health for
  CoE teams.

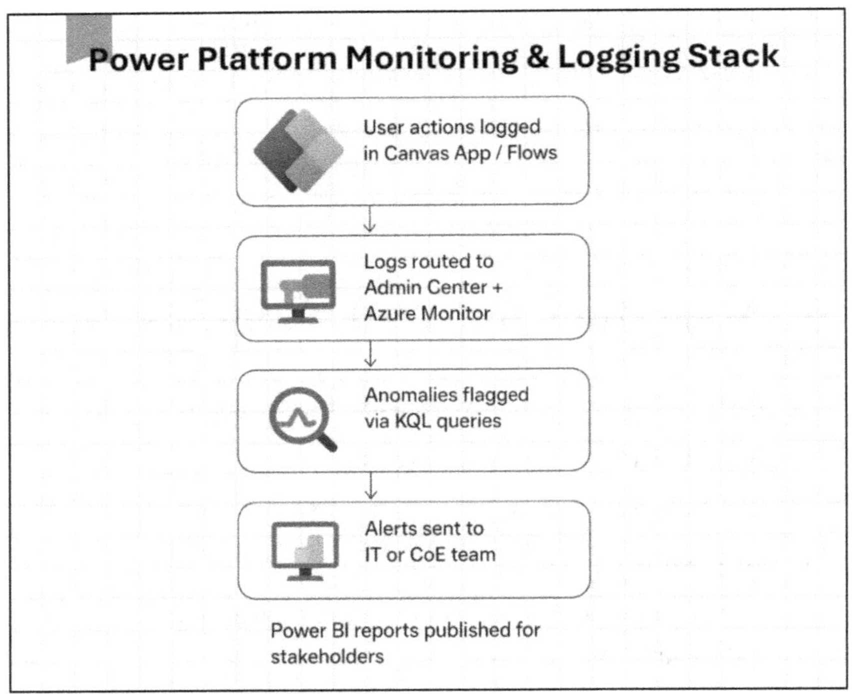

Figure 17-1. *Power Platform Monitoring and Logging Stack*

CHAPTER 18

Disaster Recovery and Business Continuity Planning

18.1 Introduction

The core public services, such as public safety, licensing, benefits, and compliance, have to run 24 by 7. Cybercrimes, natural calamities, or sometimes a system outage could shut them down. Hence, very robust Disaster Recovery (DR) and Business Continuity Plan (BCP) policies need to be established over Power Platform deployments for such agencies.

This chapter presents ways to keep systems running, protect data, and bounce back fast.

18.2 Key Threats to Continuity

- Wrong setup can corrupt environments.

- Power Automate flows can fail or get deleted.

- Accidents or ransomware can cause data loss.

© Sarat Piridi 2025

S. Piridi, *GovOps with Microsoft Power Platform and Copilot*, Inside Copilot,

https://doi.org/10.1007/979-8-8688-1796-0_18

- Dependencies (e.g., APIs, connectors, on-site gateways) can break down.

- Problems at the tenant level (identity, licensing, capacity).

18.3 Framework for Business Continuity Planning

Element	Description
Risk Assessment	Spot key apps, users, data, and dependencies
Recovery Objectives	Define Recovery Time Objective (RTO) and Recovery Point Objective (RPO) Recovery Objectives)
Backup Strategy	Choose what to back up (solutions, flows, Dataverse, environments)
Failover Strategy	Plan how services will continue (other flows manual backup)
Communication Plan	Tell internal/external stakeholders about outages

18.4 Ways to Recover from Disasters in Power Platform

- **Power Platform Pipelines:** Re-deploy solution versions to rebuild environments.

- **Dataverse Backups:** Restore database using environment-level backups.

- **Flow Version History:** Bring back older versions of cloud flows.

- **Solution Export:** Export managed solutions regularly to safe storage.

- **PowerShell Scripts:** Automate environments export, list apps/flows, and assign roles.

18.5 Azure Capabilities for DR

- **Azure Backup:** Backs up on-premises connectors and shared gateways.

- **Azure API Management Failover:** Automatically reroute traffic to other endpoints when needed.

- **Geo-Replication:** Works with Dataverse for key workloads (needs Premium license).

- **Azure Site Recovery:** Protects mixed setups that work with Power Platform.

18.6 Tabletop Testing and Drills

- Test different scenarios: "API down," "system corruption," "lost flow."

- Check how long it takes to recover and documentation quality.

- Involve IT, app creators, and business leaders.

- Keep track of what went wrong and how to fix it next time.

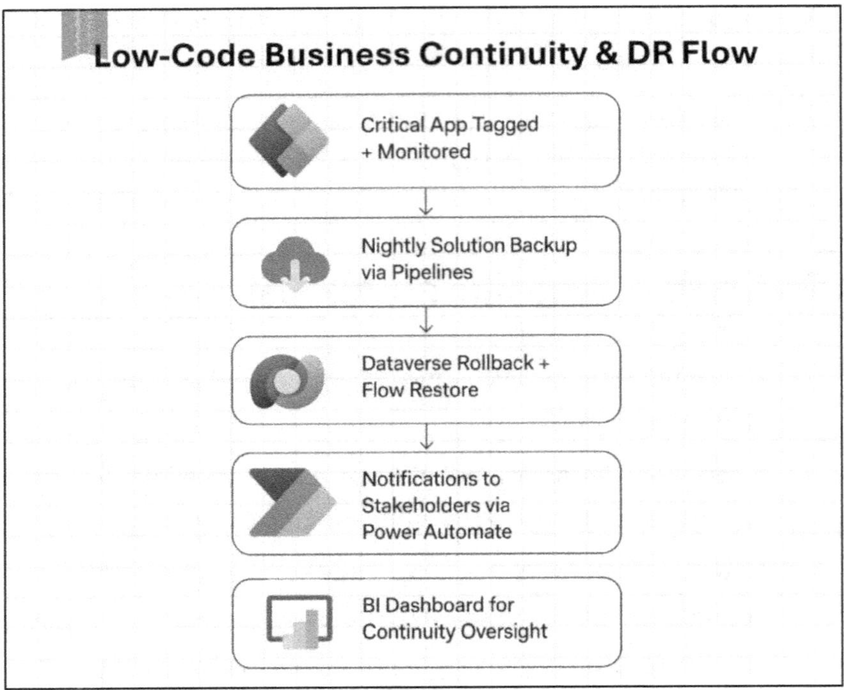

Figure 18-1. *Low-Code Business Continuity and DR Flow*

The Future of Digital Government: Trends to Watch

19.1 Introduction

Technology changes fast, and public institutions must keep up. The next wave of digital government won't just focus on automation. It will prioritize intelligence, inclusivity, and toughness. This chapter looks at new trends shaping how low-code solutions will work in government down the road.

19.2 Emerging Trends

1. **Self-running Workflows (AI + Low Code)**

   - AI systems will study workflows and offer suggestions or auto-complete them.

   - Smart routing of processes based on past case info and user behavior.

   - Systems that get better based on usage patterns.

© Sarat Piridi 2025

S. Piridi, *GovOps with Microsoft Power Platform and Copilot*, Inside Copilot,
https://doi.org/10.1007/979-8-8688-1796-0_19

2. **Citizen-Focused Digital Experiences**

- Conversational apps with voice, chat, or control with gestures

- Easy-to-build websites that work well on phones and support many languages

- Custom screens to track services, benefits, and permits

3. **AI Helpers for Policy and Law**

- AI tools to help write, sum up, and explain new laws

- Quick legal answer systems for the public and government workers

- Easy ways to search across ordinances, records, or regulations

4. **Digital IDs and mDL Integration**

- Quick sign-ups using phone-based driver's licenses and face or fingerprint scans

- Safe login across government agencies SSO using Entra ID and low-code apps

- Secure ID checks that protect your privacy

5. **Flexible Government Systems**

- Modular low-code blocks that you can reuse in different programs

- Architecture that works like microservices and links to business domains

- Connects with open data APIs, blockchain verification, and digital signatures

19.3 The Role of Cloud and Data Infrastructure

- **Hybrid Cloud Models:** Balancing data residency with cloud scalability.

- **Edge and IoT:** Apps that use data from sensors (like water quality or pollution levels).

- **Zero Trust Security:** App design includes access control based on context and risk.

- **Open Data to Ensure Accountability:** Live dashboards showing budgets, contracts, and inspection results.

19.4 Next-Gen Development Paradigms

Innovation	Description
AI Co-Development	Apps and flows created through Copilot interfaces
Human-Centered Design	Prototypes based on empathy mapping and feedback cycles
Low-Code DevOps	Pipelines, git integration, and version control for low code
Composable UX	Reusable UI parts and themes across government websites

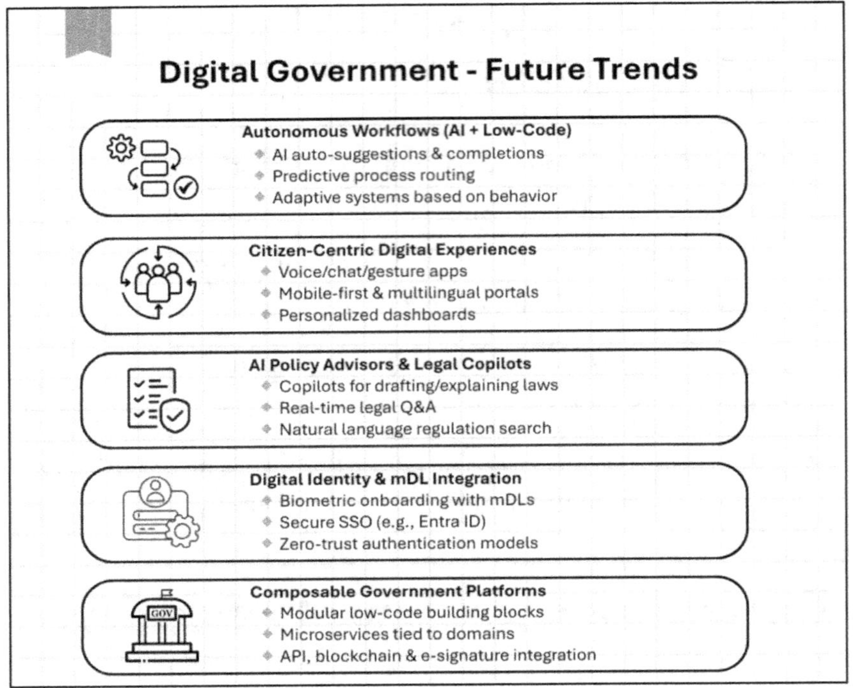

Figure 19-1. Digital Government—Future Trends

Developing a Culture of Low-Code Innovation in Government Sector

20.1 Introduction

Adopting low-code tools goes beyond technology. It represents a change in culture. Government agencies must foster an environment of ongoing innovation teamwork across departments and staff empowerment to succeed in this fast-evolving digital world.

This chapter examines how public sector organizations can establish a low-code culture that's expandable, safe, and long-lasting.

S. Piridi, *GovOps with Microsoft Power Platform and Copilot*, Inside Copilot,
https://doi.org/10.1007/979-8-8688-1796-0_20

20.2 Key Elements of an Innovation Culture

Pillar	Description
Empowerment	Enable tech and non-technical employees to fix things via sanctioned low-code tools
Governance	Direct innovation without hindering it via framework, policy, and enablement
Community	Construct internal share-hubs of knowledge, hackathons, user groups, and showcases
Recognition	Highlight impact drivers, apps enhancing ROI, and teams exhibiting top-notch innovation practices

20.3 Roles in the Low-Code Ecosystem

- **Makers/Citizen Developers:** Frontline employees develop applications to make every day work easier.

- **IT Professionals:** Support structures, security, and monitor solutions.

- **Business Analysts:** Identify needs, prototype test, and track success.

- **CoE Teams:** These teams establish standards, enable reuse, and implement policies.

- **Executives and Sponsors:** These executives support the movement and offer funds to expand.

20.4 Building a Center of Excellence (CoE)

A Center of Excellence serves as the working core of a strong low-code practice.

Important components are

- Playbooks of governance

- Catalogs of solutions

- Training Paths and Onboarding of Maker

- Tools for life cycle management apps (pipelines, approvals, reviews)

- Data on how apps are used, their value, and risks

20.5 Onboarding People and Enhancing Capabilities

- Host in-house "maker academies" to instruct Power Platform fundamentals.

- Provide templates, starter kits, and design guides.

- Team up citizen developers with professional developers for mentoring.

- Utilize examples from Microsoft Learn, LinkedIn Learning, and GitHub.

20.6 Gauging Success

Metric	Value
Time Saved	Hours reduced every week or per task due to automation
Cost Avoidance	Expense saved compared to outsourced development or legacy support
App Usage	Daily/monthly active app users and portal
Power Automate Reliability	Number of successful vs. failed runs
Maker Expansion	Number of trained active and certified makers

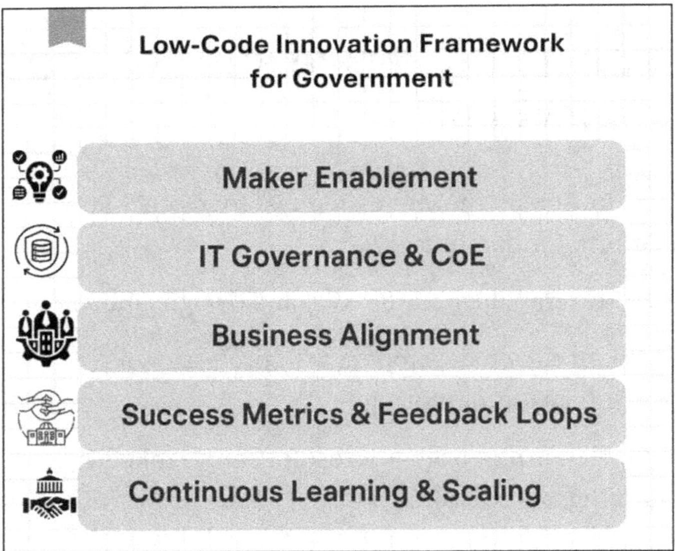

Figure 20-1. Low-Code Innovation Framework for Government

References

Microsoft Documentation and Resources

Microsoft Power Platform Architecture Icons. Microsoft
Power Platform Architecture Center.
`https://learn.microsoft.com/power-platform/`
`guidance/architecture/icons`
Microsoft Power Platform Product Documentation—
Power Apps, Power Automate, Power BI, Power Pages,
Dataverse, AI Builder, Copilot Studio.
`https://learn.microsoft.com/power-platform`
Microsoft Copilot Studio Documentation.
`https://learn.microsoft.com/copilot-studio`
Microsoft Azure AI Documentation.
`https://learn.microsoft.com/azure/ai-services`
Microsoft Responsible AI Dashboard.
`https://aka.ms/ResponsibleAI`
Microsoft Compliance Manager.
`https://compliance.microsoft.com`
Microsoft Application Lifecycle Management (ALM) for
Power Platform.
`https://learn.microsoft.com/power-platform/alm/`
Microsoft Power Platform Security and Governance
Documentation.
`https://learn.microsoft.com/power-`
`platform/admin/`
Microsoft Power BI Governance and Security.

© Sarat Piridi 2025
S. Piridi, *GovOps with Microsoft Power Platform and Copilot*, Inside Copilot,
https://doi.org/10.1007/979-8-8688-1796-0

https://learn.microsoft.com/power-bi/enterprise/
service-security

Regulatory and Industry Frameworks Referenced

FedRAMP (Federal Risk and Authorization Management
Program).

https://www.fedramp.gov

NIST (National Institute of Standards and Technology).

https://www.nist.gov

HIPAA (Health Insurance Portability and
Accountability Act).

https://www.hhs.gov/hipaa

GDPR (General Data Protection Regulation).

https://gdpr-info.eu

W3C WCAG 2.1 (Web Content Accessibility Guidelines).

https://www.w3.org/WAI/standards-guidelines/wcag

Section 508 of the Rehabilitation Act (US Federal
Government Digital Accessibility Standards).

https://www.section508.gov

European Union Artificial Intelligence Act (EU AI Act).

https://artificialintelligenceact.eu

US Executive Orders on AI and Digital Equity (White
House AI Governance).

https://www.whitehouse.gov/ostp/ai-bill-
of-rights/

Additional Sources Referenced

Microsoft Power Platform CoE (Center of Excellence)
Starter Kit.

https://learn.microsoft.com/power-platform/
guidance/coe/starter-kit

Microsoft Azure API Management Documentation.
`https://learn.microsoft.com/azure/api-management/`
Microsoft Power Platform Pipelines.
`https://learn.microsoft.com/power-platform/alm/devops-build-tools`
Microsoft Azure Event Grid and Event-Driven Architecture.
`https://learn.microsoft.com/azure/event-grid/overview`
Microsoft Azure OpenAI Service.
`https://learn.microsoft.com/azure/ai-services/openai`

References to Public Sector Practices

Throughout this book, examples are drawn from public sector best practices and real-world projects, including

- DMV Modernization Programs

- State of California—CalOES Digital Modernization Initiatives

- Microsoft Unified Premier Modernization Project

- US State and Local Public Health Agencies

- State Departments of Education (anonymous examples)

- Transportation and Infrastructure Modernization

- Department of Environmental Services—Air, Water, Waste, Sustainability

- Emergency Services and Disaster Response Automation

- Department of Justice and Corrections

- State Finance, Treasury & Accounting Systems

- Department of Human Services

- Cross-Agency Collaboration and Case Management Initiatives

These examples are built upon the author's direct experience in public sector IT modernization for state and local agencies across the United States, in addition to projects conducted in partnership with Microsoft, State of California, CalOES, DRDO, Fidelity, and Microsoft Unified Premier teams.

Additional Sources Referenced Throughout the Book

- FI$Cal—Financial Information System for California

- US Digital Services Playbook

- National Institute of Standards and Technology (NIST)

- FedRAMP Compliance

- Government Technology Magazine

- Microsoft GitHub—Power Platform Samples

Index

© Sarat Piridi 2025

S. Piridi, *GovOps with Microsoft Power Platform and Copilot*, Inside Copilot,
https://doi.org/10.1007/979-8-8688-1796-0

F

G

H

I, J

T, U

V

GPSR Compliance
The European Union's (EU) General Product Safety Regulation (GPSR) is a set
of rules that requires consumer products to be safe and our obligations to
ensure this.

If you have any concerns about our products, you can contact us on

ProductSafety@springernature.com

In case Publisher is established outside the EU, the EU authorized
representative is:

Springer Nature Customer Service Center GmbH
Europaplatz 3
69115 Heidelberg, Germany